AI and Emerging Technologies for a Sustainable Future

(Volume 2)

Technological Applications of AI in the Development of Sustainable Future

Edited by

Shilpa Gupta
Electronics and Communication Department
Chandigarh University, Gharuan, Mohali, Punjab
India

&

Ritika Sharma
Computer Science and Engineering Department
Maharaja Agrasen University, Baddi
Himachal Pradesh, India

AI and Emerging Technologies for a Sustainable Future

(Volume 2)

Technological Applications of AI in the Development of a Sustainable Future

Editors: Shilpa Gupta and Ritika Sharma

ISBN (Online): 979-8-89881-330-7

ISBN (Print): 979-8-89881-331-4

ISBN (Paperback): 979-8-89881-332-1

Published by Bentham Science Publishers Pte. Ltd. Singapore, in collaboration with Eureka Conferences, USA.

First published in 2026.

Bentham Science Publishers Pte. Ltd.
No. 9 Raffles Place
Office No. 26-01
Singapore 048619
Singapore
Email: subscriptions@benthamscience.net

BENTHAM
SCIENCE

CONTENTS

FOREWORD

In a world characterized by unprecedented technological progress and compounding global challenges, the quest for a sustainable future has never been more compelling. Artificial Intelligence (AI), which had long been the reserve of science fiction, has become an all-pervasive force across sectors and societies, presenting unparalleled opportunities to address the world's most critical sustainability challenges, ranging from global warming and environmental degradation to social injustice and resource limitation.

Where Volume I laid the groundwork by underlining seminal AI trends in energy, agriculture, water, etc., this volume builds upon that vision by pushing frontiers and giving voice to boundary-breaking thinkers across disciplines.

This volume, **"Technological Applications of AI in the Development of Sustainable Future,"** is a crucial and timely addition to the discussion regarding the applications of AI as part of the book series, **"AI and Emerging Technologies for a Sustainable Future"**, it gathers top scholars, inventors, and practitioners who examine the nexus of AI technology, and sustainability extensively and comprehensively. The chapters shed light on how AI can maximize energy systems, transform sustainable agriculture, enhance disaster relief, and facilitate smarter cities, as well as critically analyse the ethical, societal, and environmental implications of these technologies.

I hope that this book will become a go-to resource for scholars, policymakers, business leaders, and anyone dedicated to unlocking the potential of AI to make a more equitable, resilient, and sustainable future a reality.

May this work inspire collaboration between disciplines and sectors, and remind us that the future of technology can never be separated from the future of human beings and the planet we live on.

Kapil Bhatt
Department of ECE
University Institute of Information Technology
Himachal Pradesh University
Shimla, Himachal Pradesh
India

PREFACE

As sustainability becomes the solution to modern engineering, artificial intelligence has rapidly evolved from a niche technological tool to a unifying force that can address most of the complex sustainability challenges of our time. In this transformative age, Volume II of AI-Driven Technologies for Sustainable Engineering continued to explore how AI engages with sustainability, forging new avenues toward a regenerative world.

Where Volume I set the stage by highlighting foundational AI trends in energy, agriculture, water, *etc.*, this volume takes that vision further by exploring new frontiers and amplifying voices breaking boundaries across disciplines.

This volume, "Technological Applications of AI in the Development of Sustainable Future," of the book series, "AI and Emerging Technologies for a Sustainable Future", presents a wider canvas capturing how AI combines with renewable infrastructure planning, healthcare systems, fabric detection systems, and sustainable materials discovery. With the ongoing focus on interdisciplinary collaboration, the book dissects the ethical, technical, and societal implications of intelligent systems integrated into sustainable frameworks.

Chapters are enhanced with new case studies, new perspectives from developing AI methodologies, and prospective scenarios, providing a roadmap for sustainable engineering in theory and practical application. The book focuses not only on technological development but also on the cultural and institutional changes necessary for actual sustainable transformation.

Our heartfelt thanks to the authors, the visionary thinkers who are creating the next generation of sustainable engineers. Their contributions make this volume an indispensable guide for engineers, innovators, policymakers, and learners dedicated to employing AI not only as a tool but as a collaborator in creating a more sustainable world.

We wish that this book will be informative and inspirational.

Shilpa Gupta
Electronics and Communication Department
Chandigarh University, Gharuan, Mohali, Punjab
India

&

Ritika Sharma
Computer Science and Engineering Department
Maharaja Agrasen University, Baddi
Himachal Pradesh, India

List of Contributors

Abhishek Nigam	Electronics Engineering Department, IET Engineering College, Lucknow, Uttar Pradesh, India
Anil Kr. Shaw	Department of Computer Science and Engineering, JIS University, Agarpara, Kolkata, India
Anurag Verma	Electrical Engineering Department, IET Engineering College, Lucknow, Uttar Pradesh, India
Ayush Yadav	Department of UIE-Computer Science, Chandigarh University, Gharuan, Mohali, Punjab, India
Chandrmani Yadav	Department of Mechanical Engineering, Faculty of Engineering & Technology, Marwadi University Research Center, Marwadi University, Rajkot, Gujarat, India
Debdutta Pal	Department of Computer Science and Engineering, Adamas University, Kolkata, West Bengal, India
Deepti Chaudhary	University Institute of Engineering and Technology, Kurukshetra University, Kurukshetra, Haryana, India
Digant Raj	Department of UIE-Computer Science, Chandigarh University, Gharuan, Mohali, Punjab, India
Garima Thakur	Department of Electronic and Communication Engineering, Chandigarh University, Gharuan, Mohali, Punjab, India
Harmeet Singh	Department of Electronics and Communication Engineering, Chandigarh University, Gharuan, Mohali, Punjab, India
Kaushik Adhikary	Department of Computer Science and Engineering, JIS University, Agarpara, Kolkata, India
Kuldeep	University Institute of Engineering and Technology, Kurukshetra University, Kurukshetra, Haryana, India
Love Singla	Department of Biotechnology and Microbiology, Maharaja Agrasen University, Baddi, Himachal Pradesh, India
Madhu Bala	Department of Computer Science and Engineering, Lovely Professional University, Phagwara, Punjab, India
Manjunath	Department of Computer Science and Engineering, Lovely Professional University, Phagwara, Punjab, India
Nandkishor M. Sawai	Department of Mechanical Engineering, Sandip Institute of Technology and Research Centre, Nashik, Maharashtra, India
Nitin S. Patil	Department of Electrical Engineering, Sandip Institute of Technology and Research Centre, Nashik, Maharashtra, India
Om Prakash Yadav	Department of Electrical Engineering, Sandip Institute of Technology and Research Centre, Nashik, Maharashtra, India
P. Venkata Rama Sai Abhishek	Department of Electrical Engineering, Chandigarh University, Gharuan, Mohali, Punjab, India

Pallavi Dey	Department of Computer Science and Engineering, Lovely Professional University, Phagwara, Punjab, India
Paramita Sarkar	Department of Computer Science and Engineering, JIS University, Agarpara, Kolkata, India
Prabhjot Singh	Department of Electronics and Communication Engineering, Chandigarh University, Gharuan, Mohali, Punjab, India
Prashant Kumar	Department of Electrical Engineering, Chandigarh University, Gharuan, Mohali, Punjab, India
Priyanka Ghosh	Department of Computer Science and Engineering, JIS University, Agarpara, Kolkata, India
Priyanka Jangra	University Institute of Engineering and Technology, Kurukshetra University, Kurukshetra, Haryana, India
Rajni Sharma	Department of Biotechnology and Microbiology, Maharaja Agrasen University, Baddi, Himachal Pradesh, India
Ranjit Kumar Bindal	Department of Electrical Engineering, Chandigarh University, Gharuan, Mohali, Punjab, India
Rekha Devi	Department of Electrical Engineering, Chandīgarh University, Gharuan, Mohali, Punjab, India
Sarbjeet Kaur	Department of Electrical Engineering, Chandīgarh University, Gharuan, Mohali, Punjab, India
Saumya Srivastava	Department of Electronics and Communication Engineering, Chandigarh University, Gharuan, Mohali, Punjab, India
Sayani Jana	Department of Computer Science and Engineering, JIS University, Agarpara, Kolkata, India
Sheetal	Department of Zoology, Maharaja Agrasen University, Baddi, Himachal Pradesh, India
Sherin Angelina	Department of Computer Science and Engineering, JIS University, Agarpara, Kolkata, India
Sravanth	Department of Computer Science and Engineering, Lovely Professional University, Phagwara, Punjab, India
Surbhi Gupta	Department of Electrical Engineering, Chandīgarh University, Gharuan, Mohali, Punjab, India

CHAPTER 1

Real-Time Fabric Defect Detection Utilizing Deep Learning-Based Convolutional Neural Networks

Kaushik Adhikary[1,*], Sherin Angelina[1], Anil Kr. Shaw[1] and **Sayani Jana[1]**

[1] *Department of Computer Science and Engineering, JIS University, Agarpara, Kolkata, India*

Abstract: Considering the reduction in labor costs and associated benefits, investment in automated fabric defect detection proves to be highly cost-effective. A robust and efficient algorithm is essential for the development of a fully automated web inspection system. The examination of genuine fabric flaws is particularly difficult because of the multitude of defect categories, which are defined by their ambiguity and indistinctness. This work aims to classify and describe several strategies developed for detecting fabric faults. This work also provides the inaugural survey on methodologies for fabric defect detection, referencing around 160 sources. The categorization of fabric defect detection methodologies is beneficial for assessing the characteristics of the identified features. The characterization of authentic fabric surfaces through their structure and primitive set has not yet demonstrated success. Consequently, the characteristics derived from fabric surfaces have led to the classification of the proposed methodologies into three categories: statistical, spectral, and model-based. To evaluate the state-of-the-art, the constraints of several prospective techniques have been identified, and their performance has been appraised based on demonstrated findings and proposed applications. The results of this work indicate that integrating certain statistical, spectral, and model-based methodologies may produce superior outcomes compared to any individual strategy, warranting additional investigation into this matter.

Keywords: Fabric defect detection, automation, detection accuracy, image representation, convolutional neural network.

INTRODUCTION

Fabric quality inspection plays a crucial role in the textile and yarn industries. Surface imperfections can significantly impact garment quality, leading to customer dissatisfaction and potential losses [1]. Therefore, there is an urgent need for a high-performance, fast, and reliable automated inspection system [2]. Currently, most textile manufacturers rely on manual defect identification, which

* **Corresponding author Kaushik Adhikary:** Department of Computer Science and Engineering, JIS University, Agarpara, Kolkata, India; E-mail: kaushik.adhikary@jisuniversity.ac.in

Shilpa Gupta & Ritika Sharma (Eds.)

is time-consuming and inefficient. Human inspection typically detects only 60–70% of defects in real-time systems [2, 3]. Distractions encompass visual distractions (diverting one's gaze), cognitive distractions (being preoccupied with thinking), auditory distractions (being interrupted by a colleague), and weariness during garment testing. Consequently, human agility is crucial as distractions can result in considerable losses [4, 5]. Furthermore, obstacles have escalated from an industrial perspective [6]. The industry must uphold both the quality and quantity of production to preserve its credibility in the market. Consequently, people are unable to do this inspection work for extended periods while maintaining the necessary precision.

Textile manufacturing companies globally require automation of the inspection process [7]. This inspires us to address this complex issue as a research statement. Digital image processing is utilized for the processing, storage, and display of human-interpretable visual information.

Consequently, computer vision, along with MATLAB, OpenCV, and Keras, is essential and demonstrates efficacy in addressing issues posed by the contemporary industrial landscape [8]. A portion of the fabric that fails to satisfy the specified standards or characteristics is classified as a defect, leading to customer unhappiness and potentially significant losses for the textile industry [9]. Various sorts of fabric flaws include missing yarn, broken yarn, double yarn, stains, and holes. Occasionally, the yarn becomes entangled during preparation, leading to holes, which is the most unattractive flaw. The machine's malfunction may result in problems, including absent yarn. A significant disadvantage is the presence of stain marks [10].

Deep learning is a cutting-edge approach utilized for the detection of flaws in fabric. The system employs a high-resolution camera for picture capture and a stepper motor for the conveyor mechanism. Moreover, enough illumination is crucial, as insufficient lighting can result in substandard digital photos. The suggested system will employ a neural network to recognize and categorize the photos. The implementation of neural networks can enhance system performance. Processing speed can be improved using a high-performance GPU or CPU, hence decreasing computing time [11].

Deep learning is an advanced approach utilized for identifying faults in cloth. The system employs a high-resolution camera to capture images and a stepper motor for the conveyor mechanism. Furthermore, an adequate illumination source is essential, as insufficient lighting may lead to substandard digital photos. The suggested system would employ a neural network to recognize and categorize photos. Neural networks enhance system efficiency. Utilizing advanced GPUs or CPUs can enhance processing performance and diminish computing time [12].

RELATED WORK

An efficiently automated system facilitates reduced labor costs and minimizes manufacturing time. This issue draws considerable attention from researchers, resulting in numerous articles that have developed fabric flaw-detecting systems employing diverse methodologies. Ouyang *et al.* [13] have investigated the detection of fabric defects through the utilization of an embedded convolutional neural network activation layer, employing fabric image autocorrelation to define fabric motifs and leveraging it as a prominent feature. They forecasted elevated precision and introduced PPAL-CNN.

Hanbay *et al.* [14] introduced an optical-based fabric fault detection method. The quantity of yarns and fibers functions as essential units. Nonetheless, prospective fabric imperfections can be mitigated by evaluating yarns and fibers prior to fabric production. Wenninger *et al.* [15] suggested a flaw detection system for plain woven fabrics utilizing a fully convolutional network alongside yarn tracking. A method for fabric fault identification has been described. The fibers of the fabric might be identified and monitored without any conditional parameters. Subsequently, the ripple faults were identified. This issue was previously addressed using a neural network, but was limited to grey fabric exclusively. This research introduced a sophisticated colored fabric defect detection system utilizing deep learning, featuring a camera positioned above the moving fabric at an appropriate distance, accompanied by an illumination source. The system would collect the image and input it for processing (testing). In the event of an error, the motor will cease operation instantaneously. Consequently, this system would be highly beneficial in both small-scale and large-scale textile enterprises that aim to minimize labor costs while achieving superior fabric quality in the quickest possible timeframe.

Liu *et al.* [16] conducted a systematic analysis of contemporary variants of low back pain and presented a taxonomy to more distinctly categorize the notable alternatives. The advantages and disadvantages of the different LBP traits and their interrelations were also examined. A comprehensive performance evaluation was conducted for texture classification, empirically analyzing forty texture features, which comprised thirty-two recent and promising LBP variations and eight non-LBP descriptors derived from deep convolutional networks across thirteen widely-utilized texture datasets. The tests aimed to assess their resilience to various classification problems, encompassing alterations in rotation, scale, illumination, viewpoint, class quantity, diverse forms of image degradation, and computational complexity. Hoang and Rebhi [17] examined classical color spaces to assess the impact of LBP accuracy on fabric flaw detection. They achieved 92.1% accuracy in the LUV color space using a classification of 10 classes.

METHODOLOGY

The suggested transfer learning approach employs the AlexNet architecture with suitably initialized weights. The features are subsequently input into the classifier, which predicts the corresponding labels for the vessels. Due to the inferior accuracy of existing approaches, such as Inception and ResNet, compared to AlexNet, transfer learning utilizing features collected from the AlexNet network may enhance accuracy [18]. Fig. **1** illustrates the block diagram of the proposed system based on AlexNet.

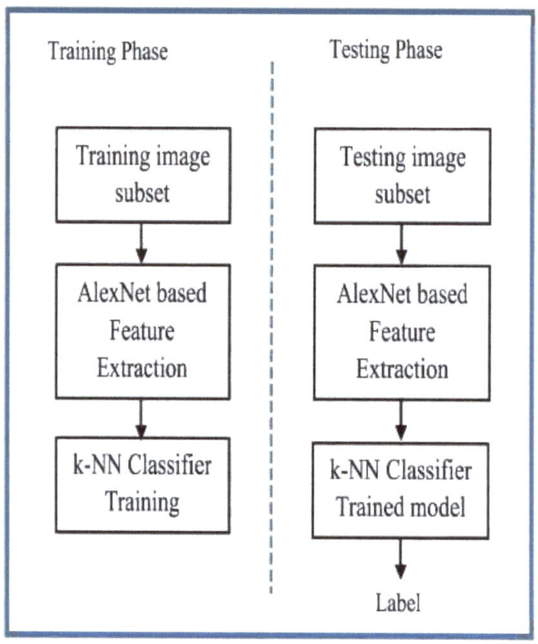

Fig. (1). Methodology of alex-based proposed system.

Imaging approaches can be categorized into two systems: those with stationary and several cameras, and those with a mobile and single camera. An example of a flaw detection system built by Uster Technologies Vision [19], featuring four stationary cameras operating concurrently, is displayed on the left. The primary benefit of utilizing stationary cameras is the mitigation of image degradation due to vibration, leading to enhanced image sharpness. Nevertheless, due to the restricted fabric area observable by a single camera, it is imperative to utilize many cameras concurrently to capture the full fabric [20]. The frame holding card aggregates data from multiple cameras. Nonetheless, increasing the quantity of cameras in the system would render it expensive and challenging to monitor problems.

DISCUSSION

The implementation of machine learning for automatic fabric defect identification has transformed quality control in the textile industry, as it is significantly faster, more consistent, and more scalable than manual inspection for faults. Current methodologies utilize deep learning models, including Convolutional Neural Networks (CNN) and object identification frameworks, such as YOLO or Faster R-CNN, to identify defects such as holes, stains, and broken threads. Traditional methods rely on manually designed feature extractors, whereas deep learning autonomously extracts features, facilitating identification across diverse textures and patterns. The primary concerns are the requirements for high-quality labeled data, computational expenses, and the ability to adapt to new fabric kinds. Transfer learning, edge computing, and hybrid models are emerging developments that facilitate real-time, cost-effective defect identification in industrial environments.

RESULTS

Hyperparameter modifications were implemented for the activation function, utilizing several combinations that encompassed the number of hidden layers, dropout probability, regularization, and learning rate. The optimal learning rate was selected when validation accuracy reached its peak. The batch size was modified for various combinations of the other hyperparameters while maintaining the optimal learning rate constant. The identical method was performed while modifying the other hyperparameters. An iterative process was conducted every 10 epochs on separate parameters in succession to identify the value that yields the maximum validation accuracy. Upon completing the training of our custom CNN, we utilized the test dataset to provide class predictions, following the presentation of training and validation loss and accuracy. This illustrated the training and validation loss for the sigmoid activation function. Fig. (**2**) illustrates the plots of loss and accuracy against epochs during the training of the optimal model. Fig. (**3**) illustrates the Confusion Matrix & Fig. (**4**) illustrates the accuracy of the proposed model.

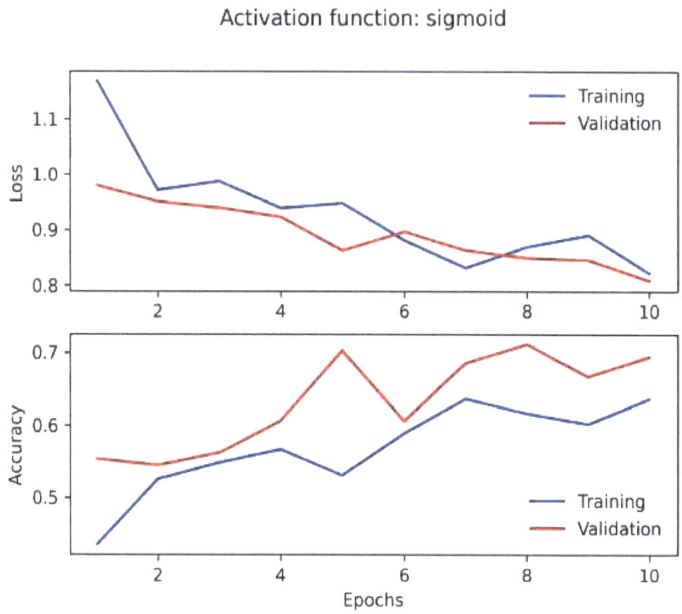

Fig. (2). Plots of loss and accuracy vs. epochs during the training of the best model.

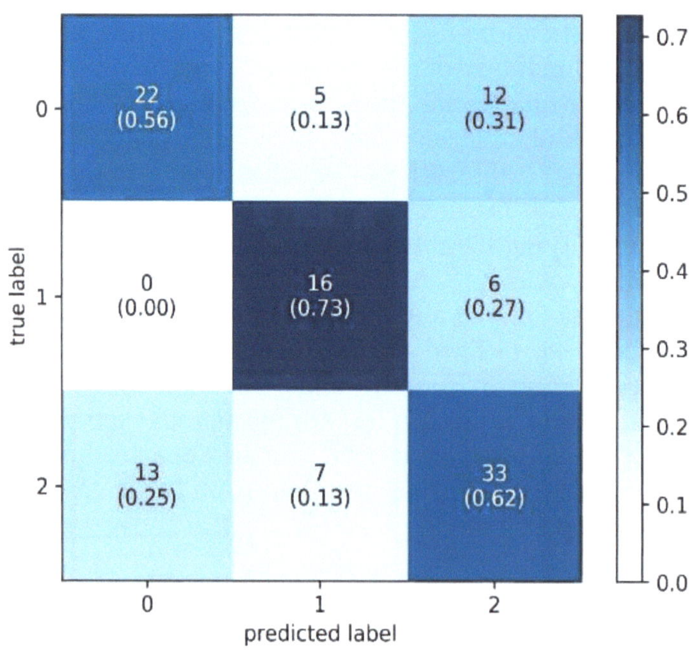

Fig. (3). Confusion matrix.

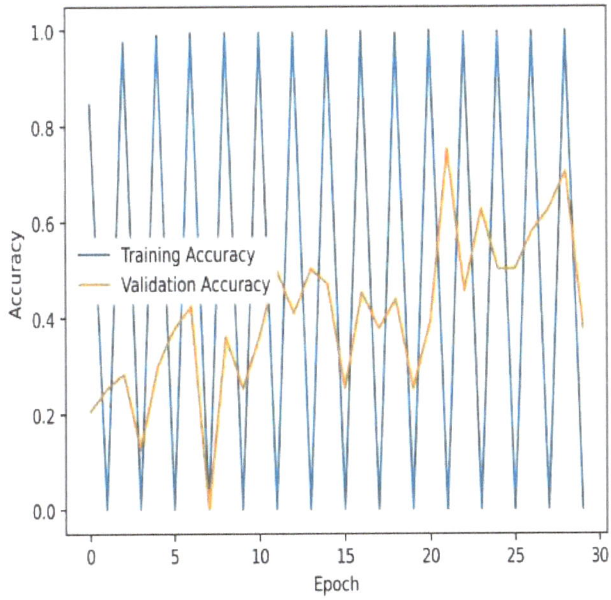

Fig. (4). Achieved accuracy.

CONCLUSION

This research introduces a system that employs an algorithm capable of precisely detecting faults in colored materials. The identification of flaws in colored textiles is demonstrated by deep learning-based convolutional neural networks to differentiate among diverse defects, including stains, holes, and absent yarns. The aforementioned section delineates experimental results utilizing diverse algorithms. The trained model demonstrates precision and yields dependable outcomes. The deployment of an automated visual inspection system for identifying faults in fabric is complex. Many previously established defect detection algorithms in this domain necessitate program adjustments to accurately identify errors when a new texture is introduced into the process. A real-time FDDS is implemented on a Texas Instruments DSP kit, utilizing input from a fabric sample. The characteristics of defect detection were evaluated utilizing the MATLAB environment. The software is entirely automated and involves no manual intervention once initiated. Based on the results, utilizing the energy feature is optimal for accurately identifying faults in the fabric texture.

REFERENCES

[1] B. Ali, H. Cheraghi Bidsorkhi, A.G. D'Aloia, M. Laracca, and M.S. Sarto, "Wearable graphene-based fabric electrodes for enhanced and long-term biosignal detection", *Sens. Actuators Rep.*, vol. 5, p. 100161, 2023.
[http://dx.doi.org/10.1016/j.snr.2023.100161]

[2] A. Rasheed, B. Zafar, A. Rasheed, N. Ali, M. Sajid, S.H. Dar, U. Habib, T. Shehryar, and M.T. Mahmood, "Fabric Defect Detection Using Computer Vision Techniques: A Comprehensive Review", *Math. Probl. Eng.,* vol. 2020, no. 1, pp. 1-24, 2020.
[http://dx.doi.org/10.1155/2020/8189403]

[3] J. Silvestre-Blanes, T. Albero-Albero, I. Miralles, R. Pérez-Llorens, and J. Moreno, "A Public Fabric Database for Defect Detection Methods and Results", *AUTEX Res. J.,* vol. 19, no. 4, pp. 363-374, 2019.
[http://dx.doi.org/10.2478/aut-2019-0035]

[4] A. Beljadid, A. Tannouche, and A. Balouki, "Automatic fabric defect detection employing deep learning", *Int. J. Electr. Comput. Eng.,* vol. 12, no. 4, pp. 4129-4136, 2022.
[http://dx.doi.org/10.11591/ijece.v12i4.pp4129-4136]

[5] K. Adhikary, and A. Kumar, "Feature Extraction and Classification Technique in Neural Network", *Int. J. Comput. Appl.,* vol. 35, no. 3, pp. 29-35, 2011.
[http://dx.doi.org/10.5120/4383-6070]

[6] R. Stojanovic, P. Mitropulos, C. Koulamas, Y. Karayiannis, S. Koubias, and G. Papadopoulos, "Real-time vision-based system for textile fabric inspection", *Real-Time Imaging,* vol. 7, no. 6, pp. 507-518, 2001.
[http://dx.doi.org/10.1006/rtim.2001.0231]

[7] M.F. Talu, K. Hanbay, and M. Hatamï Varjovï, "CNN-Based Fabric Defect Detection System on Loom Fabric Inspection", *Tekst. Konfeks. Derg.,* vol. 32, no. 3, pp. 208-219, 2022.
[http://dx.doi.org/10.32710/tekstilvekonfeksiyon.1032529]

[8] P.R. Jeyaraj, and E.R. Samuel Nadar, "Computer vision for automatic detection and classification of fabric defect employing deep learning algorithm", *Int. J. Cloth. Sci. Technol.,* vol. 31, no. 4, pp. 510-521, 2019.
[http://dx.doi.org/10.1108/IJCST-11-2018-0135]

[9] L. Liu, Z. Ma, M. Zhu, L. Liu, J. Dai, Y. Shi, J. Gao, T. Dinh, T. Nguyen, L-C. Tang, and P. Song, "Superhydrophobic self-extinguishing cotton fabrics for electromagnetic interference shielding and human motion detection", *J. Mater. Sci. Technol.,* vol. 132, pp. 59-68, 2023.
[http://dx.doi.org/10.1016/j.jmst.2022.05.036]

[10] A. Şeker, "Evaluation of Fabric Defect Detection Based on Transfer Learning with Pre-trained AlexNet", *2018 International Conference on Artificial Intelligence and Data Processing, IDAP 2018,* 2019.
[http://dx.doi.org/10.1109/IDAP.2018.8620888]

[11] W. Ji, D. Wu, W. Tang, X. Xi, Y. Su, X. Guo, and R. Liu, "Carbonized silk fabric-based flexible organic electrochemical transistors for highly sensitive and selective dopamine detection", *Sens. Actuators B Chem.,* vol. 304, p. 127414, 2020.
[http://dx.doi.org/10.1016/j.snb.2019.127414]

[12] W. Zhiyang, "A Fast Monochromatic Fabric Defect Fast Detection Method Based on Convolutional Neural Network", *J. Comput.-Aided Des. Comput. Graph,* vol. 30, no. 12, pp. 2262-2270, 2018.
[http://dx.doi.org/10.3724/SP.J.1089.2018.17173]

[13] W. Ouyang, B. Xu, J. Hou, and X. Yuan, "Fabric Defect Detection Using Activation Layer Embedded Convolutional Neural Network", *IEEE Access,* vol. 7, pp. 70130-70140, 2019.
[http://dx.doi.org/10.1109/ACCESS.2019.2913620]

[14] K. Hanbay, M.F. Talu, and Ö.F. Özgüven, "Fabric defect detection systems and methods—A systematic literature review", *Optik (Stuttg.),* vol. 127, no. 24, pp. 11960-11973, 2016.
[http://dx.doi.org/10.1016/j.ijleo.2016.09.110]

[15] L. Weninger, M. Kopaczka, and D. Merhof, "Defect detection in plain weave fabrics by yarn tracking and fully convolutional networks", *I2MTC 2018 - 2018 IEEE International Instrumentation and*

Measurement Technology Conference: Discovering New Horizons in Instrumentation and Measurement, Proceedings, pp. 1-6, 2018. [http://dx.doi.org/10.1109/I2MTC.2018.8409546]

[16] L. Liu, P. Fieguth, Y. Guo, X. Wang, and M. Pietikäinen, "Local binary features for texture classification: Taxonomy and experimental study", *Pattern Recognit.,* vol. 62, pp. 135-160, 2017. [http://dx.doi.org/10.1016/j.patcog.2016.08.032]

[17] V.T. Hoang, and A. Rebhi, "On comparing color spaces for fabric defect classification based on local binary patterns", *2018 IEEE 3rd International Conference on Signal and Image Processing, ICSIP 2018,* pp. 297-300, 2018. [http://dx.doi.org/10.1109/SIPROCESS.2018.8600419]

[18] Bodin, "Improving network approaches to the study of complex social–ecological interdependencies", *Nature Sustainability,* vol. 2, no. 7, pp. 551-559, 2019. [http://dx.doi.org/10.1038/s41893-019-0308-0]

[19] F. Pereira, V. Carvalho, F. Soares, R. Vasconcelos, and J. Machado, "Computer vision techniques for detecting yarn defects", In: W.K. Wong (Ed.), *Applications of Computer Vision in Fashion and Textiles,* no. Jan, pp. 123-145, 2018. [http://dx.doi.org/10.1016/B978-0-08-101217-8.00006-3]

[20] W. Wei, D. Deng, L. Zeng, and C. Zhang, "Real-time implementation of fabric defect detection based on variational automatic encoder with structure similarity", *J. Real-Time Image Process.,* vol. 18, no. 3, pp. 807-823, 2021. [http://dx.doi.org/10.1007/s11554-020-01023-5]

CHAPTER 2

Revolutionizing Learning: The Role of AI in Modern Education

Nandkishor M. Sawai[1,*], **Om Prakash Yadav**[2] and **Chandrmani Yadav**[3]

[1] *Department of Mechanical Engineering, Sandip Institute of Technology and Research Centre, Nashik, Maharashtra, India*

[2] *Department of Electrical Engineering, Sandip Institute of Technology and Research Centre, Nashik, Maharashtra, India*

[3] *Department of Mechanical Engineering, Faculty of Engineering & Technology, Marwadi University Research Center, Marwadi University, Rajkot, Gujarat, India*

Abstract: Artificial intelligence is revolutionizing education by enhancing learning results, accessibility, and engagement. AI is changing education by fostering diversity, streamlining administrative tasks, and enabling individualized learning. AI-powered tools that simplify complex subjects and provide individualized learning include virtual reality, adaptive learning platforms, and intelligent tutoring systems. This chapter explores the applications, benefits, challenges, and ethical quandaries of artificial intelligence as it relates to education. It investigates how teaching strategies in educational institutions are impacted by care ethics. These methods have been found to improve accuracy, efficiency, and resource allocation. Teachers may spend more time discussing concepts and communicating with students because administrative automation reduces administrative burden. Additionally, with the help of AI-supported simulation, students can practice technologies, evaluate ideas, and work through issues in a dynamic yet controlled setting. It imagines a future where artificial intelligence enhances human creativity and collaboration by looking at these opportunities and challenges, making education an inclusive, learner-centered, and lifelong experience.

Keywords: Artificial Intelligence, Virtual Reality, Digital Transformation, Lifelong Learning, Learning Analytics, Educational Equity.

INTRODUCTION

Artificial intelligence is transforming education by offering methods and technologies that enhance training, personalize learning, and make knowledge more accessible. AI can be applied to solve global problems, such as democratizing access to high-quality education, assisting children with disabi-

* **Corresponding author Nandkishor M. Sawai:** Department of Mechanical Engineering, Sandip Institute of Technology and Research Centre, Nashik, Maharashtra, India; E-mail: sawai.nm@gmail.com

Shilpa Gupta & Ritika Sharma (Eds.)

lities, and bridging the digital divide. Social constructivism, which emphasizes a student-centered approach to learning, is where the ethics of care can be found. This allows teachers to engage pupils in learning in a reciprocal relationship. It looks at how normative ethics of care practices, which are portrayed in schools as culturally neutral, maintain social reproduction. It argues for a critical examination of how the teaching-learning relationship is shaped and constrained by the white ethics of care paradigm in education [1]. The paradigm is changing in favor of services that are driven by problem-solving and assessed by the attainment of favorable results. Examine key policy and reform statements, compare and contrast various approaches to the planning and provision of school psychology services, and assess issues with the conventional delivery system, the body of information, fundamental ideas, and methods that support psychological services that prioritize functional evaluation, problem-solving, and educational responsibility. The Best Practices in School Psychology theme was a paradigm shift. We were before because several states have successfully implemented system reform; research has shown that IQ is irrelevant in identifying students with high incidence disabilities, which make up 85–90% of all students with disabilities; It is learning more about effective academic and social/behavioral interventions; reputable reports and the government is increasingly supporting systems that use non-categorical eligibility and functional assessment [2]. The dynamics of embracing changes in the educational system, such as shifting toward digital solutions, adopting a new paradigm, and changing delivery methods, it is the online learning management system's difficulties, problems, obstacles, and success criteria. The degree is significant from the planning stage to the real deployment of the learning system in higher education. The commercial sector stepped up to provide learning continuity by offering basic, secondary, and higher education [3]. The ability of a teacher to impart knowledge in their field of expertise was the main criterion used to evaluate their excellence in previous pedagogies. The development of pedagogical capacity in educational institutions was of secondary importance. The majority of the time, "teaching strategies" referred to direct instruction. Technology has been used for content distribution in recent years, mostly to help students grasp the material that is required for their courses. A relevant education extends outside the classroom to contextualize the issues by the local communities and individuals as elements of the learning environment. With the advent of ICT and online learning, there is an abundance of possibilities for growth and a shift from basic classrooms to sophisticated virtual learning environments where students may work together at any time or location [4]. AI is computer software that simulates human intellect. It is composed of several algorithms, including reinforcement learning, machine learning, decision support systems, and deep learning. Models that reflect knowledge about the real world are created using these methods. Models are created in digital education to comprehend the subject being acquired (learning), assess the learner's understanding, and comprehend the teacher's expertise (teaching). AI is used to generate digital learning, as shown in Fig. (**1**). AI is made up of several algorithms, including DSS, ML, DL, and RL. The teaching, learning, and assessment process is supported by these algorithms in terms of feedback analysis, adaptive and personalized learning, learning analytics and knowledge distribution, and course assessment. In order to comprehend the function of AI in education from the standpoints of instruction, learning, and evaluation, six data analysis goals are outlined [5]. Table **1** lists the emphasis and study objectives in addition to the dataset mapping, which is shown in Fig. (**1**).

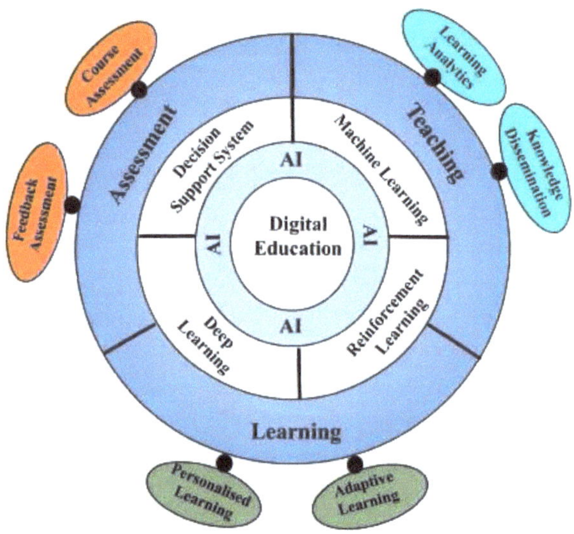

Fig. (1). Role of AI in education [5].

Table 1. Intelligence Assistance in Teaching, Learning, and Assessment [5].

Perspective	Focus	Study objective
Teaching	Learning analytics	To examine how various teaching philosophies affect students' arithmetic performance.
	Knowledge dissemination	To comprehend the reactions to various Udemy course levels.
Learning	Adaptive learning	To forecast exam results at the end of the semester.
	Personalized learning	To comprehend how test preparation affects students' performance.
Assessment	Feedback assessment	To comprehend how students behave online and how they are graded in advance of class.
	Course assessment	To use a virtual learning environment to forecast students' success in online courses.

It is emphasized by adaptive educational systems that every learner has a unique learning process. The particular educational strategy aims to incorporate the ability to identify each person's unique learning demands to guarantee that study materials and E-learning services are customized for adaptive learning [6]. Personalized and customized learning experiences are the primary benefit of adaptive learning for students. To optimize learning outcomes, algorithms for AIML might alter the tempo, content, and delivery techniques by examining each learner's unique learning preferences, strengths, and shortcomings. This individualized approach improves motivation, engagement, and retention of information, which eventually results in better academic achievement [7, 8]. As an adaptive learning platform, Smart Sparrow demonstrated a great deal of promise for motivating and involving students as well as enhancing their perceived knowledge and test scores. These are particularly significant results, particularly during the COVID-19 pandemic and in the post-COVID-19 era, as educational institutions move either permanently or temporarily away from in-person instruction to online learning in order to maintain social distance and adhere to guidelines and directives from the Health Authorities [9].

The last few years have seen a thriving field of artificial intelligence research due to intelligent teaching systems. In field studies, it has been shown that some of these systems significantly affect educational outcomes, such as motivation, asymptotic learning levels, and effective learning rate. As technology costs fall, we are just entering a period where intelligent tutoring systems may truly have an influence on the educational industry [10, 11]. A general introduction to Intelligent Tutoring Systems, a method of integrating Artificial Intelligence (AI) into education, is provided here. It presents ITSs and the reasons behind them. It examines its past: its progression from instruction aided by computers [12]. Test scores increased by 0.66 standard deviations over traditional levels, or from the 50th to the 75th percentile, as the median result of intelligent tutoring in the 50 assessments. However, whether change was measured on locally produced or standardized tests significantly influenced the amount of improvement discovered in an evaluation, indicating that test and instructional objectives alignment is a crucial factor in determining evaluation findings [13]. Based on the degree of granularity of the user interface interaction, the computer tutoring systems were divided into answer-based, step-based, and sub-step-based systems. Most intelligent tutoring systems have step-based or sub-step-based granularities of interaction, whereas most other tutoring systems have answer-based user interfaces. It is generally accepted that teaching becomes more successful as its level of detail diminishes [14]. Education is not an exception to the revolutionary period that artificial intelligence has brought about in a number of industries. AI offers creative ways to close gaps and rethink educational paradigms as conventional teaching and learning approaches struggle to satisfy the varied needs of contemporary students. AI is revolutionizing education by bringing forth greater accessibility, adaptability, and efficiency through a variety of methods, including personalized learning and intelligent teaching systems. The goal of this revolution is to rethink education in general, not only the use of technology in the classroom. AI has the potential to increase student investment, empower educators, and provide data-driven insights that inform instructional techniques. Beyond automation, artificial intelligence in education aims to create lifelong learners prepared for the challenges of the twenty-first century. The advantages, issues, and possible uses of AI in education are covered in detail in this chapter. Examining the real-world applications and recent advancements, we show that AI is more than just a tool; it is a force that is revolutionizing the world. This chapter explores a wide range of topics related to artificial intelligence in modern education, including its benefits, drawbacks, and possible uses. Examining the real-world applications and recent advancements, we show that AI is more than simply a tool; it is the force behind global educational change. Incorporating AI into contemporary education not only enhances the educational setting but also gives students the tools they will need in the future.

PERSONALIZED LEARNING: CUSTOMIZING EDUCATION FOR EACH LEARNER

In the era of technology, personalized education has emerged as a transformative approach that places the needs of the students at the heart of the learning process. Technology like artificial intelligence, big data, and flexible technology is used in personalized education to tailor instruction to the requirements, interests, and learning styles of each student. Acknowledging the uniqueness of every learner is the fundamental objective of individualized education. Traditional education is defined by this approach, which uses data insights to guide teachers, intelligent tutoring systems that adapt in real time, or AI-based suggestions for standard materials. It not only enhances academic performance but also promotes more involvement, self-motivation, and a passion for lifelong learning.

Adaptive Learning Environments

The rise of adaptive learning platforms is fundamentally altering how education is delivered by offering students individualized strategies to maximize their potential. These AI-supported systems assess preferences in learnt behavior, performance, and real-time to create personalized learning experiences that effectively adapt to each student's demands. With its one-size-fits-all approach, the Adoptive Learning Platform ensures that each student advances at their own pace and understands concepts before moving on to more difficult content.

Through interactive classrooms, personalized tests, or customized study plans, these platforms help make learning more engaging and successful. As illustrated in Fig. (**2**), adaptive learning environments dynamically adapt to learner profiles, content, tools, and ongoing evaluations to establish a feedback loop for continuous progress.

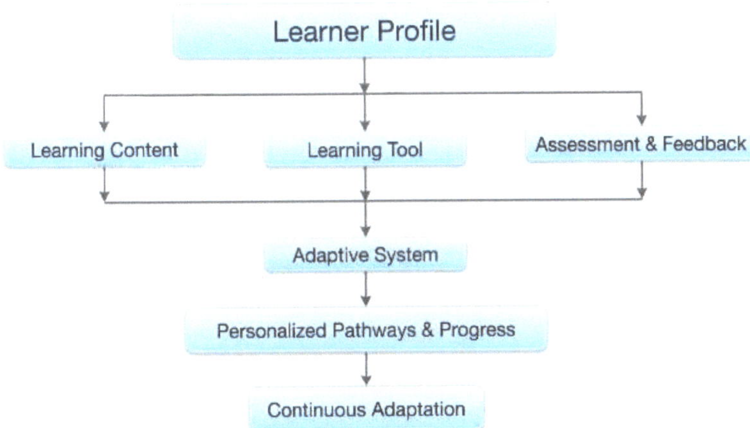

Fig. (2). Adaptive learning.

Intelligent Systems for Tutoring

Through the provision of individualized, one-on-one training that was previously only achievable with human tutors. These artificial intelligence-powered devices mimic a tutor, helping students understand difficult ideas, providing personalized feedback, and instantly adjusting to each student's needs. These kids are given the time and resources they require to succeed by Intelligent Tutoring Systems, which bridges the gap between specialized support and traditional classroom learning.

The ability of Intelligent Tutoring Systems to examine a student's learning habits, pinpoint problem areas, and modify education accordingly is at its core. These systems frequently use real-time feedback, natural language processing, and interactive problem solving to produce an interesting and productive learning environment. Intelligent Tutoring Systems increases access to high-quality education by offering scalable, affordable solutions, particularly for students in underserved or rural places. Fig. (**3**) illustrates the components of an intelligent tutoring system, emphasizing how student data, teaching models, and a knowledge base work together to deliver customized and flexible education. Overcoming Algorithmic Bias in AI-Powered Education Ensures Vitality and Disparity. Fairness Ware Machine Learning Restrictions Encourage Equitable Opportunities and Prevent AI from Increasing Prejudices. To ensure Equitable decision-making, biased training data is removed, biased outputs are corrected post-prostate, and algorithms are adjusted throughout processing. Transparency in AI systems, regular audits, and ethical norms all contribute to greater fairness. By implementing these systems, which provide equitable access to adaptive testing, intelligent tutoring, and tailored learning, artificial intelligence can be utilized to enhance education by lowering the likelihood of systemic prejudice and discrimination.

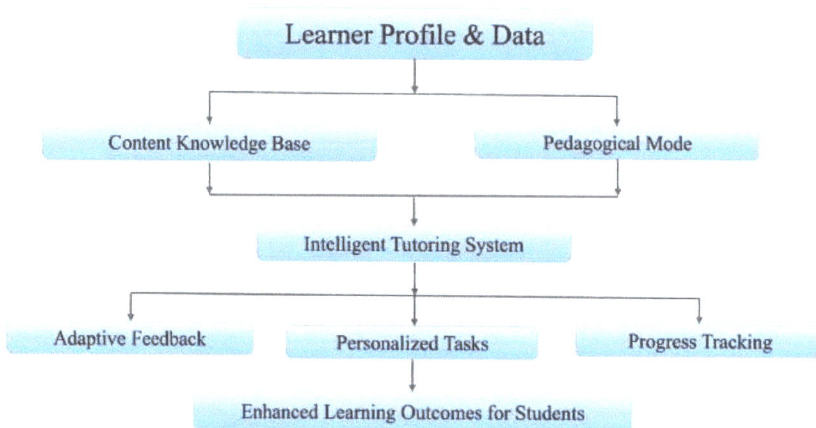

Fig. (3). Intelligent systems for tutoring.

REDEFINING THE ROLE OF THE TEACHER

The emergence of artificial intelligence in education has implications for both the function of instructors and how they learn. Since students are responsible for teaching, assessing, and guiding their educational path, teachers have traditionally been the most important individuals. Systems like material distribution, grading, and customization were made possible by AI. As a result of this acceptance, educators are no longer the sole providers of information, resources, and collaborators. Teachers' roles as the primary creators of educational experiences have changed, but their significance has not diminished. Emphasizing the human elements of social skills, emotional intelligence, critical thinking, and education has been made simpler by AI. By allowing AI to take care of time-consuming administrative duties, teachers may promote intellectual curiosity while also attending to thc needs of each individual student and devoting more time to personalized recommendations.

Automation in Administration

Administrative tasks like scheduling, grading, and recordkeeping have long been a burden and a common source of stress for educators and school administrators.

However, the administrative duty for the development of automation technologies and artificial intelligence rests with the educational institution. Their methods allow for better accuracy, efficiency, and resource allocation. Because administrative automation lessens the administrative strain, teachers may devote more time to student communication and ideas. AI-supported systems can automate time-consuming operations for instructors, administrators, and students, such as processing applications, keeping track of attendance, and grading coursework. The administrators' duties change from overseeing these administrative duties to creating courses that prioritize strategic planning and learning community assistance as the educational environment grows more automated.

AI-Powered Perspectives

In addition to transforming education, artificial intelligence is also enabling strong tools for data analysis and decision-making through its insights. Large volumes of student data, including behavioral trends, engagement patterns, and performance indicators, are used in these insights to find important patterns and trends that could otherwise go overlooked. With the aid of an AI assistant insight, educators, administrators, and legislators may increase organizational effectiveness, customize training, and improve educational outcomes by turning raw data into actionable intelligence. Based on real-time data, AI-powered tactics can evaluate the analytics system, identify children who are at risk, and offer a suitable remedy. This manifests as quick and concentrated attempts to improve instrumental technique, maximize resource utilization, and shorten the learning distance.

Development of Professionalism

The educational landscape is being altered by digital tools and artificial intelligence, but it is more crucial for educators to keep up their professional growth. By providing individualized, data-driven learning experiences that cater to each teacher's goals and requirements, AI-powered professional development programs are emerging as crucial resources for assisting educators in this process. AI-based systems may assess teachers' learning preferences, areas of strength, and areas for improvement, allowing them to offer individualized resources, courses, and interactive modules that support lifelong learning. AI may analyze progress over time, give educators insightful criticism, and suggest future actions to help them refine their approaches. This individualized strategy retains the meaningful, relevant, and accessible commercial development guarantee.

EXTENSION OF INCLUSION AND ACCESS

Students face challenges that traditional educational institutions cannot effectively handle, such as specific needs, regional barriers, and economic imbalance. Technology integration, especially artificial intelligence, is breaking down barriers and granting equal access to education for all. Through solutions like adaptive platforms that accommodate different educational processes, assistive technologies for students with disabilities, and linguistic support, artificial intelligence may strengthen educational consensus. Furthermore, because of online and remote learning platforms, no student in the disadvantaged and neglected areas will be denied access to high-quality education and instruction.

Translation of Languages

Language difficulties have long been a problem for educators, students, and increasingly involved multinational organizations. However, language translation is getting more precise, effective, and widely available as artificial intelligence develops quickly. Artificial intelligence is changing the field of AI-supported language translations by facilitating smooth communication across linguistic boundaries and providing information and experiences to a wide audience. By encouraging variety and eliminating linguistic barriers, this technology guarantees that language will never be an obstacle to education. Artificial intelligence improves verbal and written communication by providing pertinent translations through neural machine translation, such as a supported language translation tool. Furthermore, language translation technology promotes international collaboration, cross-cultural communication, and the preparation of students for a multicultural and globalized society.

The Use of Assistive Technologies

Auxiliary technology is a crucial instrument for supporting students who struggle and ensuring equal access to educational opportunities. The advancement of artificial intelligence, which offers a fresh method of assisting pupils with a range of learning needs, has accelerated the development of this technology. From AI-powered reading assistants and personalized education platforms to speech-to-text ups, assistant technologies are becoming more sophisticated, accessible, and effective to offer a full learning environment.

Artificial intelligence-powered auxiliary equipment assesses each person's unique style, adjusts to particular needs, and offers beneficial support to pupils who struggle with cognitive, sensory, or physical challenges. For instance, students with AI visual cognitive deficits can benefit from cognitive support from visual AIDS, which can also provide real-time speech recognition and education for students with auditory inadequacies. As illustrated in Fig. (**4**), assistive technologies are crucial in fulfilling a range of needs pertaining to education, mobility, and communication, thus advancing inclusivity and accessibility.

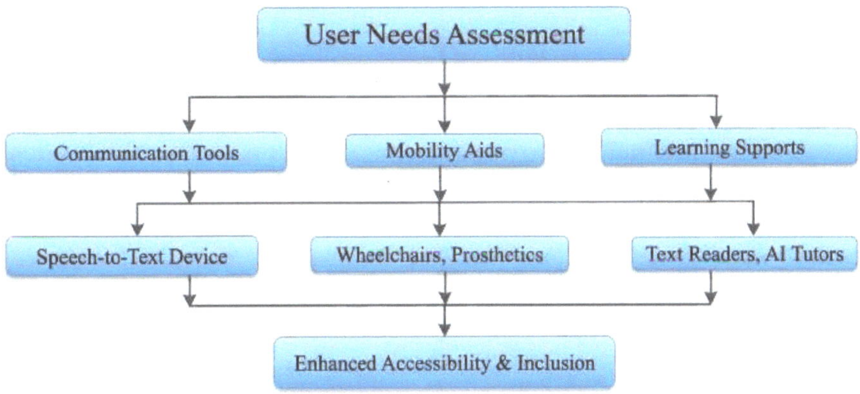

Fig. (4). The use of assistive technologies.

Economical Education

A significant barrier for many families and students worldwide is the rising expense of education, which has made tuition, textbooks, and other resources unaffordable for pupils. However, AI is playing a significant role in lowering the cost of education while offering innovative ways to do so without compromising the caliber of instruction attained. Because AI can automate administrative tasks, streamline resource distribution, and provide scalable, personalized learning experiences, it is helping to lower the cost of education and increase access to it. Artificial intelligence can take the place of students' priceless textbooks and other learning materials, expanding access to high-quality education.

Research and inventions should be combined to provide a comprehensive grasp of AI developments in education. Improvements in AI-driven assessments, adaptive learning, and individualized tutoring have improved engagement and learning outcomes. Developments in Fairness Ware, Reinforcement Learning, and Dynamic Bayesian Networks by expanding systems, AI enhances intelligent tutoring systems. Explainable AI research ensures that educational decisions are transparent. AI-planted learns analytics and multimodal learning environments are two more emerging trends in personalized education. By incorporating these advancements, a forward-looking perspective of artificial intelligence's revolutionary significance in contentious education is offered, highlighting the most recent innovations.

EXPERIENTIAL AND IMMERSION LEARNING

When education is memorable, interesting, and relevant to everyday life, it is most effective. AI-driven simulation, virtual reality, augmented reality, and other cutting-edge technologies are used in immersive and empirical education methodologies to provide a dynamic and captivating learning environment. This approach surpasses traditional textbooks and lectures by giving students the opportunity to engage with the virtual world, work through real-world issues, and get valuable but controlled practical experience. Fosters thorough assessment and long-term memory, which is followed by taking virtual science experiments, gaining professional skills in the field of images, or touring historical locations.

The Use of Simulated Environments

Students can now change and adapt the learning process through the use of virtual reality, augmented reality, and artificial intelligence simulations of immersion technology. With the help of this AI-supported simulation, students can practice technologies, evaluate ideas, and work through issues in a dynamic yet controlled setting. It enables students to learn in ways that are not possible with traditional methods, such as analyzing historical events, conducting scientific experiments, or reenacting complex real-world scenarios. Artificial Intelligence Finding Simulation helps students explore and improve their comprehension in the virtual environment by giving them instant feedback and pre-made instructions. These environments allow students to experiment, make mistakes, and learn from them without the risks or constraints of the actual world in a variety of subjects, such as history, engineering, medicine, and the arts.

Learning through Gaming

Gamification makes students' innate motivations more lively and enjoyable by appealing to their sense of dominance and achievement through the use of student stimulation, challenges, competitions, and artistic gaming. This change has been made possible by a variety of artificial intelligence technologies, which allow for the development of gaming experiences that are customized to the tastes and needs of certain students. Artificial intelligence-powered gaming learning platforms can assess students in real time based on their performance, as well as on the material, rewards, and level of difficulty. In addition to providing students with entertainment, this leads to a more engaging and personalized learning environment where they are continuously challenged and supported. In addition to introducing sports like leaderboards, medals, and attributes, gaming learning motivates students to complete their studies and collaborate with their peers.

CHALLENGES AND ETHICAL CONSIDERATIONS

Education is becoming more digital and data-driven, which is raising concerns about privacy, racism, access inequities, and artificial intelligence. The risk of student data being misused is a major concern, and the AI system makes data, privacy, and security even more vulnerable. Furthermore, by giving somc learning groups unfair opportunities, AI applications that power algorithms may inadvertently perpetuate discrimination. A further ethical conundrum is balancing automated and human communication.

Data Security

A huge quantity of data from vulnerable children is integrated, saved, and assessed because schooling uses digital tools and increasingly sophisticated artificial intelligence. This data includes everything from personal information to behavioral patterns and academic performance. Although there is a desire to improve academic achievement and personalize training, there are serious privacy and security concerns with this data. Protecting private student data from abuse, illegal access, and violations has become a top responsibility for educational institutions, digital companies, and others.

AI-supported systems can identify data management mistakes despite their fluctuating capabilities. Data breaches, unlawful data sharing, and misuse of third-party information pose a threat to students' safety and reputation. Furthermore, the absence of precise laws and regulations pertaining to the privacy of data in education has made these issues worse by leaving individuals and organizations unsure of their rights and obligations.

Algorithm Bias

Artificial intelligence has the potential to transform both the academic experience and outcomes of modern education. The AI system may still be impacted by bias, and students in particular demographic groups may experience unfair outcomes. Defective assumptions, unpleasant training data, or institutional injustice can all pose a severe threat to the algorithm's partisanship in terms of inclusion and impairment in schooling. These preconceptions have the power to worsen rather than to increase the existing distance if left unchecked.

In the academic AI system, prejudice can manifest itself in a variety of ways, such as unfair access to educational resources, inaccurate representations of students, or unintentional bias based on socioeconomic, gender, or racial characteristics. These biased AI-supported teaching tools harm the efficiency and legality, in addition to harming particular pupils. The development, implementation, and assessment of the AI system must be done to minimize, minimize, and avoid these problems.

In AI-Powered Education, Overcoming Algorithmic Bias Ensures Vitality and Disparity. Learning outcomes may differ when debasing strategies like rewiring and divorce dataset creation are used. Fairness Ware Limitations in Machine Learning Promote Fair Opportunities and Stop AI from Strengthening Prejudices. Biased outputs are rectified post-prostate, biased training data is draped, and algorithms are modified during processing to guarantee Equitable decision-making. More fairness is facilitated by ethical standards, frequent audits, and transparency in AI systems. Artificial intelligence can be used to improve education by reducing the possibility of systemic prejudice and discrimination through the implementation of these systems, which offer fair access to adaptive testing, intelligent tutoring, and customized learning.

The Digital Divide

Digital partitions, or the gap between those who have access to modern technology and those who do not, are a significant barrier to educational equality in the era of artificial intelligence. Even if AI-enabled solutions have the potential to completely transform educational outcomes and experiences, they run the risk of widening the already existent disparity in dependable internet connectivity and unequal access. Students in low-income, rural, or disadvantaged environments often lack access to personalized, innovative, and scalable artificial intelligence solutions.

Addressing digital divides calls for a multifaceted approach that takes into account infrastructure expenses as well as equal and consensus policies. Closing this gap not only ensures that all students have access to digital resources and AI devices but also fosters a more equitable learning environment where kids from all socioeconomic backgrounds may thrive.

ARTIFICIAL INTELLIGENCE IN EDUCATION'S FUTURE

As artificial intelligence continues to advance, its impact on education is anticipated to surpass all prior projections. From virtual teachers and immersion simulations to personalized adaptive learning systems, artificial intelligence has the potential to fundamentally alter how, where, and what. This revolutionary technology anticipates the requirements of future students in addition to addressing present issues, empowering them to thrive in an increasingly interconnected and complex environment.

In the future of education, it will offer more possibilities than just new technologies. It perfectly captures the ambiance of an educational setting where accessibility, customization, and involvement are at their highest levels. With growing complexity, AI will propose a standard approach to estimating learning outcomes, assessing intricate student performance patterns, and developing a more effective and rational learning environment. In response to the ever-evolving needs of workers, AI is anticipated to support lifelong learning, assisting individuals in retraining and skilling.

LIFELONG EDUCATION

The idea of lifelong learning is less significant than the speed and rapid change of today's world. Professionals from many industries must continuously adjust to changing circumstances, learn new skills, and continue creating trends to remain competitive in their field. Artificial intelligence plays a significant role in this shift by enabling customization, requiring distinct learning methods, and professional goals. Platforms with AI support ensure that users may access relevant and useful content at any point in their careers through personalized training, skill assessments, and dynamic resources.

AI encourages lifelong learning by identifying skill gaps, identifying each learner's unique learning habits, and developing a customized skill development path. With this technology, students can receive fast feedback and ideas while moving at their own pace, thanks to real-time adaptation. Artificial intelligence allows professionals to relearn skills with the efficiency, elasticity, and flexibility of previously learned abilities through certification programs, virtual simulations, or micro-learning modules.

Worldwide Collaboration

In an increasingly interconnected society, international collaboration is more crucial in education. Artificial intelligence is removing barriers based on geography and culture by developing a cross-border learning platform that connects professionals, educators, and students worldwide. These AI-powered platforms foster multicultural, varied learning environments where individuals may collaborate on projects, share ideas, and cope with different methods, all of which improve students' educational experiences.

AI facilitates global collaboration by offering flexible teaching resources that accommodate online meetings, several educational systems, linguistic and cultural requirements, and real-time translation capabilities. These platforms not only improve cross-cultural understanding but also prepare students for the global workforce. Through international skill-sharing networks, global research initiatives, and shared virtual courses, AI-supported education provides the chance to engage with people from diverse backgrounds and specialists, enhancing their educational and social capabilities.

Emerging Innovations

Innovative concepts that have the potential to fundamentally alter teaching, learning, and information evaluation approaches are emerging as a result of advanced technology integration in education. Blockchains and quantum computing are two of them that are upending schooling. The credentials are being converted by the blockchain, which can safely record and validate the data and the administration of educational records. Meanwhile, quantum computing can handle complicated educational modeling. The course provides unconnected insights into learning patterns, resource optimization, and building.

By ensuring the legitimacy of educational diplomas, their transparency, and their portability, blockchain technology eradicates fraud and improves the verification process for both students and institutions. It allows people to display their duty globally and allows credentials to be stored in a safe, decentralized manner for lifetime education. Though it is still in its infancy, quantum computing promises enormous computational power that will enable it to solve optimization issues, replicate intricate educational systems, and enhance personalized education algorithms beyond current capabilities.

CONCLUSION

AI in education aims to empower individuals, not only to introduce new technology. The advantages of AI can be combined with the expertise of educators to produce an all-encompassing, adaptable, and forward-thinking educational ecosystem. Since the advent of artificial intelligence in the classroom, learning and usage patterns have evolved. AI's demonstrated ability to empower teachers, improve accessibility, and personalize learning experiences has made traditional education more flexible, inclusive, and engaging. It is difficult to ignore the moral and useful questions these developments present. Ensuring that all students, regardless of their circumstances or backgrounds, benefit from AI requires careful consideration of data privacy, algorithm bias, and proper access. Looking to the future, artificial intelligence has immense potential in education. In addition to satisfying the needs of the modern world, educators and technologists can use this game-changing technology to develop a learning environment system that encourages creativity, curiosity, and critical thinking. Along with advancing technology, AI's potential to transform education presents a huge chance to empower future generations and build a society that is more informed and just.

REFERENCES

[1] B. MacGill, "A paradigm shift in education: pedagogy, standpoint and ethics of care", *International Journal of Pedagogies and Learning,* vol. 11, no. 3, pp. 238-247, 2016. [http://dx.doi.org/10.1080/22040552.2016.1272531]

[2] D. J. Reschly, and J. E. Ysseldyke, "Paradigm shift: The past is not the future",

[3] A. Maqsood, J. Abbas, G. Rehman, and R. Mubeen, "The paradigm shift for educational system continuance in the advent of COVID-19 pandemic: Mental health challenges and reflections", *Current Research in Behavioral Sciences,* vol. 2, p. 100011, 2021.

[4] P.D. Khedkar, and P. Nair, "Transformative pedagogy: A paradigm shift in higher education", In: *Proceedings of Third International Conference on Multidisciplinary Research & Practice*, 2016, pp. 332-337.

[5] A.K. Janardhanan, K. Rajamohan, K.S. Manu, and S. Rangasamy, "Digital education for a resilient new normal using artificial intelligence—applications, challenges, and way forward", In: *Digital Teaching, Learning and Assessment* Chandos Publishing, 2023, pp. 21-44.

[6] K. Colchester, H. Hagras, D. Alghazzawi, and G. Aldabbagh, "A survey of artificial intelligence techniques employed for adaptive educational systems within e-learning platforms", *J. Artif. Intell. Soft Comput. Res.,* vol. 7, no. 1, pp. 47-64, 2017. [http://dx.doi.org/10.1515/jaiscr-2017-0004]

[7] I. Gligorea, M. Cioca, R. Oancea, A.T. Gorski, H. Gorski, and P. Tudorache, "Adaptive learning using artificial intelligence in e-learning: A literature review", *Educ. Sci. (Basel),* vol. 13, no. 12, p. 1216, 2023. [http://dx.doi.org/10.3390/educsci13121216]

[8] D. Tsolis, S. Stamou, P. Christia, S. Kampana, T. Rapakoulia, M. Skouta, and A. Tsakalidis, "An adaptive and personalized open source e-learning platform", *Procedia Soc. Behav. Sci.,* vol. 9, pp. 38-43, 2010. [http://dx.doi.org/10.1016/j.sbspro.2010.12.112]

[9] M. Yakin, and K. Linden, "Adaptive e□learning platforms can improve student performance and engagement in dental education", *J. Dent. Educ.,* vol. 85, no. 7, pp. 1309-1315, 2021. [http://dx.doi.org/10.1002/jdd.12609] [PMID: 33825184]

[10] M.G. Helander, Ed., *Handbook of human-computer interaction.* Elsevier, 2014.

[11] R. A. John, C. F. Boyle, and B. J. Reiser, "Intelligent Tutoring Systems", *Computer,* vol. 3, no. 4, .

[12] H. Nwana, "Intelligent tutoring systems: an overview", *Artif. Intell. Rev.,* vol. 4, no. 4, pp. 251-277, 1990. [http://dx.doi.org/10.1007/BF00168958]

[13] J.A. Kulik, and J.D. Fletcher, "Effectiveness of intelligent tutoring systems: a meta-analytic review", *Rev. Educ. Res.,* vol. 86, no. 1, pp. 42-78, 2016. [http://dx.doi.org/10.3102/0034654315581420]

[14] K.U.R.T. VanLEHN, "The relative effectiveness of human tutoring, intelligent tutoring systems, and other tutoring systems", *Educ. Psychol.,* vol. 46, no. 4, pp. 197-221, 2011. [http://dx.doi.org/10.1080/00461520.2011.611369]

CHAPTER 3

Heart Stroke Disease Prediction Using Metaheuristic Techniques of Machine Learning

Madhu Bala[1,*], **Pallavi Dey**[1], **Manjunath**[1] and **Sravanth**[1]

[1] *Department of Computer Science and Engineering, Lovely Professional University, Phagwara, Punjab, India*

Abstract: Heart disease remains one of the most prevalent causes of death worldwide, highlighting the critical need for early diagnosis and preventive measures. This chapter focuses on developing a heart stroke risk prediction system using machine learning-based models. A publicly accessible heart disease dataset that includes important health markers like age, sex, type of chest pain, resting blood pressure, cholesterol, fasting blood sugar, electrocardiogram readings, maximum heart rate, and other pertinent variables is used to train the algorithms. Several machine learning algorithms, including Random Forest, Logistic Regression, and SVM, were used to analyze the dataset that contained all of the patients' health-related data in order to determine which one best fit the data and could most effectively forecast risk. The study's main conclusion is that the Random Forest algorithm performs the best, as shown by important metrics including accuracy, precision, recall, and f1-score.

Keywords: Heart stroke disease, Logistic regression, SVM, cross-validation, Machine learning.

INTRODUCTION

One of the most serious consequences of cardiovascular illness, heart stroke, continues to be a major source of morbidity and death worldwide. Early detection of individuals at risk of heart stroke can significantly reduce the rate of severe health complications and fatalities. Clinical examinations based on a number of health markers, including age, blood pressure, cholesterol, and other cardiovascular variables, are traditionally used to determine the risk of stroke [1]. However, it is frequently challenging to reliably predict stroke using traditional approaches due to the complexity and variability of these clinical variables. With its capacity to evaluate vast datasets, find trends, and offer predictive insights, machine learning has become a potent instrument in the medical field in recent

* **Corresponding author Madhu Bala:** Department of Computer Science and Engineering, Lovely Professional University, Phagwara, Punjab, India; madhucse0105@gmail.com

Shilpa Gupta & Ritika Sharma (Eds.)

years [2]. These capabilities can be applied to the early detection and prevention of heart attacks. Heart stroke is hard to forecast because it's a complicated condition. The risk of stroke is influenced by a wide range of clinical factors, many of which are interrelated and vary significantly from patient to patient. The models that are now in use are either too basic or not sufficiently generalizable to other populations. Additionally, the need for an accurate, interpretable, and scalable model to predict heart stroke risk is critical for healthcare providers to make informed decisions and prioritize patients at high risk [3]. The complexity of analysing clinical data remains a significant hurdle in developing reliable prediction models, particularly in identifying which variables have the most predictive power [4].

According to WHO data, heart attacks or strokes account for four out of five fatalities, with one-third of those deaths occurring before the age of 70. According to another 2016 report, approximately 17.9 million individuals died that year, accounting for 31% of all deaths, with heart attacks and strokes accounting for 85% of these deaths. Factors that mostly increase the chance of a stroke or any heart disease in a person include blood pressure, blood sugar level, cholesterol level, obesity, lifestyle, and any blood flow abnormalities like thalassemia. Also, it can happen all of a sudden without any of these factors or symptoms.

Literature Review

Stroke is one of the leading causes of mortality across the globe, thereby requiring a critical need for accurate and early prediction systems. Machine learning algorithms, when combined with metaheuristic optimization algorithms, result in enhanced predictive accuracy, feature selection, and model generalizability in healthcare applications [5]. In 2019, several researchers demonstrated the effectiveness of various classifiers, such as SVM, logistic regression, decision trees, and random forest, on the UCI heart disease dataset. It was found that these models often face challenges in terms of feature redundancy and parameter tuning. Table **1** shows the various works along with the different methodologies used by researchers for the prediction of heart stroke.

METHODOLOGY

Dataset Description

This heart illness dataset, which includes details on the characteristics associated with cardiovascular health, was extracted from the UCI Machine Learning Repository for the purpose of studying and analyzing the prediction of heart stroke, typically for a classification job. The collection includes information on 14 distinct traits from 1500 individuals. Age, gender, kind of chest discomfort, cholesterol, fasting blood sugar, maximum heart rate attained, thalassemia, and other characteristics are included. In feature engineering, data is generated synthetically as the available dataset is only of 300 rows, and for better accuracy of the models, we needed a large dataset. Moreover, no real data is readily available, so we generated synthetic data. Scaling of data is done as a preprocessing step by applying normalization and an integrated mean cross-validation score.

Table 1. Methodologies used by various researchers for the prediction of heart stroke, along with the accuracies obtained.

S.No	Paper Title	Authors	Objective	Method Used	Parameter	Accuracy
1	Machine Learning Developments for Stroke Prediction: An Extensive Analysis [6]	F. Mohammed Arshad; K. Sharmila	To assess and contrast different machine learning models' performance in predicting strokes.	K-Nearest Neighbors (KNN), Random Forest, and Logistic Regression are the three main machine learning models.	Age, BMI, Hypertension, Heart Disease, Smoking Status, and Glucose Levels	Random Forest: 96.97%
2	A comparative analysis of machine learning methods for predicting heart attacks [1]	Sharmistha Bhattacharjee; Miraz Al Mamun; Partha Pratim Pandit; Fariha Tabassum; Fatema Tabassum Liza; Madhab Chandra Das	To identify the most accurate algorithm for predicting stroke risk.	Decision Tree, k-Nearest Neighbor	Depth, minimum samples split, Number of neighbors (k)	~85%-90%

(Table 1) cont.....

S.No	Paper Title	Authors	Objective	Method Used	Parameter	Accuracy
3	Evaluation of Machine Learning Methods' Performance in Stroke Prediction [7]	Md. Mahfujur Rahman; M Shamim Al Mamun; M Shamim Kaiser; Tamara Islam Meghla; Maria Sultana Keya; Minhaz Uddin Emon	To use machine learning methods based on health-related characteristics to suggest an early prediction model for stroke disorders.	Collected 5,110 patient records from hospitals in Bangladesh. Conducted data preprocessing (normalization, encoding, and dataset splitting). Applied ten algorithms and a weighted voting classifier.	Age, sex, heart disease, high blood pressure, marital status, type of job, type of home, BMI, average blood sugar, and smoking status.	Evaluation of Machine Learning Methods' Performance in Stroke Prediction
4	A Thorough Analysis of Machine-Learning Applications for Stroke Risk Identification and Prediction and Post-Stroke Outcomes [8]	Teopolina Nantinda; Attlee M Gamundani; Maria N Kanyama	To present a thorough analysis of machine learning applications used to forecast stroke risk and post-stroke outcomes.	Among the models examined were supervised learning techniques, including decision trees, logistic regression, and SVM.	Lifestyle factors, post-stroke parameters include physical recovery rates, cognitive function, and quality of life.	Decision trees and ensemble methods often performed well, with some studies reporting up to 92% accuracy in stroke prediction.
5	Machine Learning Analysis of an Uneven Stroke Prediction Dataset [9]	Atul Kumar Uttam	To evaluate and enhance the performance of machine learning models for stroke prediction using datasets that show class imbalance.	Techniques such as resampling methods (oversampling and undersampling) were employed to mitigate the effects of imbalance.	Key clinical factors	Some models achieve accuracies exceeding 90% after adjustment for class imbalance.
6	Machine Learning-Based Predictive Modeling for Stroke Risk Assessment [10]	Ayush Mishra, Gurmeet Saini, Vikas Thakur, Inderdeep Kaur, and Muskan Sharma	To enhance early detection and prevention strategies.	preprocessing steps (including data normalization and feature selection)	cholesterol, diabetes, and high blood pressure.	90%, suggesting that they could be useful in clinical evaluations of stroke risk.

(Table 1) cont.....

S.No	Paper Title	Authors	Objective	Method Used	Parameter	Accuracy
7	Using Machine Learning Methods to Predict Strokes in Patients [11]	W. Jaisingh, S.R. Sujithra, and R.K. Kavitha	To investigate and use various machine learning algorithms to forecast a patient's risk of stroke in order to develop a tool for early identification and healthcare prevention	The research involved collecting a dataset from medical records, preprocessing the data (including cleaning and normalization)	clinical indicators	SVM 92-95%
8	Detection of Brain Stroke Using Machine Learning Algorithm [12]	E Sujatha; Monica D K	To create a machine learning-based model that uses a variety of health markers to accurately detect brain strokes and help with prompt medical interventions.	Artificial Neural Networks (ANN), Random Forest, and Support Vector Machines (SVM).	To ensure a thorough evaluation of the models' prediction skills, metrics such as accuracy, precision, recall, F1-score, and AUC were used to gauge their performance.	Metrics like as accuracy, precision, recall, F1-score, and AUC were used to measure the models' performance and provide a thorough evaluation of their predictive power.

(Table 1) cont.....

S.No	Paper Title	Authors	Objective	Method Used	Parameter	Accuracy
9	Enhancing the Prediction of Cardiovascular Disease: Machine Learning and Cross-Fold Validation [13]	N. Komal Kumar; A. Kalyan Kumar; G. Thorani; L. Sahithi; P. Pujitha	To use robust validation methods and machine learning algorithms to enhance the predictive performance of models for cardiovascular disease.	The models were evaluated based on their accuracy, precision, recall, F1-score, and AUC, and cross-fold validation was implemented to ensure reliability and mitigate overfitting.	This study considered various algorithms, such as Logistic Regression, Decision Trees, Random Forest, Support Vector Machines (SVM), and others, and analyzed their performance in forecasting CVD.	The findings showed that the most accurate models were the Random Forest and SVM, which were both able to exceed 90% accuracy for reliably predicting the risks of cardiovascular disease.
10	Machine Learning Models Based on Grid-Search Optimization and Shapley Additive Explanations (SHAP) for Early Stroke Prediction [14]	Rabia Emhamed Al Mamlook; Fathia Lahwal; Najat Elgeberi; Muhammad Obeidat; Qais Al-Na'amneh; Ahmad Nasayreh	To propose an algorithm that utilizes grid-search optimization for hyperparameter tuning and SHAP for explainability of model predictions	This research consisted of gathering a dataset from stroke patients, performing the necessary data preprocessing, conducting a grid-search for model parameter optimization, and interpreting model outputs with SHAP.	The predictive power of several machine learning techniques, such as Random Forest, Support Vector Machines (SVM), Gradient Boosting, and Logistic Regression, was assessed.	The results demonstrated the advantages of grid-search and SHAP in enhancing model reliability and interpretability, showing that the optimized models attained high accuracy rates, with Random Forest and Gradient Boosting performing especially well.

(Table 1) cont.....

S.No	Paper Title	Authors	Objective	Method Used	Parameter	Accuracy
11	eXplainable AI Makes It Possible to Forecast Upper Limb Rehabilitation Results for Patients with Subacute Strokes [15]	Rudy Gasparin Pavan; Federica Cruciani; Nicola Valè; Alessandro Picelli; Marialuisa Gandolfi; Ilaria Boscolo Galazzo	To predict rehabilitation results for sub-acute stroke patients' upper limb recovery using explainable AI approaches, offering insights into factors influencing recovery.	Their predictive performance was examined while looking at the use of machine learning explainability techniques like SHAP (Shapley Additive Explanations). A variety of algorithms were employed alongside the predictive performance, and Shapley was explained and used for interpretation in the models.	Along with the other metrics, effectiveness was measured by accuracy, precision, recall, F1-score, and some value in the clarity of results based on XAI.	Providing both high accuracy and valuable insights into patient recovery processes.
12	A Combination Artificial Intelligence Method for Predicting Strokes Early [16]	Irnatene Dahbia, Chouiref Zahira, and Lacene Belinda.	To develop a hybrid artificial intelligence model that enhances the prediction accuracy for early detection of stroke, aiming to assist in timely medical intervention.	To improve prediction performance, a variety of machine learning and artificial intelligence approaches are used, such as ensemble methods or neural networks.	Metrics like accuracy, sensitivity, specificity, and perhaps AUC-ROC are used to evaluate model performance, allowing for a thorough assessment of prediction efficacy.	The results indicate that the hybrid model outperforms conventional techniques in early stroke prediction, highlighting the advantages of integrating several AI techniques for medical diagnostics.

(Table 1) cont.....

S.No	Paper Title	Authors	Objective	Method Used	Parameter	Accuracy
13	Using Recurrent Neural Networks and Optimization Techniques to Predict Stroke Disease [17]	Moatamad Refaat Hassan, Ali Mohamed Hussien, Hager Saleh, and Abdelmgcid A. Ali	To develop a predictive model using RNNs optimized with advanced techniques to accurately predict stroke occurrences based on patient data.	The research employs RNN architectures, likely combined with optimization algorithms such as genetic algorithms or particle swarm optimization, to improve the model's training and performance.	The study examines various clinical features, which may include demographic data, medical history, and specific health metrics relevant to stroke risk assessment.	accuracy improvements in stroke prediction compared to conventional methods,
14	Improvement of Machine Learning Algorithms' Performance on Heart Stroke Prediction Applications by the Use of Sampling and Feature Selection Methods [4]	Sree Harrsha Singara, Naga Sreeharsha Reddy Ambati, Syam Sukesh Konjeti, and Selvi C	To predict heart stroke using an unbalanced dataset from Kaggle, enhancing prediction accuracy through comparative analyses of resampling techniques and feature selection methods across various machine learning algorithms.	Data Preprocessing: Filling missing values (e.g., using mean for BMI), converting categorical data to numerical format.. - Feature Selection Methods: Information Gain, Fisher Score, Exhaustive FS, etc..	With an emphasis on improving their performance through data preprocessing, a variety of machine learning algorithms are examined, including but not limited to logistic regression, decision trees, Support Vector Machines (SVM), and ensemble methods.	the highest accuracy of 97.9%

(Table 1) cont.....

S.No	Paper Title	Authors	Objective	Method Used	Parameter	Accuracy
15	Predicting Atrial Fibrillation Attacks using a Semi-supervised Algorithm Using Convolution Auto-encoder of Time Series Data [18]	Dakun Lai, Peirong Zheng, and Yuchen Jiang	To combine convolutional autoencoder (CAE) and Long Short-Term Memory (LSTM) models to create a new two-stage semi-supervised prediction approach for Paroxysmal Atrial Fibrillation (PAF).	**Stage 1**: Unsupervised learning with CAE to compress and reconstruct RR interval time series. -**Stage 2**: Supervised learning using LSTM for classification based on encoded features.	Ten ECG records from the AFDB and NSRDB were used for testing, together with 20 PAF segments and 20 normal heart rates from the AFPDB.	Ten-fold cross-validation was used to achieve 0.004 root mean square error and 93.56% average accuracy; the F1 score was 0.9345.
16	Optimizing Neural Network Performance to Predict Coronary Heart Stroke Disease	Azat Kabdullin; Maxat Kabdullin; Lyazat Naizabayeva	The study utilizes various optimization techniques, such as hyperparameter tuning and regularization methods, to improve the neural network's training process and overall predictive capabilities.	The research likely focuses on several neural network architectures and optimizers (e.g., Adam, SGD) to determine which model configuration is best for coronary heart disease prediction.	Key clinical parameters may include age, gender, cholesterol levels, blood pressure, smoking status, and family history of heart disease. These factors contribute to assessing an individual's risk for CHD.	Use the area under the ROC curve (AUC) to assess how well the suggested prediction model works.

(Table 1) cont.....

S.No	Paper Title	Authors	Objective	Method Used	Parameter	Accuracy
17	Learning vector quantization for the extraction of tiny strokes in videos [19]	Mauridhi Hery Purnomo, Surya Sumpeno, and Aviv Yuniar Rahman	To develop a method for automatically detecting minor strokes in video sequences, which could aid in early diagnosis and treatment by providing timely alerts to healthcare providers.	The study employs Learning Vector Quantization (LVQ), a supervised machine learning algorithm, to analyze video data and classify occurrences of minor strokes based on predefined features.	Video data likely includes clinical recordings or publicly available datasets that contain examples of minor strokes, possibly annotated for training the model.	The findings may demonstrate the ability of the LVQ-based approach to accurately detect and extract instances of minor strokes from video, contributing to advancements in stroke monitoring and prevention strategies.
18	A voting system for machine learning based on ensemble learning for the prediction of chronic diseases [20]	Soualihou Ngnamsie Njimbouom; Jeong-Dong Kim; Candra Zonyfar; Hyun Lee; Taek Lee; Jung-Been Lee	To improve chronic disease prediction accuracy by developing an ensemble classifier (ELVot-CroDiP) that utilizes multiple machine learning algorithms through a majority voting mechanism.	- Ensemble Learning - Various ML algorithms (RF, DT, Extra Trees, LR, AdaBoost, SVM, XGBT) - Grid Search for hyperparameter tuning - Voting mechanism (majority voting)	health repositories, containing relevant health metrics and patient data.	90% worked effectively

(Table 1) cont.....

S.No	Paper Title	Authors	Objective	Method Used	Parameter	Accuracy
19	HypGB: Using LASSO FS and the HyperOpt HPO Framework, a High Accuracy GB Classifier for Heart Disease Prediction [21]	Method Abbas Jafar; Myungho Lee	To use the LASSO feature selection and a gradient boosting classifier supplemented with hyperparameter optimization (HyperOpt) to create a high-accuracy predictive model for heart disease.	The approach utilizes the Gradient Boosting algorithm, employing HyperOpt for hyperparameter tuning to achieve better model performance. LASSO (Least Absolute Shrinkage and Selection Operator) is used for feature selection to enhance model interpretability and reduce overfitting.	The accuracy, precision, recall, and F1-score are among the measures used to assess the model's performance.	Demonstrating the effectiveness of hyperparameter tuning and feature selection in heart disease prediction.
<u>20</u>	Multiple Parallel U-Nets and a Pixel-Level Classifier for Predicting Ischemic Stroke Lesion in CT Perfusion Scans [22]	Russell Greiner, Pierre Boulanger, Brian Buck, and Mohsen Soltanpour	The primary goal is to use a pixel-level classification method in conjunction with several parallel U-Net architectures to predict ischemic stroke lesions in CT perfusion scans.	The study utilizes U-Net models, which are effective for biomedical image segmentation. The approach involves training several U-Net models in parallel and subsequently employing a pixel-level classifier to refine lesion predictions.	The dataset consists of CT perfusion scans from stroke patients, which are used to train and validate the U-Net models and pixel-level classifier.	Reliability of ischemic stroke lesion predictions compared to traditional methods,

(Table 1) cont.....

S.No	Paper Title	Authors	Objective	Method Used	Parameter	Accuracy
21	LP Analysis for Tabla Stroke Onset Detection [23]	K.Sri Rama Murty and R Gowriprasad.	Suggest an onset detection method for tabla strokes that overcomes the difficulties caused by the resonance properties of the instrument and increases accuracy.	Analysis of Linear Predictions (LP); Hilbert Envelope (HE); onset detectors based on energy and spectrum flux; and onset detectors based on machine learning (HELP method)	F-measure for evaluation of detection accuracy.	When compared to the performance on raw tabla signals, the HELP-based method demonstrated a 12% relative improvement in F-measures.

Machine Learning Models

Different professions are using machine learning models for a variety of tasks, such as clustering and classification. The dataset's properties influence the model selection. Three supervised machine learning models—logistic regression, random forest, and SVM—are used in this work to determine the accuracy of the heart stroke.

Logistic Regression

The main use of this supervised machine learning approach is binary classification. By estimating the probabilities using the logistic function and predicting the likelihood of one outcome based on the other, this technique uses two attributes of the data to determine their relationship. Because of its ease of interpretation, this method is mostly useful in domains like as the social sciences, healthcare, and finance.

Random Forest

This supervised machine learning approach is mostly employed for regression and classification tasks. Because it generates several decision trees while training the dataset, this approach is often referred to as a random decision forest. Random Forest generates distinct decision trees during training by selecting data points and characteristics at random. Based on the input data, each tree generates its own predictions. Random Forest is less likely to overfit than individual decision trees because, once all the trees have been trained, the algorithm aggregates their outputs to produce a single final tree. This approach's capacity to handle huge datasets makes it popular in industries like banking, e-commerce, and stock trading.

Support Vector Machine (SVM)

Classification and outlier detection issues are addressed by this supervised machine learning method, which can be adjusted for regression. It operates by identifying a line that best divides the various classes in the data and crosses the mean of the classes. It is a popular option for categorizing emails, photos, and even medical data because it can clearly distinguish between different classifications (shown in Fig. **1**).

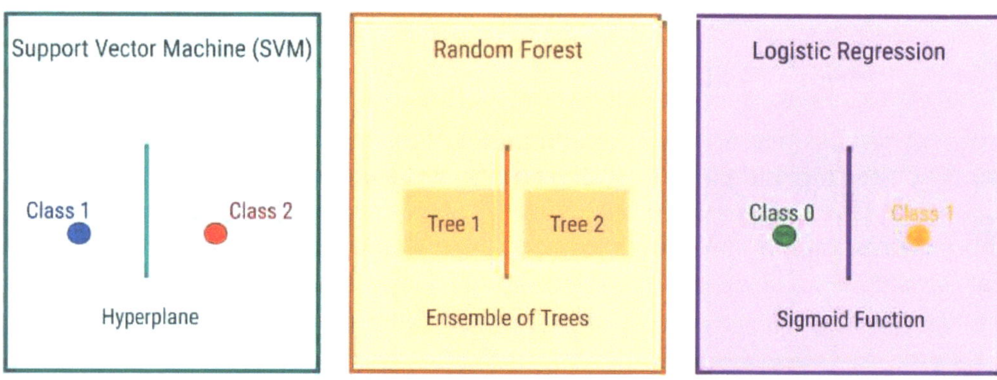

Fig. (1). The operation of the SVM, Random Forest, and Logistic Regression algorithms.

Model Evaluation

In healthcare, predicting heart attacks is a crucial task, and how effectively we assess machine learning models' performance determines how effective they are. This section examines the accuracy, precision, recall, F1-score, AUC-ROC, and validation methods, including train-test split and cross-validation are the main metrics used to evaluate these models.

Evaluation Parameters

The current study uses a number of crucial measures to assess how well our models work:

- Accuracy: Accuracy is equal to the sum of the accurate positive predictions and the imprecise negative predictions divided by the total number of predictions.
- Precision: Precision is calculated by dividing the number of accurate positive predictions by the number of imprecise positive predictions. It is the proportion of real positive cases to true positive expectations.
- F1-Score: The F1-score offers a fair assessment of the model's performance by providing a harmonic mean of precision and recall:
  F1= 2×(Precision×Recall)/(Precision+Recall).
- ROC: At different threshold settings, the ROC curve shows the true positive rate versus the false positive rate.

Validation Strategies

To ensure the models are reliable and accurate, this study uses various strategies: Splitting the dataset into two sections—one for training the model and the other for testing its performance, which is known as the "train-test split."

- Cross-validation: Dividing the dataset into subsets improves the model evaluation. This process is repeated several times, with the model being trained on some folds and validated on others.
- K-Fold Cross-Validation: K equal portions of the dataset are separated. Every time the model is trained, a different fold is used for validation.
- K-Fold stratified: This version is especially useful for datasets that are unbalanced since it guarantees that each fold has a comparable distribution of classes.

This study evaluated the performance of the machine learning models using 5-fold cross-validation (Fig. **2**) to guarantee a strong assessment of the prediction models. Each of the five equal sections of the dataset was utilized as a validation set, while the other four sections were used for training. This procedure was carried out five times, enabling one validation use for each subset.

RESULTS

Five-fold cross-validation was used to assess the heart stroke prediction models' outcomes. Accuracy, precision, recall, F1-score, and ROC are among the performance indicators. Random Forest, Support Vector Machine (SVM), and Logistic Regression are among the models evaluated in this study. Table **2** highlights the average performance metrics derived from the 5-fold cross-validation.

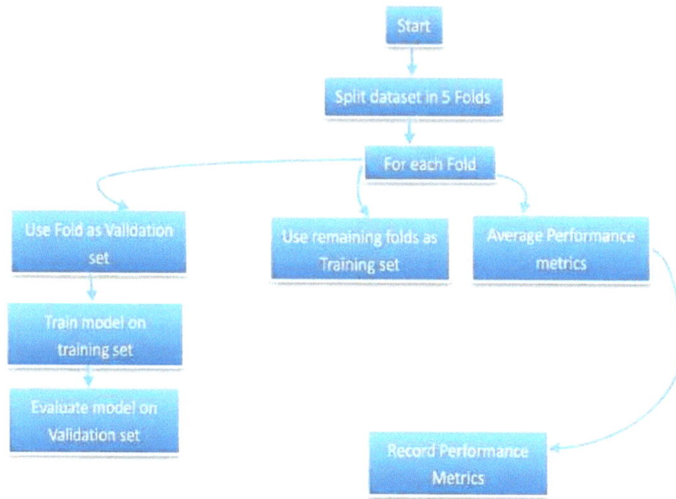

Fig. (2). Applying the 5-fold cross-validation method to the provided dataset.

Table 2. Performance indicators from the 5-fold cross-validation.

Model	Accuracy	Precision	Recall	F1 -Score	Cross-Validation
Random Forest Method	1.00	1.00	1.00	1.00	0.99
Support Vector Machine	1.00	0.96	1.00	0.98	0.92
Logistic Regression	0.96	1.00	00.50	0.95	0.94

Confusion matrices were created in order to assess each model's performance in more detail. • The true positive, true negative, false positive, and false negative rates are all revealed by these matrices. Fig. (**3**) demonstrates the confusion matrix of Random Forest.

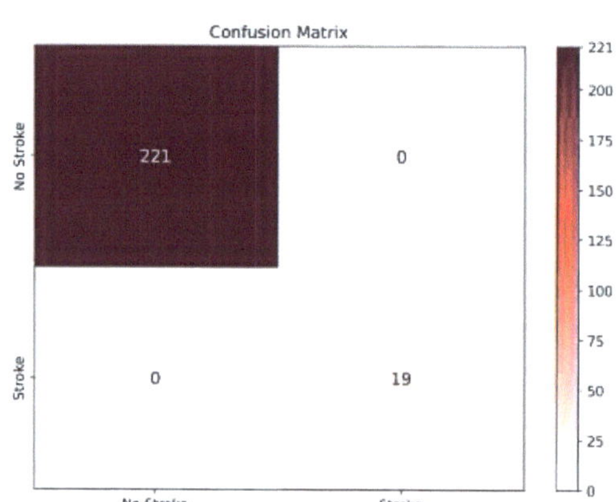

Fig. (3). Confusion matrix of random forest.

- True Negatives: 221 cases had the accurate prediction of "no stroke."
- True Positives: 19 cases had the accurate prediction of "stroke."
- FN stands for False Negatives, where 0 cases were mispredicted as "no stroke."
- False Positives: nothing was mislabeled as a "stroke."

The logistic regression confusion matrix is shown in Fig. (**4**). 275 cases of True Negatives (TN) were accurately forecasted as "no stroke." In terms of True Positives (TP), 24 cases were accurately identified as "stroke." False Negatives (FN): One case was misdiagnosed as "no stroke." FP (False Positives): 0 cases were misclassified as "stroke."

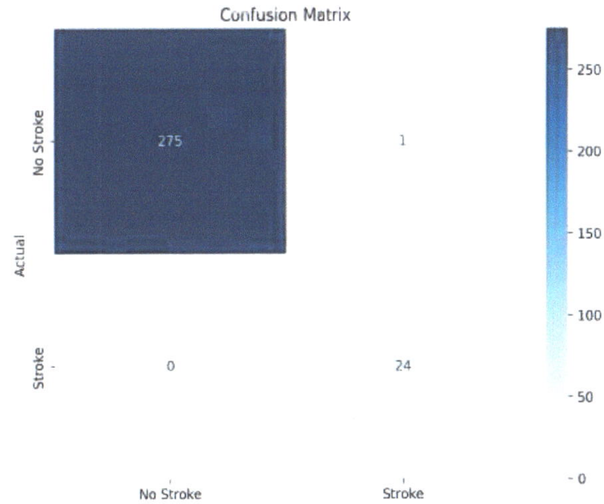

Fig. (4). Confusion matrix of Logistic regression.

Fig. (**5**) shows the SVM's confusion matrix. There were 276 True Negatives (TN) that were accurately predicted to be "no stroke." In terms of True Positives (TP), 12 cases were accurately identified as "stroke." False Negatives (FN): zero cases were misdiagnosed as "no stroke." False Positives (FP): Twelve cases were mislabelled as "stroke."

The receiver operating characteristic curve is used to evaluate the performance of a classification model. It was determined that the area under the ROC curve (AUC) was 0.99 (Fig. **6**), which is exceptionally well, and indicates that the model is able to differentiate between stroke and non-stroke cases well.

The Random Forest model performed flawlessly on every metric, including an F1-score of 1.00, accuracy, precision, and recall of 100%. Its robustness and dependability in predicting cardiac strokes are demonstrated by its cross-validation score of 0.99. With a 100% accuracy rate, the SVM likewise showed excellent performance. Recall was flawless at 100%, although precision was marginally worse at 96%. With an F1-score of 0.98, precision and recall are well-balanced. Although it shows a little more unpredictability than the Random Forest, the cross-validation score of 0.92 indicates good generalization. In the case of logistic regression, the accuracy of 96% was marginally worse. Even while it had 100% flawless precision, its recall was noticeably lower at 50%, suggesting that it might have missed a substantial portion of positive cases. Good dependability is indicated by a cross-validation score of 0.94, while an F1-score of 0.95 implies reasonable performance overall. While the SVM also demonstrated impressive results, the Random Forest model outperformed the others overall, and the recall of Logistic Regression was noticeably weak.

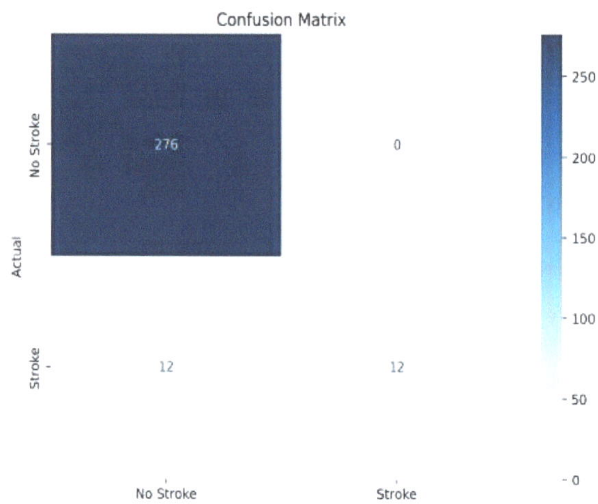

Fig. (5). Confusion matrix of SVM.

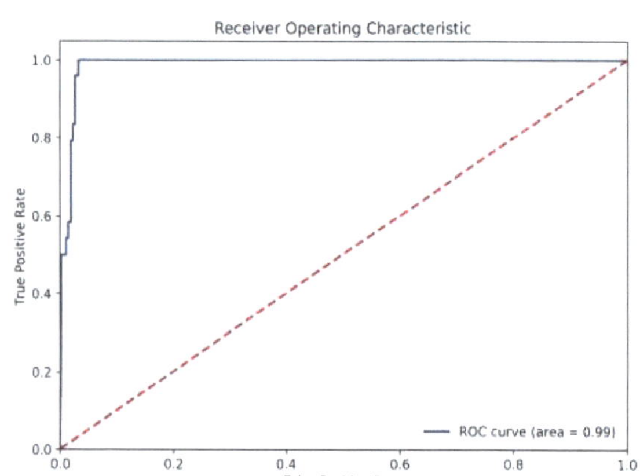

Fig. (6). Receiver operating characteristics curve.

CONCLUSION

The study is focused on the implementation of various classification models for the prediction of heart stroke diseases. Support vector machine, logistic regression, and random forest are the models that are used to evaluate the patient health on the UCI data set to identify the individuals who are at risk of stroke based on the number of clinical features. Among all the models implemented, the results show high classification accuracy in the case of logistic regression. The near-perfect ROC curve shows very low false positive and false negative rates, which is very important in healthcare applications where accurate detection can help in significantly improving the patient outcomes. Overall, the study underscores the potential of various classification machine learning algorithms to support clinical decision-making processes.

REFERENCES

[1] M.C. Das, "A comparative study of machine learning approaches for heart stroke prediction", *2023 International Conference on Smart Applications, Communications and Networking (SmartNets),* IEEE, pp. 1-6, 2023.
[http://dx.doi.org/10.1109/SmartNets58706.2023.10216049]

[2] E. Dritsas, and M. Trigka, "Stroke Risk Prediction with Machine Learning Techniques", *Sensors (Basel),* vol. 22, no. 13, p. 4670, 2022.
[http://dx.doi.org/10.3390/s22134670] [PMID: 35808172]

[3] I. Mishra, and S. Mohapatra, "An enhanced approach for analyzing the performance of heart stroke prediction with machine learning techniques", *Int. J. Inf. Technol.,* vol. 15, no. 6, pp. 3257-3270, 2023.
[http://dx.doi.org/10.1007/s41870-023-01321-8]

[4] N. S. R. Ambati, S. H. Singara, and S. S. Konjeti, "Performance Enhancement of Machine Learning Algorithms on Heart Stroke Prediction Application using Sampling and Feature Selection Techniques", *in 2022 International Conference on Augmented Intelligence and Sustainable Systems (ICAISS),* IEEE, pp. 488-495, 2022.
[http://dx.doi.org/10.1109/ICAISS55157.2022.10011040]

[5] M. Bala, and S.K. Bansal, "Investigating a Spectrum of Machine Learning Methods for Leaf Disease Detection in Pepper, Potato, and Tomato", *ECS J. Solid State Sci. Technol.,* vol. 13, no. 10, p. 107003, 2024.
[http://dx.doi.org/10.1149/2162-8777/ad83f2]

[6] F.M. Arshad, and K. Sharmila, "Advances in Machine Learning for Stroke Prediction: A Comprehensive Review", *in 2024 8th International Conference on I-SMAC (IoT in Social, Mobile, Analytics and Cloud) (I-SMAC),* IEEE, pp. 1798-1802, 2024.
[http://dx.doi.org/10.1109/I-SMAC61858.2024.10714900]

[7] M. U. Emon, M. S. Keya, T. I. Meghla, Md. M. Rahman, M. S. Al Mamun, and M. S. Kaiser, "Performance Analysis of Machine Learning Approaches in Stroke Prediction," *in 2020 4th International Conference on Electronics, Communication and Aerospace Technology (ICECA),* IEEE, Nov. 2020, pp. 1464–1469.
[http://dx.doi.org/10.1109/ICECA49313.2020.9297525]

[8] T. Nantinda, A.M. Gamundani, and M.N. Kanyama, "Machine-Learning Application for Detection and Prediction of Stroke Risk and Post-Stroke Outcomes: A Comprehensive Review", *2024 International Conference on Artificial Intelligence, Big Data, Computing and Data Communication Systems (icABCD),* IEEE, pp. 1-9, 2024.

[http://dx.doi.org/10.1109/icABCD62167.2024.10645285]

[9] A.K. Uttam, "Analysis of Uneven Stroke Prediction Dataset using Machine Learning", *6th International Conference on Intelligent Computing and Control Systems (ICICCS),* pp. 1209-1213, 2022.
[http://dx.doi.org/10.1109/ICICCS53718.2022.9788309]

[10] M. Sharma, I. Kaur, G. Saini, V. Thakur, and A. Mishra, "Predictive Modeling for Stroke Risk Assessment Using Machine Learning", *International Conference on Intelligent Systems for Cybersecurity (ISCS),* pp. 1-6, 2024.
[http://dx.doi.org/10.1109/ISCS61804.2024.10581155]

[11] R.K. Kavitha, W. Jaisingh, and S.R. Sujithra, "Applying Machine Learning Techniques for Stroke Prediction in Patients", *2021 International Conference on Advancements in Electrical, Electronics, Communication, Computing and Automation (ICAECA),* IEEE, pp. 1-4, 2021.
[http://dx.doi.org/10.1109/ICAECA52838.2021.9675652]

[12] R. Sujatha, J.M. Chatterjee, N.Z. Jhanjhi, and S.N. Brohi, "Performance of deep learning vs machine learning in plant leaf disease detection", *Microprocessors and Microsystems,* vol. 80, p. 103615, 2021.
[http://dx.doi.org/10.1016/j.micpro.2020.103615]

[13] N.K. Kumar, A. Kalyan Kumar, G. Thorani, L. Sahithi, and P. Pujitha, "Improving Cardiovascular Disease Prediction: Machine Learning and Cross-Fold Validation", *2024 IEEE International Conference on Interdisciplinary Approaches in Technology and Management for Social Innovation (IATMSI),* IEEE, pp. 1-6, 2024.
[http://dx.doi.org/10.1109/IATMSI60426.2024.10503072]

[14] R.E. Al Mamlook, "Machine Learning Models Based on Grid-Search Optimization and Shapley Additive Explanations (SHAP) for Early Stroke Prediction", *in 2024 4th Interdisciplinary Conference on Electrics and Computer (INTCEC),* IEEE, pp. 1-7, 2024.
[http://dx.doi.org/10.1109/INTCEC61833.2024.10602984]

[15] M. Gandolfi, I. Boscolo Galazzo, R. Gasparin Pavan, F. Cruciani, N. Vale, A. Picelli, S.F. Storti, N. Smania, and G. Menegaz, "eXplainable AI Allows Predicting Upper Limb Rehabilitation Outcomes in Sub-Acute Stroke Patients", *IEEE J. Biomed. Health Inform.,* vol. 27, no. 1, pp. 263-273, 2023.
[http://dx.doi.org/10.1109/JBHI.2022.3220179] [PMID: 36343005]

[16] L. Belinda, I. Dahbia, and C. Zahira, "A Hybrid Artificial Intelligence Approach for Early Stroke Prediction", *in 2023 5th International Conference on Pattern Analysis and Intelligent Systems (PAIS),* IEEE, pp. 1-8, 2023.
[http://dx.doi.org/10.1109/PAIS60821.2023.10322003]

[17] L.A. Gabralla, A.M. Hussien, A. AlMohimeed, H. Saleh, D.M. Alsekait, S. El-Sappagh, A.A. Ali, and M. Refaat Hassan, "Automated Diagnosis for Colon Cancer Diseases Using Stacking Transformer Models and Explainable Artificial Intelligence", *Diagnostics (Basel),* vol. 13, no. 18, p. 2939, 2023.
[http://dx.doi.org/10.3390/diagnostics13182939] [PMID: 37761306]

[18] Y. Jiang, P. Zheng, and D. Lai, "A Semi-supervised Algorithm for Atrial Fibrillation Attack Prediction Using Convolution Auto-encoder of Time Series Signal", *45th Annual International Conference of the IEEE Engineering in Medicine & Biology Society (EMBC),* IEEE, pp. 1-4, 2023.
[http://dx.doi.org/10.1109/EMBC40787.2023.10339988]

[19] M. Rajora, M. Rathod, and N.S. Naik, *Stroke Prediction Using Machine Learning in a Distributed Environment.*, 2021, pp. 238-252.
[http://dx.doi.org/10.1007/978-3-030-65621-8_15]

[20] S.N. Njimbouom, J-D. Kim, C. Zonyfar, H. Lee, T. Lee, and J-B. Lee, "An ensemble learning-based machine learning with voting mechanism for chronic disease prediction", *2024 International Conference on Artificial Intelligence, Computer, Data Sciences and Applications (ACDSA),* IEEE, pp. 1-6, 2024.
[http://dx.doi.org/10.1109/ACDSA59508.2024.10467844]

[21] A. Jafar, and M. Lee, "Enhancing Kidney Disease Diagnosis Using ACO-Based Feature Selection and Explainable AI Techniques", *Appl. Sci. (Basel),* vol. 15, no. 6, p. 2960, 2025. [http://dx.doi.org/10.3390/app15062960]

[22] M. Soltanpour, R. Greiner, P. Boulanger, and B. Buck, "Improvement of automatic ischemic stroke lesion segmentation in CT perfusion maps using a learned deep neural network", *Comput. Biol. Med.,* vol. 137, p. 104849, 2021. [http://dx.doi.org/10.1016/j.compbiomed.2021.104849] [PMID: 34530336]

[23] R. Gowriprasad, and K.S.R. Murty, "Onset detection of Tabla Strokes using LP Analysis", *2020 International Conference on Signal Processing and Communications (SPCOM),* IEEE, pp. 1-5, 2020. [http://dx.doi.org/10.1109/SPCOM50965.2020.9179587]

CHAPTER 4

AI-guided Agriculture Shaping the Future of Farming Practices

Om Prakash Yadav[1,*], **Nandkishor M. Sawai**[2] and **Nitin S. Patil**[1]

[1] *Department of Electrical Engineering, Sandip Institute of Technology and Research Centre, Nashik, Maharashtra, India*

[2] *Department of Mechanical Engineering, Sandip Institute of Technology and Research Centre, Nashik, Maharashtra, India*

Abstract: The agriculture industry is severe suffering due to climate variation, high investment, low returns, and manpower shortage. Furthermore, agricultural land is contracting due to rapid industrialization and urbanization. These challenges have affected the sustainable agricultural growth and raised a serious concern about food security for growing populations. Therefore, investing in innovative tools and techniques in agricultural practices has become a necessity to reduce farming costs, minimize labour dependency, optimize water needs in irrigation, and enhance crop yield. The learning capabilities of AI algorithms can significantly analyze historical patterns of environmental data to predict weather patterns and anticipate climate change impacts. The integration of IOT with AI technology provides valuable insights into soil quality, seed selection, irrigation scheduling, weed management, and pesticide use. AI-enabled farming robots and drones are improving the detection of weeds and crop diseases, and enabling precise pesticide application, thereby reducing farming costs and enhancing crop yields. Research has shown that AI-enabled robots and drones can enhance crop productivity by up to 30%. In this context, this chapter highlights the transformative role of AI in crop monitoring, irrigation management, yield prediction, disease and pest detection, weed control, and weather forecasting.

Keywords: AI algorithms, crop disease detection, pest detection, irrigation management, imaging robots, precision farming, weather forecasting, weed control.

INTRODUCTION

Agriculture is the backbone of the economy for many developing countries, providing food to over one billion people worldwide. In India, the agricultural sector itself employs nearly half of the population and contributes approximately

* **Corresponding author Om Prakash Yadav:** Department of Electrical Engineering, Sandip Institute of Technology and Research Centre, Nashik, Maharashtra, India; E-mail: opnit05@gmail.com

Shilpa Gupta & Ritika Sharma (Eds.)

18% to the national Gross Domestic Product (GDP) [1, 2]. Over the past decade, modern tools and technologies have been progressively adopted in agriculture to boost crop yields and meet growing global food demands. With the world population expected to touch ten billion by 2050, ensuring food security has become more critical than ever [3]. However, increasing crop yield is a complex challenge, mired by factors such as climate change, global warming, declining soil fertility, and unpredictable weather conditions [4, 5]. The integration of Artificial Intelligence (AI) with the Internet of Things (IoT) offers promising solutions to these challenges. AI-powered algorithms can analyze vast and complex agricultural datasets to support informed decision-making, helping farmers optimize resource utilization and enhance productivity [6]. Agriculture 4.0, which clamped cutting-edge technologies such as machine learning, deep learning, blockchain, and smart autonomous systems, is revolutionizing traditional farming practices [7, 8]. These innovations are paving the way for more efficient, sustainable, and resilient agricultural systems.

AI technology has emerged as a powerful data processing tool through Machine Learning (ML) algorithms such as Artificial Neural Networks (ANN) and Support Vector Machines (SVM), Deep Learning (DL), computer vision, chatbots, and Natural Language Processing (NLP) [9]. Advanced AI algorithms, such as generalized AI, have led to more accurate and effective weather forecasting, irrigation management, disease and pest detection, and yield prediction [10]. Generative AI algorithms process complex datasets collected from high-resolution imagery obtained through drones, robots, satellites, and field sensors to generate insightful solutions for farmers [11]. AI-powered robots are accurately performing manual tasks such as weeding, harvesting, and fruit picking, thus significantly reducing labour costs [12, 13]. Thus, innovative tools and computer technologies in farming systems have mitigated crop losses while ensuring sustainable agricultural practices [14, 15]. Research has shown that AI and IoT applications, along with drip-based irrigation systems, have improved water efficiency by up to 50% [16 - 18]. Ongoing research continues to focus on developing more versatile and reliable IoT-based irrigation systems to minimize water wastage.

Thus, the recent advancements in farming practices, utilizing the analytical and statistical potential of advanced AI algorithms, can further enhance crop productivity, promote sustainability in agriculture, and ensure food security for future generations. Thus, AI-powered solutions could help to improve agricultural yields and ultimately enhance farmers' income in countries like India, where most of the population is based on agriculture for their livelihood [19, 20]. By systematic solving the challenges in the agriculture sector with the power of AI-based innovations, it can switch from reactive solving to proactive and sustainable methods. In this context, this chapter presents a comprehensive overview of the progress and applications of AI in agriculture, along with the associated challenges and potential solutions.

INNOVATIONS IN PRECISION FARMING USING AI

Precision farming, utilizing the analytical and predictive solutions of AI and IoT applications, enhances agricultural practices and helps farmers shift from losses to profitability. Fig. (**1**) presents the extensive usage of AI technology across different sectors of agriculture. The figure shows that weather forecasting, smart irrigation, disease detection and pest management, weed detection, crop monitoring, and yield prediction are the key areas where AI is revolutionizing farm practices.

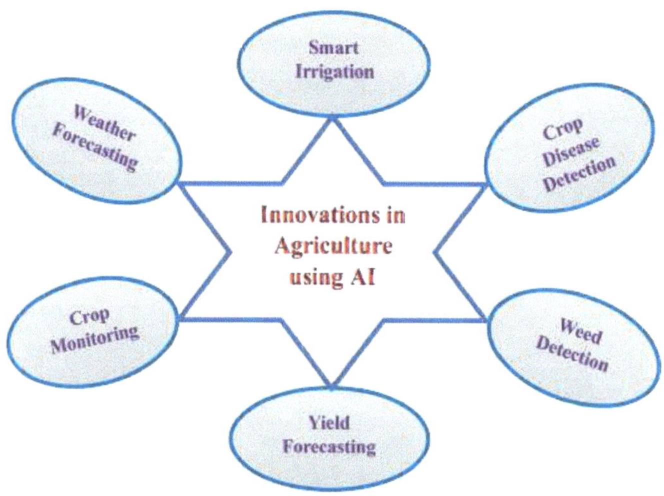

Fig. (1). Transformative AI applications across agricultural domains.

AI-DRIVEN CROP MONITORING

Drones and robots with high pixel cameras and AI enable decision-making capabilities, assist farmers in detecting crop health, soil quality, weather conditions, and eventually crop yield. Using multispectral and hyperspectral cameras, the drones take high-resolution aerial images that are analysed by AI algorithms to detect crop diseases, water stress, and pest infestations [11, 14]. Firms like Precision Hawk in the US use AI technology to give farmers actionable information that minimizes crop loss and reduces pesticide use. Fig. (**2**) illustrates a drone-based crop monitoring system developed by Zena Drones. It has a high-definition camera for capturing images, video, and data for smart surveillance solutions. All-Terrain Vehicles (ATVs) having multiple sensors and imaging technology offer ground-level information on crop health conditions. These autonomous vehicles and drones are assembled with advanced sensors to monitor field parameters like soil moisture, environment temperature, and nutrient levels of the crop [21]. These vehicles utilize machine learning algorithms to detect crop conditions like leaf colour, stress, and bugs, which helps in real-time crop disease diagnosis, helps farmers to make decisions on pesticides, and the requirement of irrigation [22].

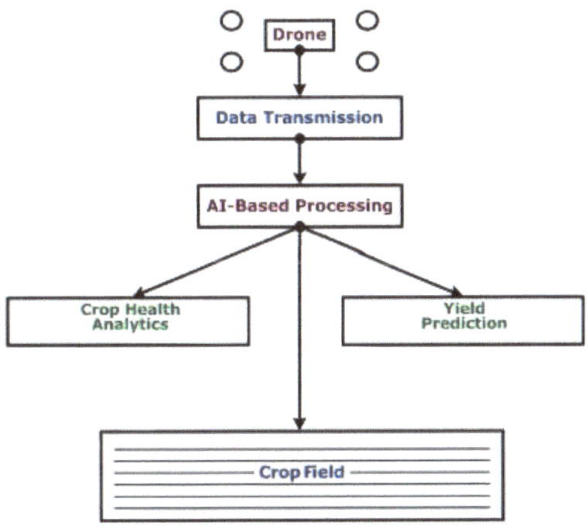

Fig. (2). Drone imaging system for crop monitoring [Source: Available from: https://www.zenadrone.com].

Using data from soil sensors, drones, and satellite imagery, an AI-based system evaluates critical soil parameters like humidity, pH level, and nutrients [16]. Data fusion methods combine information collected from multiple sources, sensors, and image analysis to provide a holistic picture of farm land health. Big data analysis and deep learning models operate on this complex dataset, extracting patterns, forecasting trends, and agricultural practices [11]. The Explainable AI (XAI) techniques, such as SHapley Additive Explanations (SHAP) and Local Interpretable Model-Agnostic Explanations (LIME), enhance the transparency of ML models. This transparency allows the model's learned farming patterns to be compared with the expertise of farmers and agronomists [20]. This helps in generating more trustworthy information about crop health and the growth of the crop. Trace Genomics uses AI to analyse soil samples, yielding in-depth reports on soil microbiomes and nutrient deficiencies. Similarly, tools like CropX merge sensor data and ML algorithms to forecast soil temperature and moisture, planning fertilization schedules and watering for to crop [18].

In India, the adoption of drone-based crop monitoring is advancing through initiatives of government schemes like the Sub-Mission on Agricultural Mechanization (SMAM). Collaborations with startups such as Fasal and Skymet provide smallholder farmers with affordable drone technology and predictive tools for informed decisions on irrigation, health and pest control, and fertilizer application. Under the SMAM scheme, financial support is provided by the Indian government for purchasing of drones. Institutions like ICAR, KVKs, and SAUs receive up to 100% assistance (up to Rs. 10 lakhs), while FPOs are granted 75% for demonstrations by the Indian government [23].

AI-POWERED SMART IRRIGATION SYSTEMS

For years, traditional methods of irrigation have supported agriculture with flood and surface irrigation, but bring inefficiencies in the form of over-irrigation, under-irrigation, soil erosion, and nutrient leaching. These add to costs, reduce yields, and make water scarcity even worse, considering that agriculture absorbs around 85% of the freshwater available in the world [11]. To meet these challenges, AI has been seen as the next big wave of change. It optimizes water management, boosts productivity by real-time analysis of data, and uses superior algorithms.

AI-based irrigation systems monitor key parameters like type of crop, weather conditions, soil humidity, and evapotranspiration rates to accurately determine aquatic requirements. It requires a humidity sensor placed near the plant root to detect real-time soil moisture [17]. This moisture information facilitates real-time decisions on irrigation, hence avoiding overwatering and increasing resource management. Microcontrollers like Arduino and Raspberry Pi process sensor data to control water pumps based on environmental and soil conditions, minimizing human intervention [18]. Drip and subsurface drip irrigation systems further enhanced efficiency by delivering water directly to roots, reducing evaporation and runoff. Subsurface systems, with buried pipelines, ensure targeted hydration and minimize surface water loss. Fig. (**3**) illustrates an AI-enabled IoT system for smart irrigation of farms. It analyses the weather forecast data with soil moisture, humidity, and environmental temperature to activate the irrigation pump system for the best watering of farms.

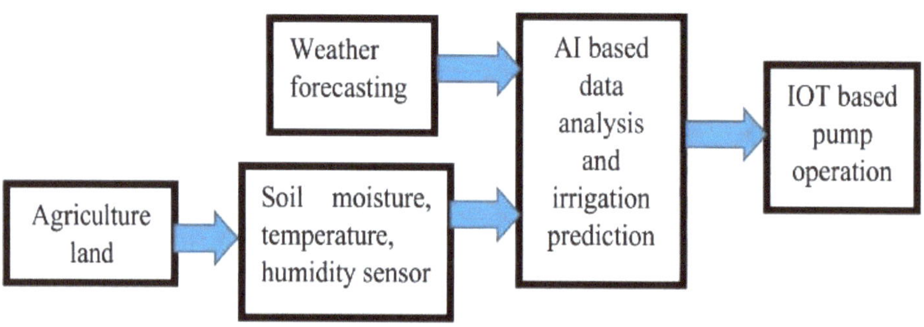

Fig. (3). Smart irrigation system using an artificial intelligence system.

AI-powered leak detection systems also emerged, monitoring water flow and pressure to identify and address leaks early, reducing wastage. Precision water management advanced further with AI and Internet of Things (IoT) integration. Techniques such as dielectric measurement measure soil moisture based on its dielectric constant. Neutron moderation measures water content at different depths by observing the interaction of neutrons with the water molecules. These techniques enable farmers to formulate specific irrigation plans that will prevent root rot and waterlogging [16]. Drones and ground-based sensors made irrigation a multi-dimensional technique. Drones are equipped with AI-powered imaging technologies that detect water stress or uneven irrigation across fields, while ground sensors provide localized monitoring [18].

In India, government initiatives, such as the "Per Drop More Crop" program under PMKSY, encourage the use of AI-driven irrigation technologies. Start-ups like DeHaat use AI and IoT to provide actionable insights on irrigation and nutrient management for farmers. It enables small-scale farmers to increase productivity while conserving resources. Studies indicate they could cut water consumption by as much as 40%, tackling two of the main challenges facing mankind: food growth and scarcity of water resources [24, 25].

YIELD FORECASTING USING AI

Crop yield prediction is an essential aspect of contemporary agriculture, from crop cultivation, resource allocation, and market strategy decisions. Improvements in artificial intelligence have drastically changed this aspect by providing methods for precise and efficient forecasting. AI algorithms such as ANN, SVM, and deep learning analyses vast datasets extracted from sensors to derive non-linear relationships among variables such as weather patterns, soil conditions, crop management practices, and historical yields [25]. This assists farmers in making predictive decisions on soil class-based seed selection, crop health and pest management, fertilizers, and irrigation, which ultimately enhances agriculture yield.

High-resolution multispectral data from satellites, with vegetation indices such as the Normalized Difference Vegetation Index (NDVI) and Enhanced Vegetation Index (EVI), help in assessing crop health, identifying stress, and estimating biomass. These indices act as a backbone for precise yield predictions, with real-time knowledge of crop conditions [26 - 28]. Remote sensing captures spectral reflectance, and indices like NDVI analyze vegetation health through near-infrared and visible light reflectance. In addition, AI supports market strategies by predicting optimal harvest times, thereby reducing post-harvest losses by up to 30% and improving overall harvest efficiency [29]. Case studies further validate the impact of AI in agriculture, for instance, platforms like CropIn in India and global tools such as Sentinel-2 facilitate yield forecasting and precision farming across diverse agro-climatic regions [17]. Despite its great potential, crop yield prediction through AI is plagued by challenges like limited accessibility of data, inconsistency in datasets, and scalability. These can only be overcome through the integration of diverse data sources, improving the transparency of the model, and validation AI tools in diverse contexts. Models that are transparent and interpretable will be the only way to establish trust among farmers and policymakers. The refinement of AI-driven tools and their practical utility will depend on collaborative efforts from agricultural scientists, data engineers, and policymakers.

ENHANCING PEST AND DISEASE MANAGEMENT

Artificial Intelligence in agriculture is ushering in the latest tools in pest and disease management, considered one of the biggest challenges faced by farmers today. With advanced technologies such as drones, multispectral imaging, predictive analytics, and precision spraying systems, farmers will be able to prevent threats beforehand, increase yields, and further promote sustainable agriculture [29, 30]. These technological advancements make better use of available resources, have less impact on the environment, and result in higher yields-the potential of artificial intelligence in agriculture. Unlike traditional satellite-based systems, which often fail in adverse weather conditions, drones provide high-resolution imagery regardless of environmental settings [31, 32]. Operating at altitudes of 400–500 feet, drones capture detailed field data, enabling the early detection of diseases, pest outbreaks, and nutrient deficiencies.

Multispectral imaging technology further enhances monitoring capabilities. Utilizing vegetation indices, such as NDVI, to identify stressed or infected areas, even before any symptoms can appear, is an added benefit in which the drone approach can prevent further losses on farmland [27]. As the literature presents, these technologies are also proven to evaluate crop biomass, nitrogen levels, and early-stage diseases, thereby bringing valuable information that could optimize yield and field management [33]. Collaborative efforts, such as predictive models developed with the Indian Council of Agricultural Research (ICAR), have successfully anticipated locust invasions, enabling timely preventive actions. Agritech platforms like CropIn and mobile applications like PlantVillage Nuru offer region-specific pest control advice and instant crop health diagnoses [34].

An AI-based decision support system integrates various sources of data, like satellite imagery, real-time sensors, and ground observations, to further advance integrated pest management strategies. The hybrid AI models are further enhancing disease detection and pest control. A hybrid model based on Convolutional Autoencoder (CAE) network and Convolutional Neural Network (CNN) used by the author to detect peach plant disease using leaf image with a prediction accuracy of approximate 99% [35]. These systems promote targeted interventions and reduce reliance on traditional, broad-spectrum pesticide applications. Precision spraying systems, for example, have been transformed with the advent of IoT capabilities and AI vision technologies [36, 37]. They are able to pinpoint areas that need to be treated with greater accuracy, reducing waste and cost, as well as the negative environmental impact. Deep learning algorithms optimize droplet distribution and ensure uniform and targeted chemical spraying by identifying crops and weeds. In India, products such as Plantix and AI-driven mobile apps make diagnostic tools more accessible to smallholder farmers, giving them near-instant disease identification. In Andhra Pradesh, drones with AI cameras are being tested for the detection of pests in cotton fields. Tools such as TartanSense's BrijBot, which reduces the use of pesticides by as much as 60%, illustrate how AI can help farmers increase sustainability while boosting profitability. AI-based technology further supports crop spatial mapping and disease monitoring from space using platforms such as Landsat imagery. It results in greater market prices of healthier crops that raise farmer income and livelihood. According to studies, 20–30% losses in crops and an increase of 15–20% in farmers' net incomes are reported among the users of AI solutions. Fig. (**4**) presents the Ecorobotix plant-by-plant AI system, which offers a prototype model designed to enhance the process of crop disease detection and treatment. The new system uses smart sensors to identify crop diseases on individual plants and to intervene accordingly, in a targeted and efficient manner.

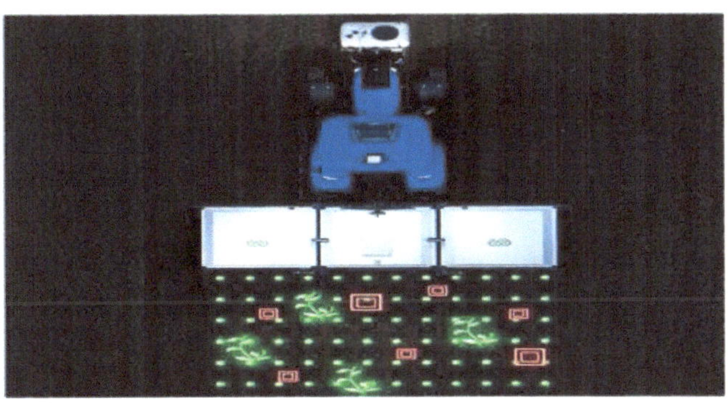

Fig. (4). Ecorobotix's Plant-by-Plant AI detection and treatment System (Source: https://ecorobotix.com/en/plant-by-plant-ai-software/).

WEED MANAGEMENT AND CONTROL

Weed management is an important part of sustainable farming, as weeds compete with crops for water, nutrients, and sunlight. Traditional methods, such as manual removal and blanket herbicide applications, are often labour-intensive, environmentally detrimental, and economically inefficient. AI-driven systems have brought precision to weed management by allowing targeted interventions. For example, Blue River Technology's See and Spray system uses computer vision and machine learning to distinguish crops from weeds [38]. This innovation applies herbicides selectively, thereby reducing chemical use and operational costs while improving crop health and minimizing environmental damage [39]. Similarly, Ecorobotix, an autonomous AI-powered robot from Europe, uses GPS and advanced sensors to detect and spray weeds directly. Most importantly, these systems dramatically minimize chemical wastage, thereby achieving the principles of sustainable farming.

TartanSense's BrijBot robot, developed by TartanSense in India, is a low-priced AI-powered automotive vehicle designed especially for small-level farmers. The Bengaluru-based startup company Cropin has designed an App to help farmers map their field boundaries with GPS-enabled smartphones and weather analysis. With the reduction of herbicide use up to 60%, and raising net incomes by 15–20% with AI-driven weed detection and planting systems, it helps and motivates farmers to enter the business of agriculture.

REVOLUTIONIZING WEATHER FORECASTING

Climate change and weather uncertainty are the major sources of agricultural distraction, so advanced precision tools are required to monitor and forecast the weather patterns for better agricultural output. In this context, AI algorithms can be a valuable tool for analyzing historical weather patterns, predicting future weather conditions, and providing innovative solutions to address its challenges. AI algorithms analyse large and complex datasets of past weather patterns and satellite imagery, providing precise and real-time information regarding weather conditions to assist farmers [40]. Such informative prediction enables farmers to take optimised decisions on irrigation, fertilization, pest management, and harvest scheduling. Based on past weather patterns, ML algorithms offer analytical solutions for forecasting rainfall, temperature, and extreme weather patterns [3].

For instance, precise rainfall prediction avoids over-irrigation, conserves water, and saves money, and environment temperature prediction enables planning of planting and harvesting to avoid heat stress. It enables early warning for severe weather conditions to take preventive measures in advance and avoid crop losses. The meteorological prediction model improves data quality by employing sophisticated data pre-processing methods. Cloud computing, IoT, and Wireless Sensor Networks (WSNs) are utilized to enhance structured data for prediction precision [41]. Hybrid models utilize machine learning and deep learning methods to analyze statistical characteristics, such as autoregressive integrated moving average (ARIMA) in data, for enhancing weather forecast accuracy. By integrating Recurrent Neural Networks (RNNs) for temporal analysis and Convolutional Neural Networks (CNNs) for feature extraction, these models are able to capture short-term fluctuations as well as long-term trends, enhancing forecasting reliability and coping with complex meteorological data. By guaranteeing strong model performance, these pre-processing procedures enhance computational efficiency and forecasting accuracy.

CASE STUDY: AI APPLICATIONS IN AGRICULTURE

AI-enabled tools in farming have significantly enhanced the prediction of soil quality, weather conditions, crop yield, and profitability for farmers worldwide. The market for AI in agriculture is projected to grow at a CAGR of 23.1% from USD 1.7 billion in 2023 to USD 4.7 billion by 2028. In America, AI is revolutionizing agriculture to overcome labour shortages and climate change effects. For instance, Iowa State University's AI Institute for Resilient Agriculture is creating AI solutions to promote the green revolution and farmer profit, aimed at minimizing the use of resources while enhancing crop yields. Autonomous tractors and drones are in common use today, and AI is being included in machinery by John Deere for restructuring agriculture. In India, Microsoft teamed up with the Karnataka Agricultural Price Commission (KAPC) to build an AI model for predicting prices of the Tur crop. PepsiCo India promotes regenerative farming in Uttar Pradesh through AI-based solutions that enhance potato cultivation. In the same way, IBM's Watson Decision Platform has been deployed across states such as Madhya Pradesh, Gujarat, and Maharashtra for hyperlocal weather forecasting and soil moisture detection. The other initiative includes the AI-based drones implemented by Garuda Aerospace in Tamil Nadu. These drones enable precision pesticide spraying, significantly reducing costs, labour dependency, and the environmental impact of chemical use. Collectively, these technologies demonstrate the transformative potential of AI in enhancing agricultural productivity, reducing losses, and promoting sustainable practices. These technologies highlight how AI is driving productivity, conserving resources, and increasing profitability in agriculture worldwide. AI continues to confront key challenges with groundbreaking solutions that open the way for a more productive and environmental friendly agricultural future.

CHALLENGES AND OPPORTUNITIES OF AI IMPLEMENTATION IN AGRICULTURE

There are certain challenges and opportunities involved in the application of AI in agricultural practices. The high cost of implementing AI and the education of farmers are the major constraints for small farmers, especially in developing nations, since these technologies require a large number of sensors, drones, and IoT devices. In addition, the majority of farmers, and particularly those in rural environments, are not trained to the extent of digital literacy needed to operate AI tools and interpret results properly. Data security and privacy are also issues since AI platforms will capture sensitive farm information in large volumes, and robust measures of data protection, along with transparency, are needed to establish farmer trust. Rural connectivity and infrastructure problems, such as an unreliable power supply and a lack of decent internet connectivity, also affect the deployment of real-time AI systems.

Despite all these issues, AI presents an enormous potential for contemporary agriculture. It enhances efficiency and productivity using data-based methods in tracking soil, weather, and crop health, thereby raising yields and reducing waste. AI also assists in sustainability through green practices in the precise use of chemicals and water. Lastly, AI can assist in the early identification of pests and diseases so that farmers can act early to prevent them while reducing the application of pesticides. The activities of agriculture are manual and involve planting, weeding, and harvesting, making it hard to manage manually, hence the possibility of operational inefficiency. Overcoming these challenges and exploiting opportunities through AI will assist in shaping agriculture as a sustainable and resilient sector.

THE FUTURE SCOPE OF AI IN ADVANCING AGRICULTURE

The AI algorithm helps farmers to predict weather conditions by analysing complex data of climate and environment patterns, and provides informative solutions to planting calendars, crop choice, and irrigation planning to reduce the adverse effects of climate uncertainties. With genomics, AI enhances the creation of crops with desired traits like disease and drought tolerance, making it easier to secure food in varying climates. Urban and vertical agriculture would be optimized by AI, using limited areas dictated by environmental factors like humidity, temperature, and light to create efficient urban food production without consuming much. Future research should explore the integration of multi-sensor data like soil and leaf health conditions, plant type, and weather patterns, deployment of edge AI for faster decision-making, and development of collaborative robotic swarms to improve efficiency. Advancements in adaptive learning models and smart IOT devices will further enhance the reliability and accuracy of precision farming. Collectively, all these innovations guarantee a sustainable and resilient future for agriculture.

CONCLUSION

The AI applications are revolutionizing agriculture by addressing the challenges of climate change, soil quality testing, labour shortages, and resource inefficiencies. AI-based technologies, such as machine learning, deep learning, and generative AI, analyze complex datasets related to weather, environment, soil quality, humidity, and leaf colours, providing informative solutions to farmers. Furthermore, AI-enabled and IoT-based robotic systems, drones, and autonomous vehicles continuously enhance farming practices through automated decision-making and cultivation to improve productivity and crop management. Predictive information based on AI optimizes fertilizer and pesticide usage, thus lowering health risks for consumers and reducing environmental footprint. In the future, hybrid AI technologies can be integrated with IoT and robotics to enhance cultivation and farming methodologies.

REFERENCES

[1] R. Kumar, S. Yadav, M. Kumar, J. Kumar, and M. Kumar, "Artificial intelligence: New technology to improve Indian agriculture", *Int. J. Chem. Stud.,* vol. 8, no. 2, pp. 2999-3005, 2020. [http://dx.doi.org/10.22271/chemi.2020.v8.i2at.9208]

[2] Available from: https://cfo.economictimes.indiatimes.com/news/46-of-indias-workforce-in-agriculture-contributes-only-18-to-gdp-report/115655625

[3] M.C. Hunter, R.G. Smith, M.E. Schipanski, L.W. Atwood, and D.A. Mortensen, "Agriculture in 2050: Recalibrating targets for sustainable intensification", *Bioscience,* vol. 67, no. 4, pp. 386-391, 2017. [http://dx.doi.org/10.1093/biosci/bix010]

[4] R. Agrawal, and R.C. Jain, "Composite model for forecasting rice yield", *Indian J. Agric. Sci.,* vol. 52, no. 3, pp. 189-194, 1982.

[5] L. Kouadio, M. El Jarroudi, Z. Belabess, S.E. Laasli, M.Z.K. Roni, I.D.I. Amine, N. Mokhtari, F. Mokrini, J. Junk, and R. Lahlali, "A review on UAV-based applications for plant disease detection and monitoring", *Remote Sens. (Basel),* vol. 15, no. 17, p. 4273, 2023. [http://dx.doi.org/10.3390/rs15174273]

[6] S. Panwar, "Pre harvest forecasting of crop yield using non-linear regression modelling : A concept",

[7] K.G. Arvanitis, and E.G. Symeonaki, "Agriculture 4.0: The role of innovative smart technologies towards sustainable farm management", *Open Agric. J.,* vol. 14, no. 1, pp. 130-135, 2020. [http://dx.doi.org/10.2174/1874331502014010130]

[8] B. Fasciolo, L. Panza, and F. Lombardi, "Exploring the integration of Industry 4.0 technologies in agriculture: A comprehensive bibliometric review", *Sustainability (Basel),* vol. 16, no. 20, p. 8948, 2024. [http://dx.doi.org/10.3390/su16208948]

[9] R.I. Mukhamediev, Y. Popova, Y. Kuchin, E. Zaitseva, A. Kalimoldayev, A. Symagulov, V. Levashenko, F. Abdoldina, V. Gopejenko, K. Yakunin, E. Muhamedijeva, and M. Yelis, "Review of Artificial Intelligence and Machine Learning Technologies: Classification, Restrictions, Opportunities and Challenges", *Mathematics,* vol. 10, no. 15, p. 2552, 2022. [http://dx.doi.org/10.3390/math10152552]

[10] S.A. Bhat, and N.F. Huang, "Big data and AI revolution in precision agriculture: Survey and challenges", *IEEE Access,* vol. 9, pp. 110209-110222, 2021. [http://dx.doi.org/10.1109/ACCESS.2021.3102227]

[11] M.J. Bashir, and R. Mumtaz, "“A Review of Advances in Computer Vision, Multi/Hyperspectral Imaging, UAVs, and Agri-Bots,” in Generative AI Foundations", In: *Developments, and Applications*, 2025, pp. 149-190.

[12] A.R. Onteddu, R.R. Kundavaram, A. Kamisetty, J.C.S. Gummadi, and A. Manikyala, "Enhancing Agricultural Efficiency with Robotics and AI-Powered Autonomous Farming Systems", *Malaysian Journal of Medical and Biological Research,* vol. 12, no. 1, pp. 7-22, 2025.

[13] D.S. Dayana, T. Venkatamuni, A. Bhagyalakshmi, T.N. Malleswari, and S. Ushasukhanya, *AI-Controlled Robotics in Smart Agricultural Systems: Enhancing Precision, Sustainability, and Productivity*, 2025.

[14] R. Kumar Kasera, S. Gour, and T. Acharjee, "A comprehensive survey on IoT and AI based applications in different pre-harvest, during-harvest and post-harvest activities of smart agriculture", *Comput. Electron. Agric.,* vol. 216, p. 108522, 2024. [http://dx.doi.org/10.1016/j.compag.2023.108522]

[15] Y. Yang, Y. Han, S. Li, Y. Yang, M. Zhang, and H. Li, "Vision based fruit recognition and positioning technology for harvesting robots", *Comput. Electron. Agric.,* vol. 213, p. 108258, 2023. [http://dx.doi.org/10.1016/j.compag.2023.108258]

[16] H. Wei, W. Xu, B. Kang, R. Eisner, A. Muleke, D. Rodriguez, P. deVoil, V. Sadras, M. Monjardino, and M.T. Harrison, "Irrigation with Artificial Intelligence: Problems, Premises, Promises", *Human-Centric Intelligent Systems,* vol. 4, no. 2, pp. 187-205, 2024. [http://dx.doi.org/10.1007/s44230-024-00072-4]

[17] M.F. Aslan, K. Sabanci, and B. Aslan, "Artificial intelligence techniques in crop yield estimation based on Sentinel-2 data: A comprehensive survey", *Sustainability (Basel),* vol. 16, no. 18, p. 8277, 2024. [http://dx.doi.org/10.3390/su16188277]

[18] H. Zia, A. Rehman, N.R. Harris, S. Fatima, and M. Khurram, "An Experimental Comparison of IoT-Based and Traditional Irrigation Scheduling on a Flood-Irrigated Subtropical Lemon Farm", *Sensors (Basel),* vol. 21, no. 12, p. 4175, 2021. [http://dx.doi.org/10.3390/s21124175] [PMID: 34204584]

[19] K. Amankulova, N. Farmonov, E. Abdelsamei, J. Szatmári, W. Khan, M. Zhran, J. Rustamov, S. Akhmedov, M. Sarimsakov, and L. Mucsi, "A novel fusion method for soybean yield prediction using Sentinel-2 and PlanetScope imagery", *IEEE J. Sel. Top. Appl. Earth Obs. Remote Sens.,* vol. 17, pp. 13694-13707, 2024. [http://dx.doi.org/10.1109/JSTARS.2024.3402114]

[20] A. Cartolano, A. Cuzzocrea, and G. Pilato, "Analyzing and assessing explainable AI models for smart agriculture environments", *Multimedia Tools Appl.,* vol. 83, no. 12, pp. 37225-37246, 2024. [http://dx.doi.org/10.1007/s11042-023-17978-z]

[21] P. Das, G.K. Jha, A. Lama, and R. Parsad, "Crop yield prediction using hybrid machine learning approach: A case study of lentil (Lens culinaris Medik.)", *Agriculture,* vol. 13, no. 3, p. 596, 2023. [http://dx.doi.org/10.3390/agriculture13030596]

[22] G. Mohyuddin, M.A. Khan, A. Haseeb, S. Mahpara, M. Waseem, and A.M. Saleh, "Evaluation of Machine Learning Approaches for Precision Farming in Smart Agriculture System—A Comprehensive Review", *IEEE Access,* 2024.

[23] Available from: https://pib.gov.in/PressReleaseIframePage.aspx?PRID=1985470

[24] E. Bwambale, F.K. Abagale, and G.K. Anornu, "Smart irrigation monitoring and control strategies for improving water use efficiency in precision agriculture: A review", *Agric. Water Manage.,* vol. 260, p. 107324, 2022. [http://dx.doi.org/10.1016/j.agwat.2021.107324]

[25] R. Sitharthan, M. Rajesh, S. Vimal, E. Saravana Kumar, S. Yuvaraj, A. Kumar, I. Jacob Raglend, and

K. Vengatesan, "A novel autonomous irrigation system for smart agriculture using AI and 6G enabled IoT network", *Microprocess. Microsyst.,* vol. 101, p. 104905, 2023. [http://dx.doi.org/10.1016/j.micpro.2023.104905]

[26] Q. Ilyas, M. Ahmad, and A. Mehmood, "Automated Estimation of Crop Yield Using Artificial Intelligence and Remote Sensing Technologies", *Bioengineering (Basel),* vol. 10, no. 2, p. 125, 2023. [http://dx.doi.org/10.3390/bioengineering10020125] [PMID: 36829619]

[27] T. Hu, X. Zhang, G. Bohrer, Y. Liu, Y. Zhou, J. Martin, Y. Li, and K. Zhao, "Crop yield prediction via explainable AI and interpretable machine learning: Dangers of black box models for evaluating climate change impacts on crop yield", *Agric. For. Meteorol.,* vol. 336, p. 109458, 2023. [http://dx.doi.org/10.1016/j.agrformet.2023.109458]

[28] L. Ale, A. Sheta, L. Li, Y. Wang, and N. Zhang, "Deep learning-based plant disease detection for smart agriculture", In: *in 2019 IEEE Globecom Workshops (GC Wkshps)*Waikoloa, HI, USA, 2019, pp. 1-6.

[29] H.W. Gammanpila, M.A.N. Sashika, and S.V.G.N. Priyadarshani, "Advancing Horticultural Crop Loss Reduction Through Robotic and AI Technologies: Innovations, Applications, and Practical Implications", *Adv. Agric.,* vol. 2024, no. 1, p. 2472111, 2024. [http://dx.doi.org/10.1155/2024/2472111]

[30] M. Padhiary, D. Saha, R. Kumar, L.N. Sethi, and A. Kumar, "Enhancing precision agriculture: A comprehensive review of machine learning and AI vision applications in all-terrain vehicle for farm automation", *Smart Agricultural Technology,* vol. 8, p. 100483, 2024. [http://dx.doi.org/10.1016/j.atech.2024.100483]

[31] A. Saksena, R.C. Jain, and R.L. Yadav, "Development of early warning and yield assessment models for rainfed crops based on agro-meteorological indices", In: *Project Report New Delhi* IASRI, 2001.

[32] D. Xia, P. Chen, B. Wang, J. Zhang, and C. Xie, "Insect detection and classification based on an improved convolutional neural network", *Sensors (Basel),* vol. 18, no. 12, p. 4169, 2018. [http://dx.doi.org/10.3390/s18124169] [PMID: 30486481]

[33] D.J. Leybourne, N. Musa, and P. Yang, "Can artificial intelligence be integrated into pest monitoring schemes to help achieve sustainable agriculture? An entomological, management and computational perspective", *Agric. For. Entomol.,* vol. 27, no. 1, pp. 8-17, 2025. [http://dx.doi.org/10.1111/afe.12630]

[34] Available from: https://bigdata.cgiar.org/digital-intervention/plantvillage-nuru-pest-and-diease-monitoring-using-ai/

[35] P. Bedi, and P. Gole, "Plant disease detection using hybrid model based on convolutional autoencoder and convolutional neural network", *Artificial Intelligence in Agriculture,* vol. 5, pp. 90-101, 2021. [http://dx.doi.org/10.1016/j.aiia.2021.05.002]

[36] A. Subeesh, and C.R. Mehta, "Automation and digitization of agriculture using artificial intelligence and internet of things", *Artificial Intelligence in Agriculture,* vol. 5, pp. 278-291, 2021. [http://dx.doi.org/10.1016/j.aiia.2021.11.004]

[37] W. Alazzai, B. Sh. Z. Abood, H. Al-Jawahry, and M. Obaid, "Precision farming: The power of AI and IoT technologies", *E3S Web of Conferences,* vol. 491, p. 04006, 2024. [http://dx.doi.org/10.1051/e3sconf/202449104006]

[38] M. Vasileiou, L.S. Kyrgiakos, C. Kleisiari, G. Kleftodimos, G. Vlontzos, H. Belhouchette, and P.M. Pardalos, "Transforming weed management in sustainable agriculture with artificial intelligence: A systematic literature review towards weed identification and deep learning", *Crop Prot.,* vol. 176, p. 106522, 2024. [http://dx.doi.org/10.1016/j.cropro.2023.106522]

[39] N. Rai, Y. Zhang, B.G. Ram, L. Schumacher, R.K. Yellavajjala, S. Bajwa, and X. Sun, "Applications of deep learning in precision weed management: A review", *Comput. Electron. Agric.,* vol. 206, p.

107698, 2023.
[http://dx.doi.org/10.1016/j.compag.2023.107698]

[40] R.M. Pujahari, S.P. Yadav, and R. Khan, "Intelligent farming system through weather forecast support and crop production", In: *Application of Machine Learning in Agriculture.* Academic Press, 2022, pp. 113-130.
[http://dx.doi.org/10.1016/B978-0-323-90550-3.00009-6]

[41] Y. Varshney, and N. Ram, "Weather forecasting: A systematic review using AI approaches", *Weather,* vol. 4, no. 10, 2024.

CHAPTER 5

AI-Powered Maintenance Planning and Hydrogen Energy Performance in Cargo Drones

Surbhi Gupta[1,*], **Rekha Devi**[1] and **Sarbjeet Kaur**[1]

[1] *Department of Electrical Engineering, Chandīgarh University, Gharuan, Mohali, Punjab, India*

Abstract: Drones powered by hydrogen fuel cells, which have longer flight durations and emit less carbon emissions, are emerging as a sustainable alternative for intercity cargo transportation. However, there are still issues related to reliability and fuel efficiency, as well as achieving optimal fuel efficiency. This study examines the development and application of hydrogen-powered drones for cargo delivery between cities. Because of their high energy density and zero emissions, hydrogen fuel cells provide an attractive alternative to traditional modes of transportation, which have decreased their sustainability benefits due to worries regarding carbon emissions. Because of the development, construction, and operation of hydrogen-powered drones, this endeavour aims to reduce dependency on conventional air and road transportation, and these drones will be able to transport supplies between cities. The study begins with a presentation of current drone technology, emphasizing the limitations of battery-powered drones in terms of range and cargo capacity. After that, a thorough analysis of hydrogen fuel cell technology is presented, with a focus on how it might improve drone endurance and operation. The challenges and useful benefits of implementation are illustrated through case studies and real-world applications. The findings of this study support the broader goal of developing effective and environmentally friendly transportation networks and set the stage for future developments in drone technology.

Keywords: Drone technology, Hydrogen Fuel cells, Intercity cargo transport.

INTRODUCTION

Rapid developments in drone technology are opening new avenues for creative thinking across a range of sectors, including logistics and transportation. Among these developments, the creation of hydrogen-powered drones for intercity cargo transportation stands out as a potentially practical replacement for traditional drones that are battery-operated.

* **Corresponding author Surbhi Gupta:** Department of Electrical Engineering, Chandīgarh University, Gharuan, Mohali, Punjab, India; E-mail: surbhi.e9023@cumail.in

Shilpa Gupta & Ritika Sharma (Eds.)

Utilizing the benefits of hydrogen fuel cells, this novel approach improves the efficiency, range, and sustainability of cargo drone operations. Hydrogen fuel cells- potentially more effective and environmentally friendly power sources than lithium-ion batteries are used in drones that run on hydrogen. These drones are designed to transport goods between cities, meeting the growing need for faster and greener delivery methods in the logistics sector. By using drones with hydrogen fuel cells, there is a reduction in carbon emissions, an increase in the flight distance and a reduction in downtime.

In the logistics industry, there is a growing need for prompt and dependable delivery services due to the growth of e-commerce and rising customer expectations. Traditional drones that run on batteries have been crucial in meeting these expectations by offering quick delivery choices over short distances.

However, the limitations of alternative fuels in terms of flying time and payload capacity have prompted research into them. Hydrogen fuel cells offer a potential solution to those problems because of their increased electricity density and faster refuelling times. Hydrogen-powered drones are superior to battery-powered drones in several ways.

Hydrogen fuel cells offer a higher energy density than lithium-ion batteries, which enables longer flight times and greater payload sizes. Hydrogen-based drones are therefore the best option because intercity goods delivery requires greater flying ranges. Additionally, hydrogen fueling takes a lot less time than battery recharging, which reduces downtime and increases operational efficiency. Rechargeable lithium-ion or lithium-polymer batteries, which are lighter and simpler to charge than other battery types, are used in drones that run on batteries. They often only fly for 20 to 30 minutes, though they are suited for lighter payloads and shorter trips. Hydrogen fuel cells, which have a higher energy density and enable longer flight time enable longer flight times, often several hours, are used by drones that run on hydrogen. These drones are ideal for longer missions and larger payloads, but they face more complex challenges for refuelling. Also, manufacturing batteries and disposal pose a risk to the environment. Since hydrogen fuel cells only emit water vapour, a more environmentally friendly option than batteries, which have a large environmental impact due to mining and disposal issues.

This is in line with international initiatives to promote sustainable technologies and reduce carbon footprints. Drones driven by hydrogen have the potential to drastically reduce greenhouse gas emissions during cargo delivery, which will aid in the shift to more environmentally friendly logistics systems. Drones, having greater flight ranges, faster refuelling, and less of an environmental impact, probably overcome the shortcomings of their battery-powered competitors. The use of drones powered by hydrogen could be crucial to determining the future of freight delivery and advancing greener and more effective modes of transportation as logistics continually develop.

LITERATURE REVIEW

The literature survey shows differing opinions from various authors. The first paper, based on Hybrid Fuel Cell Powered Drones, focuses on the challenges in the fuel economy while extending the sources' lifespans in persistent missions. The off-the-shelf drone powered by a 650 W fuel cell can be extended by 37 minutes. The study involved using an electric fuel cell/battery-based drone. The paper outcome shows that power sources operated below their rated capacity, leading to 5.1% of fuel consumption. The Operating cost was achieved at 1450€ for one fuel cell stack lifecycle [1]

Hybrid fuel cell-powered drones have attracted a great deal of attention based on the prospect of extended flight times and improved efficiency. This review combines recent literature in the field to emphasize the principal developments, system architectures, and performance studies.

Energy Management Strategies: Efficient energy management is important for maximizing the performance of hybrid fuel cell drones. Energy management strategies for hydrogen conservation and efficiency enhancement. Based on real flight test data, they proved that a more advanced energy management system could extend drone endurance by about 21.81 minutes [1].

System Architectures: To balance the supply and demand of power, several hybrid system architectures have been studied. Three topologies using lithium-polymer batteries and proton exchange membrane fuel cells (PEMFCs) were examined in a 2020 study by an unnamed author. The study indicated the design factors that must be considered for fixed-wing UAVs to operate at their best [2, 3].

Integration with Renewable Energy: Improving UAV endurance by the integration of fuel cells with renewable energy sources has shown promise. According to recent research, tiny UAV flight times can be nearly doubled by combining solar and fuel cell technologies. For instance, Gang et al. achieved extremely long flying periods by using a hybrid system that included an 80 W solar cell system, a battery, and a 300 W PEMFC [4].

Practical applications have proven the feasibility of hybrid fuel cell drones. The Hybrid Tiger UAV by the Naval Research Laboratory combines a PEMFC system with solar panels and gliding capabilities. The design attained a specific energy of around 1200 Wh/kg, far exceeding that of conventional lithium-ion batteries [5].

Hydrogen fuel cell technology is poised as a promising alternative power source for multi-rotor drones to provide increased endurance in flight while minimizing the effect on the environment. Critical technologies revolve around structural lightweights, efficient methods of hydrogen storage, and sustainable energy management paradigms. Lighter-than-air materials, as well as improved structural configurations, play a crucial role in compensating for the heavier weight of the fuel cell apparatus. Hydrogen storage technology, including high-pressure tanks and metal hydrides, is under investigation for storing hydrogen efficiently and safely onboard. Sophisticated energy management systems are key to power supply-demand balancing for optimized overall performance. Even with these developments, issues persist with thermal management and integration of systems. Further R&D is important to overcome such issues and make full use of hydrogen fuel cell-powered multi-rotor drone capabilities [6 - 17].

METHODOLOGY

To complete the feasibility of the study, it is necessary to determine the viability and infrastructure requirements before implementing hydrogen-powered drones for intercity cargo transport. The flow diagram of the same is given in Fig. (**1**).

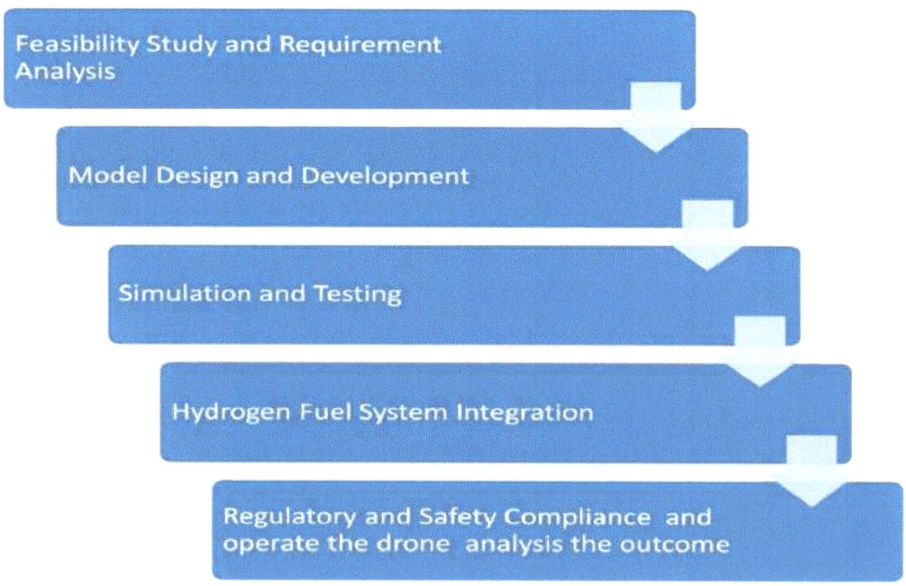

Fig. (1). Flow diagram and methodology of work.

Drone designs are created by incorporating navigation algorithms into CAD models and simulations. To improve performance and safety, prototypes are built, and they are carried out through testing. The step-by-step methodology is given below

1. Carry out a feasibility analysis of hydrogen-powered drones, considering payload, range, safety, legal, and infrastructure specifications.
2. Maximize design through CAD simulation with an emphasis on lightweight, high-power hydrogen fuel cell implementation.
3. Construct a robust, aerodynamic drone body with carbon fiber composite; ensure safe fuel system integration *via* simulation.
4. Create prototypes, undertake extensive testing, and optimize design for control, fuel efficiency, and structural integrity.
5. Comply with aviation and environmental laws; implement safety measures and obtain appropriate certifications.
6. Implement pilot projects on some intercity corridors to accumulate data, streamline operations, and expand for ecologically friendly cargo transportation.

DESIGN AND MODELLING

The newly released drone model represents a significant breakthrough in unmanned aerial vehicle (UAV) technology, showcasing a distinctive three-propeller configuration that optimizes both efficiency and stability. With a 500 kg capacity, this unique drone is designed to carry heavy payloads, making it perfect for a wide range of applications, from industrial operations and disaster relief to logistics and cargo delivery.

The drone's hydrogen fuel cell power system is one of its most notable features. This sustainable substitute for conventional battery-powered or combustion engine drones not only increases the drone's flight time but also greatly lessens its environmental impact. Because of the high energy density provided by the hydrogen fuel cells, the drone can carry out long-duration missions without the arrangement of the three propellers to improve manoeuvrability and aerodynamics. Because of its improved lift and decreased drag, this design enables the drone to fly better even when carrying large payloads. This drone model is made of high-quality materials and state-of-the-art technology, which guarantees its dependability and durability in a variety of demanding conditions. Hydrogen-based drones as an intercity cargo transporter model in CATIA V5 are represented in Fig. (**2**).

Fig. (2). Hydrogen-based drones as an intercity cargo transporter model in CATIA V5.

Functionality and safety must be maximized in the cargo container of a hydrogen-powered drone intended for interstate travel, and the cargo drone body model shown in Fig. (**3**). The drone's overall weight and flight efficiency are minimally affected by the container because it is made of lightweight yet sturdy materials like reinforced plastics or sophisticated composites. To keep cargo stable during travel and lower the chance of damage or movement, it is designed with a robust locking mechanism.

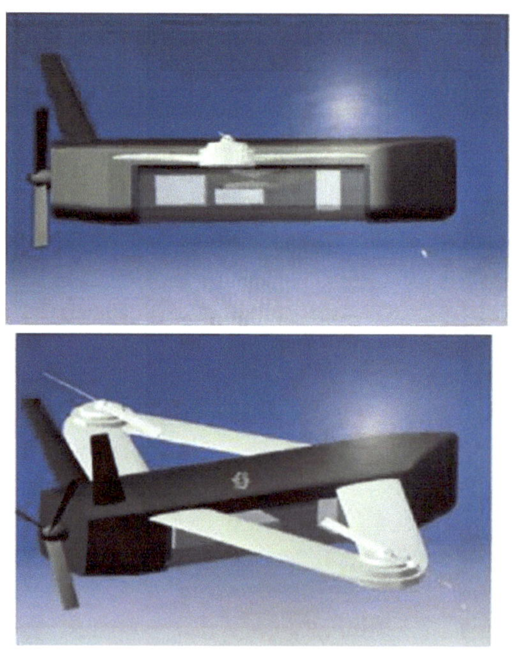

Fig. (3). Cargo drone body model.

Ventilation is very important, especially for cargo that needs precise air conditions or may be sensitive to temperature variations. To maintain the ideal atmosphere for different kinds of goods, the container should have movable ventilation systems. Furthermore, fragile items are shielded from vibration and damage by incorporated cushioning and shock-absorbing materials.

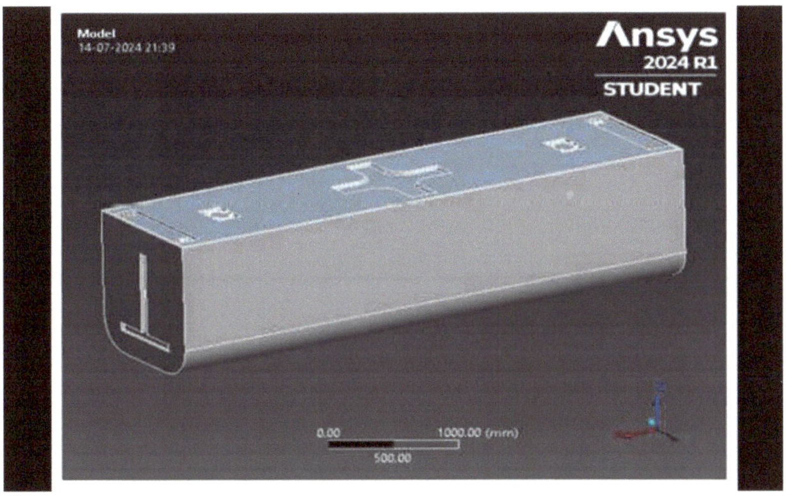

Fig. (4). container model for store product.

Modular characteristics in the container's design could make it simple to reconfigure it to accommodate different types and sizes of cargo.

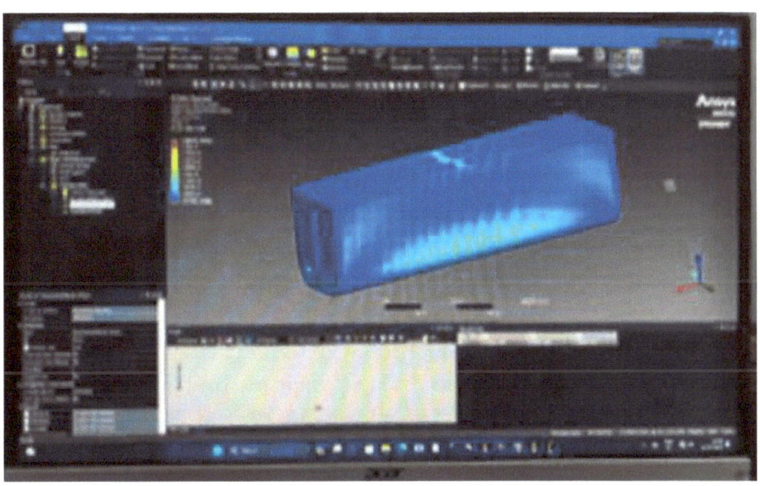

(Fig. 5) contd.....

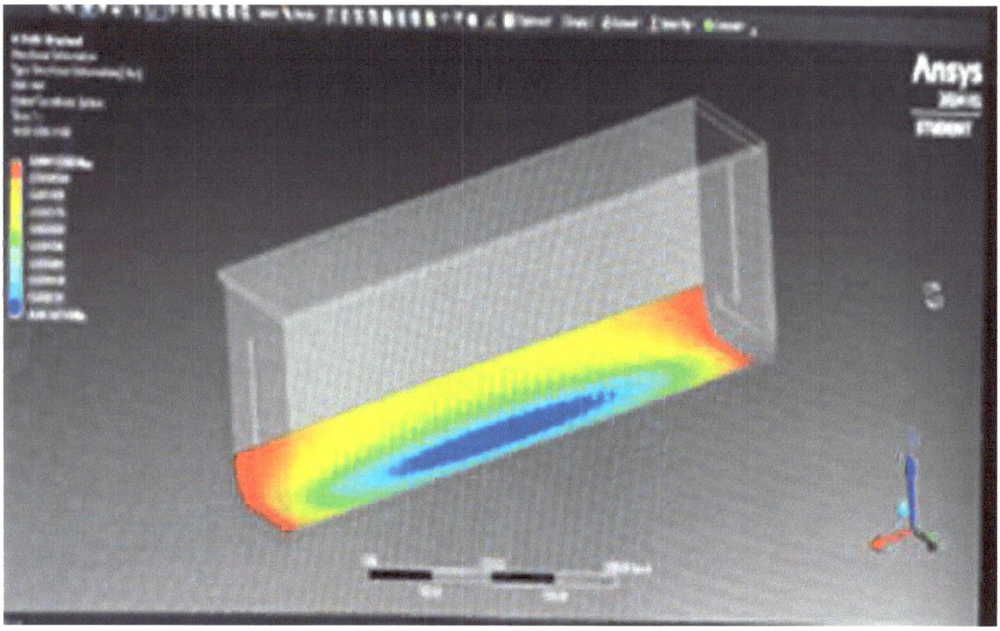

Fig. (5). Cargo container in ANSYS model.

This flexibility optimizes cargo capacity and guarantees adaptation. In addition, the container needs to have communication and GPS tracking systems installed in order to deliver cargo safely and effectively. These systems will provide for real-time updates on the cargo's location and progress. In order to meet the requirements of intercity cargo transport *via* drone, the container's design must generally strike a balance between protection, durability, and adaptability. Figs. (**4** and **5**) presenting container model and simulations in the ANSYS model.

In the literature review section, we observed differing opinions from various authors. The first paper is based on Hybrid Fuel Cell Powered Drones here the main challenge focuses on the fuel economy while extending sources lifespans in persistent missions and also off-the-shelf drone fed by a 650 W fuel cell record can be extended by about 37 minute and here used electric fuel cell/battery-based drone .In this paper outcomes allow power sources to operate off with their rated of the area, prolonging their service life and lead to 5.1% of fuel consumption reduction. Operating cost achieved at 1450€ during one fuel cell stack lifecycle [7 - 10]. Hybrid fuel cell-powered drones have attracted a great deal of attention based on the prospect of extended flight times and improved efficiency. This review combines recent literature in the field to emphasize the principal developments, system architectures, and performance studies.

Energy Management Strategies: Efficient energy management is important for maximizing the performance of hybrid fuel cell drones explored energy management strategies for hydrogen conservation and efficiency enhancement. Based on real flight test data, they proved that a more advanced energy management system could extend drone endurance by about 21.81 minutes [11 - 13].

System Architectures: A number of hybrid system architectures have been investigated in order to provide a balance of power supply and demand. Research by an unidentified author (2020) analyzed three architectures with Proton Exchange Membrane Fuel Cells (PEMFCs) and lithium-polymer batteries. The study gave indications of the design considerations required in order to achieve optimized performance within fixed-wing UAVs.

Integration with Renewable Energy: Integration of fuel cells with renewable energy sources has been promising to increase UAV endurance. Recent studies have shown that the integration of solar cells with fuel cell systems can almost double the flight time of small UAVs. For example, Gang et al. used a hybrid system that consisted of a 300 W PEMFC, a battery, and an 80 W solar cell system, and this resulted in very extended flight times [14].

Practical applications have proven the feasibility of hybrid fuel cell drones. The Hybrid Tiger UAV by the Naval Research Laboratory combines a PEMFC system with solar panels and gliding capabilities. The design attained a specific energy of around 1200 Wh/kg, far exceeding that of conventional lithium-ion batteries [15].

Hydrogen fuel cell technology is poised as a promising alternative power source for multi-rotor drones to provide increased endurance in flight while minimizing the effect on the environment. Critical technologies revolve around structural lightweights, efficient methods of hydrogen storage, and sustainable energy management paradigms. Lighter-than-air materials as well as improved structural configurations play a crucial role in compensating for the heavier weight of the fuel cell apparatus. Hydrogen storage technology, including high-pressure tanks and metal hydrides, is under investigation for storing hydrogen efficiently and safely onboard. Sophisticated energy management systems are key to power supply-demand balancing for optimized overall performance. Even with these developments, issues persist with thermal management and integration of systems. Further R&D is important to overcome such issues and make full use of hydrogen fuel cell-powered multi-rotor drone capabilities [16, 17].

One of the most important parts of a hydrogen-based drone that ensures efficiency and safety is the tank that holds hydrogen and oxygen. The tank is made of high-strength alloys or sophisticated composite materials, and its design maximizes drone performance by withstanding the high pressures involved in hydrogen storage while keeping the tank's lightweight profile. Its specifications are given in Table **1**.

Table 1. Specifications of the container fuel tank.

Parameters	**Independent**
Parameters key	Ans.DS
Attributes	No
Named selection	No
Material properties	No
Advance Geometry Properties	
Use Associativity	Yes
Coordinate System	No
Reader mode updated file saved	No
Smart CAD update	Yes
Compare parts update	No
Analysis Type	3D
Mixed Import Resolution	None
Import Facet Quality	Source
Clean Body on Imports	No
Stitch Surface on Import	None
Disjoint Geometry Decompose	Yes
Enclosure and Symmetry Processing	Yes

To keep hydrogen and oxygen apart and lower the possibility of hazardous reactions, the tank is usually separated into distinct sections, as shown in Fig. (**6**) and the fuel tank model in in Fig. (**7**).

To regulate the flow of gases and preserve ideal conditions for combustion and propulsion, each compartment is equipped with precisely designed valves and pressure regulators. In order to control the low temperatures of the hydrogen that is being kept and avoid leaks or pressure changes, the tank's design also has strong insulation and cooling systems.

Fig. (6). Hydrogen and oxygen tank model.

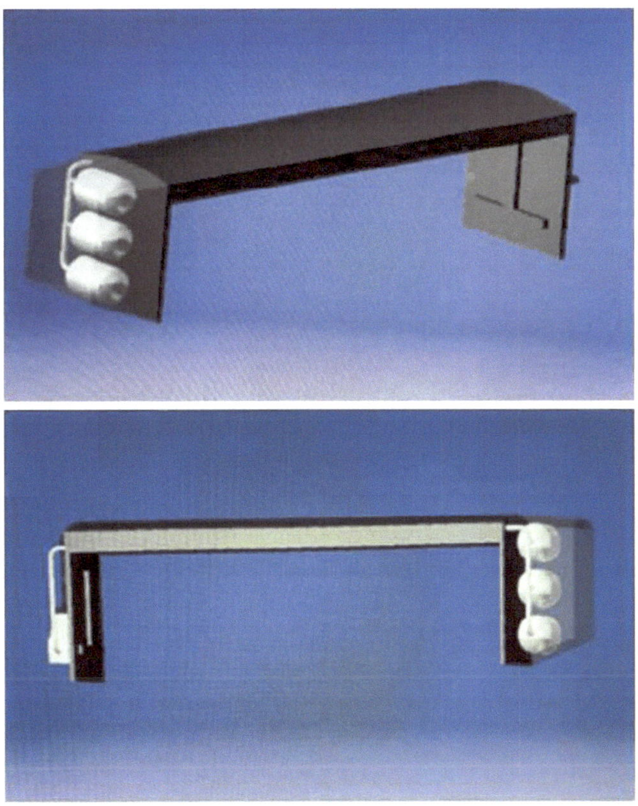

Fig. (7). Fuel tank model.

Because safety is of the utmost importance, the tank has numerous safety features, such as sophisticated leak detection systems and pressure release valves.

Furthermore, the tank's design facilitates a smooth and efficient connection with the drone's propulsion system or fuel cell. For intercity cargo transportation, the tank's design must place a high priority on efficiency, safety, and durability. Hydrogen-based drones as an intercity cargo transporter model specification given in Table **2**.

Table 2. Hydrogen-based drones as intercity cargo transporter model specification.

Design Parameter	Dimension	Material
Total Length	7m	
Wing Span	8m	
Aspect Ratio	8	
Cargo Volume	6.5m3	Aluminium Alloy
Body Height	1.3m	
Aerofoil	NACA 63415	
Motors diameter	0.3m	BLDC Motors
Wing	4	
Total Payload	500 kg	
Endurance	12 hrs	
Body		Carbon fibre

MODELING AND SIMULATIONS

This study uses MATLAB simulation to model and analyse the operation of hydrogen-powered drones for intercity cargo delivery. The simulation creates a virtual environment using MATLAB's Simulink and Aerospace Toolbox to test a number of variables, such as aerodynamics, fuel efficiency, and payload capacity. Important variables, including oxygen integration, hydrogen fuel consumption, and drone stability, are studied in order to optimise the design and operation methods.

Through simulations, the effects of several flight circumstances, including weather and payload weight, are examined in order to assess drone performance. The drone's potential for long-distance cargo transport is clarified by the ability to assess system reliability and energy efficiency, utilizing MATLAB's capabilities.

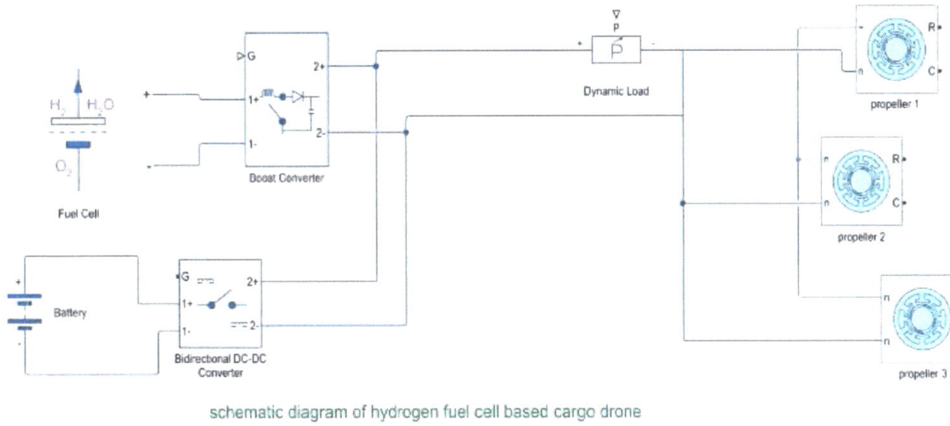

Fig. (8). Schematic diagram of model.

In the work hydrogen fuel cells are the primary power source, with batteries acting as a backup when necessary. This dual power technology ensures a constant energy supply and increases the reliability of long-distance drones. Through the integration of numerous electronic controllers, the management and distribution of electricity between the fuel cell and batteries are optimized, maintaining efficiency and stability. The drone is built with three propellers, each of which is driven by a high-efficiency motor.

The precise placement of these propellers allows the drone to control the weight and dynamics of payload carrying while providing balanced lift and movement. Propeller speeds are managed by advanced electronic controllers that adjust to variations in wind and payload, ensuring a steady and comfortable flight. In order to conduct a comprehensive study and optimize the power systems, propeller dynamics, and overall flight performance, this model mainly depends on MATLAB simulations and the schematic diagram of the aircraft displayed in in Fig. (**8**). By optimizing the ratio of battery consumption to hydrogen fuel cell usage, the simulations help extend and improve the efficiency of the flight. This creative strategy highlights the potential of hydrogen fuel cells in the future of aviation logistics by utilizing cutting-edge technology to provide an effective and sustainable intercity cargo transportation solution. Fig. (**9**) presents the fuel cell in MATLAB Simulink.

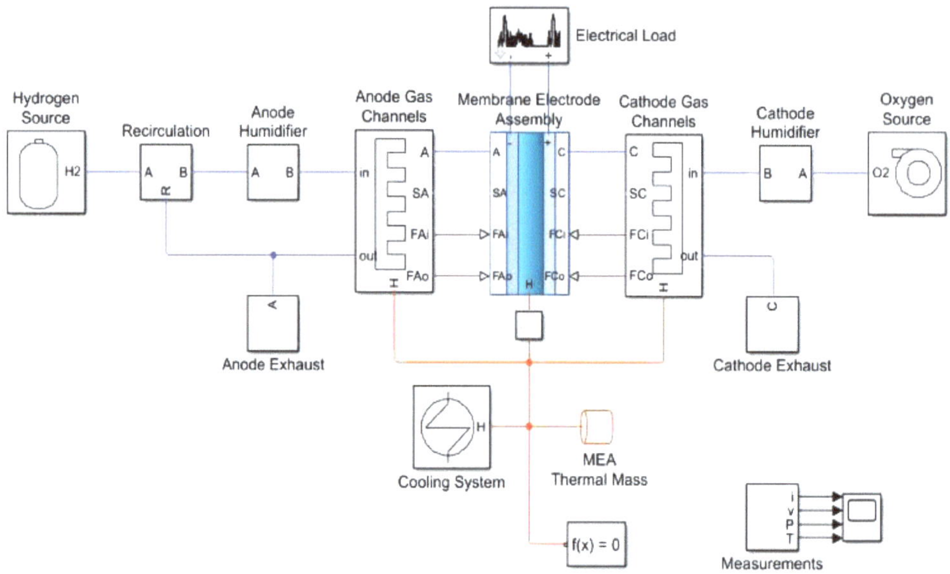

Fig. (9). Fuel cell in matlab simulink.

Hydrogen and oxygen undergo an electrochemical reaction in a hydrogen fuel cell to produce power. After entering the anode, hydrogen (H_2) molecules are divided into protons (H^+) and electrons (e^-) *via* a catalyst. While the electrons travel through an external circuit to create an electric current, the protons pass through an electrolyte membrane to the cathode. When oxygen molecules (O_2) combine with protons and electrons at the cathode, heat and water (H_2O) are created. This technique is a green power source because it is very efficient and only produces heat and water as waste.

Fig. (**10**) shows a MATLAB simulation of a hydrogen fuel cell where the oxygen component interacts with the hydrogen protons and electrons at the cathode. Simulink is used to describe the flow of oxygen using equations governing its diffusion and reaction kinetics. Protons passing across the electrolyte membrane and electrons entering through the external circuit combine with oxygen as it reaches the cathode side. The process releases water and energy. With the help of MATLAB's Simulink blocks, one may model the oxygen reduction reaction (ORR), diffusion processes, and the impact of oxygen concentration on fuel cell efficiency in general.

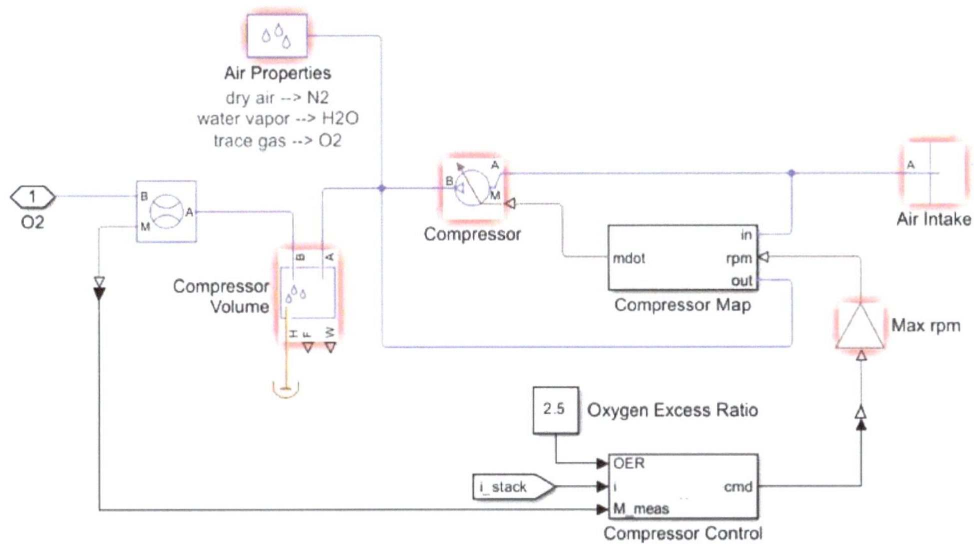

Fig. (10). Oxygen part in fuel cell.

The simulation ensures an accurate portrayal of the electrochemical processes seen in real life while adjusting parameters such as oxygen flow rate and concentration to improve the fuel cell's output and efficiency.

Fig. (**11**) illustrates the flow and reaction of hydrogen at the anode using a MATLAB fuel cell simulation. To generate an electric current, the protons travel through the electrolyte membrane to the cathode, while the electrons travel through an external circuit. Using Simulink blocks, the hydrogen flow, reaction kinetics, and the impact of hydrogen concentration on fuel cell performance are all simulated. The simulation ensures that the power output and efficiency of the fuel cell are appropriately modelled and optimized by adjusting variable (hydrogen flow rate and pressure) using an AI algorithm.

Fig. (**12**) shows the cooling technique used in a MATLAB fuel cell simulation to regulate the heat generated by the electrochemical reactions. Heat exchangers, coolant flow, and temperature control systems can all be simulated with Simulink blocks to mimic the cooling system.

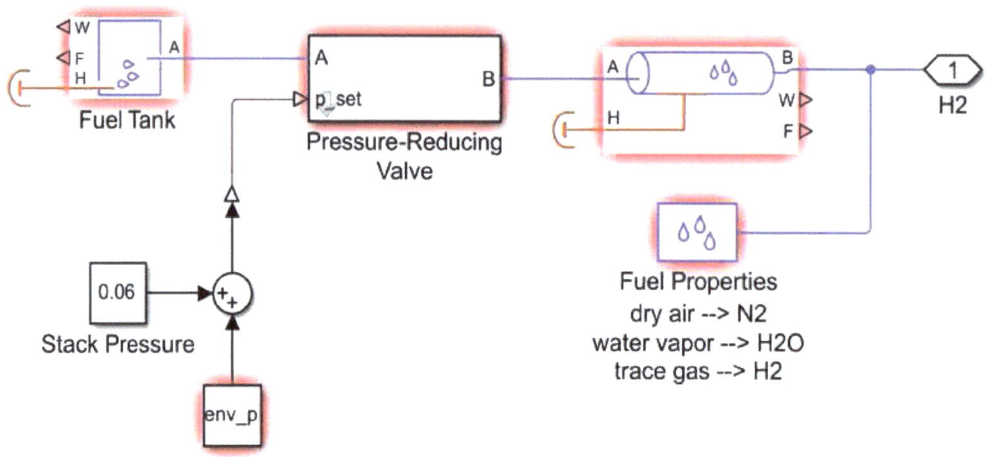

Fig. (11). Hydrogen part in fuel cell.

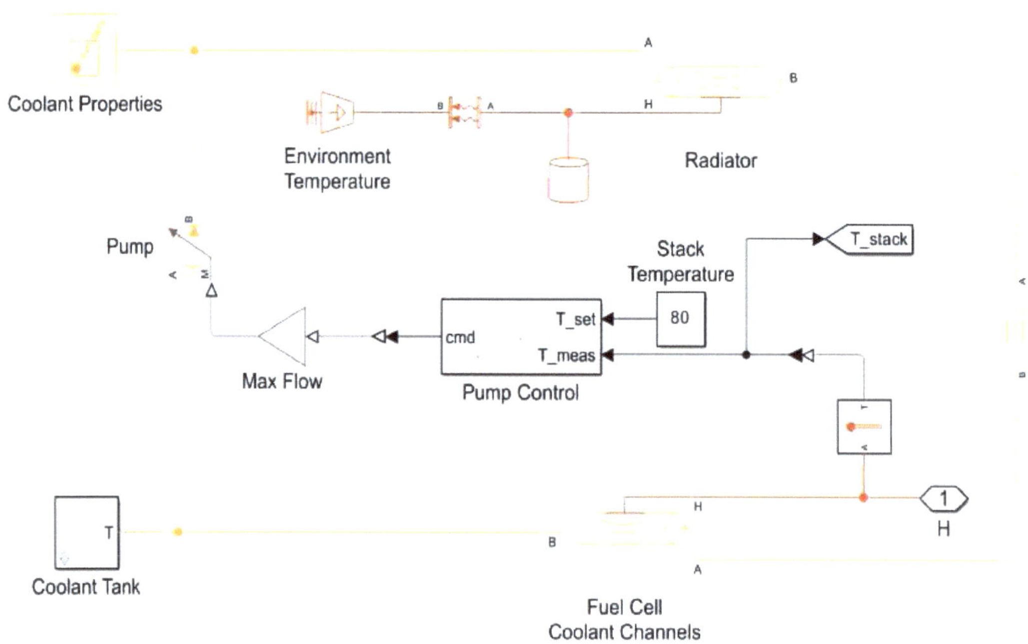

Fig. (12). cooling part of the hydrogen fuel cell.

The coolant, usually water or air, travels around the fuel cell to absorb excess heat and maintain the optimal operating temperature. The simulation incorporates flow dynamics and heat transfer equations to model the interaction between the coolant and the fuel cell components. By altering parameters such as coolant flow rate, inlet temperature, and heat exchanger efficiency, the simulation offers effective thermal control. This increases system lifetime, maintains fucl ccll pcrformancc, and prevents overheating. Fig. (**13**) shows the hydrogen fuel cell for the freight drone MATLAB simulation.

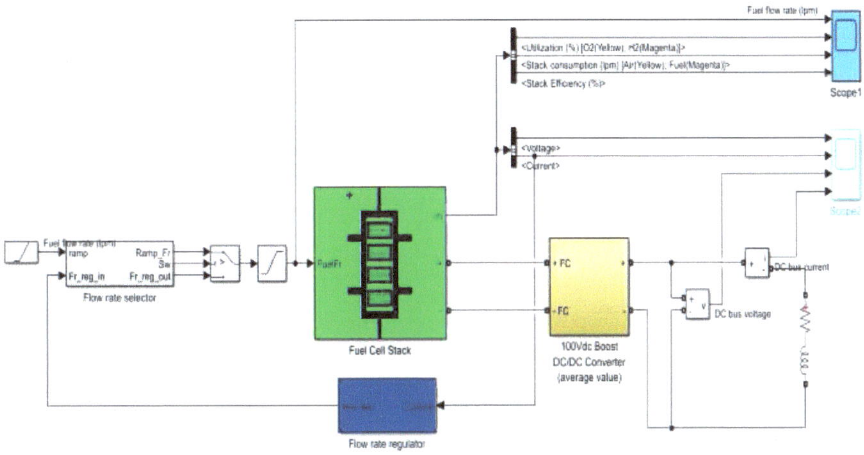

Fig. (13). Hydrogen fuel cell for cargo drone matlab simulation.

Improvements in fuel cells are making it possible for hydrogen-based drones to replace traditional delivery methods in a practical and efficient manner, completely changing the way freight is transported between cities. These drones' brains are the hydrogen fuel cell, which uses an electrochemical reaction with oxygen to convert hydrogen's chemical energy into electrical energy. The sole byproducts of this process are heat and water vapour, making hydrogen fuel cells an environmentally benign energy source.

These drones' fuel cell systems are designed, simulated, and optimized primarily using MATLAB, a high-performance technical computing language and environment. With MATLAB's comprehensive toolkit, engineers can model and simulate the complex dynamics of hydrogen fuel cells and represent key fuel cell operations like power generation, heat control, and electrochemical processes. This enables the fuel cell's behaviour to be carefully controlled, ensuring the drone's dependable and efficient operation while in flight.

In order to maintain optimal performance and safety during intercity cargo transportation missions, real-time control algorithms must be created. MATLAB's hardware interface features facilitate this process. The data analysis and visualization capabilities of MATLAB provide engineers with valuable information about the operational characteristics of hydrogen fuel cells, enabling them to promptly identify potential issues and take the necessary action. MATLAB can be used to accelerate the development of drones driven by hydrogen, which will hasten the deployment of these advanced cargo carriers.

Hydrogen-powered drones are a viable option for intercity cargo transportation because of their significant operational and environmental advantages. The development of fuel cell technology is largely due to MATLAB's strong features and capabilities, which ensure that these drones will realise their potential to transform the logistics industry.

RESULT AND ANALYSIS

In comparison to drones that run solely on batteries, the integration of hydrogen fuel cells into drones for intercity cargo transport has demonstrated notable gains in flying time and payload capacity. Reliable performance depends on stable power production and effective thermal management, which are confirmed by MATLAB simulations in Fig. (**14**) and in-person testing. Drones powered by hydrogen have a significant negative environmental impact because they only produce heat and water vapour. Lifecycle analyses show reduced environmental impact, particularly with renewable hydrogen. These results show that using drones driven by hydrogen to transport freight between cities is both feasible and sustainable.

Fuel Flow Rate and Saturation Point

Initially, the fuel flow rate to the hydrogen fuel cell increases as the system effectively absorbs and utilizes hydrogen. However, this flow rate eventually reaches a saturation point, indicating that the system has reached its maximum capacity to process additional fuel. For best performance at this point, the proper ratio of hydrogen to oxygen must be maintained.

Reaction and Balance

When the fuel cell reaches the saturation point, oxygen and hydrogen from the corresponding tanks react. Water and electrical energy are the byproducts of this electrochemical reaction, which is aided by the electrodes. In order to preserve system stability and guarantee effective power generation, this reaction must be properly managed.

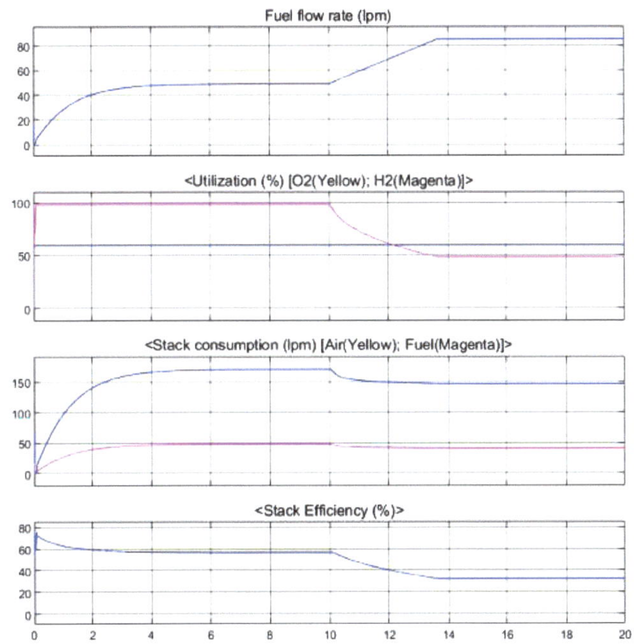

Fig. (14). Hydrogen fuel cell matlab simulation.

Air-to-Fuel Ratio

The device has an air-to-fuel mechanism that takes oxygen out of the surrounding air and combines it with hydrogen. This procedure guarantees the maintenance of the proper reactant ratio for effective energy conversion. For the fuel cell to operate at its best and produce power consistently, this ratio must be adjusted.

Efficiency

The ideal ratio of hydrogen to oxygen allows the hydrogen fuel cell to operate with high efficiency at first. However, as time progresses, the efficiency of the system decreases and stabilizes around 48%. This decline in efficiency may result from factors such as fuel cell component degradation, accumulation of impurities, or reduced effectiveness of the reaction process as the fuel cell approaches its operational limits. Figs. (**15** - **17**) show the fuel flow rate, hydrogen and oxygen rate and consumption and air. Fig. (**18**) gives the simulations of the voltage and current control rate.

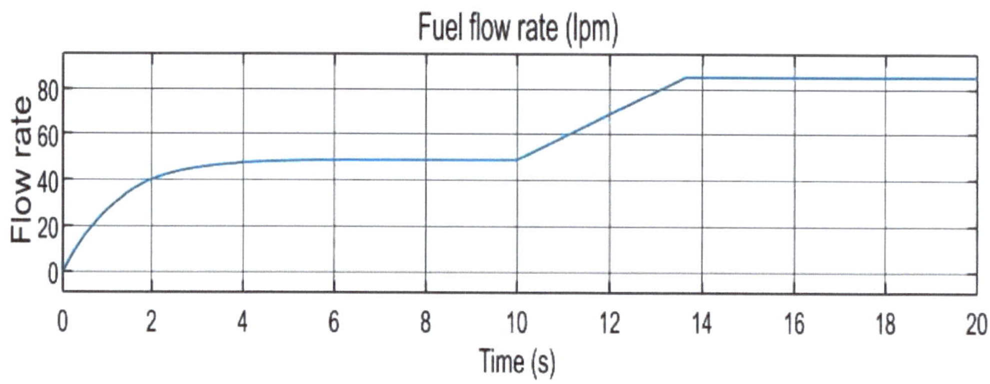

Fig. (15). Fuel flow rate.

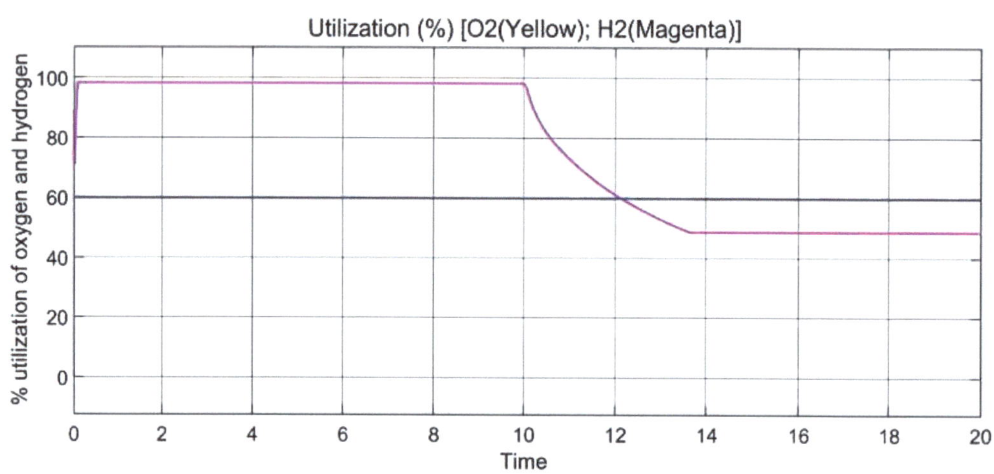

Fig. (16). Hydrogen and oxygen rate.

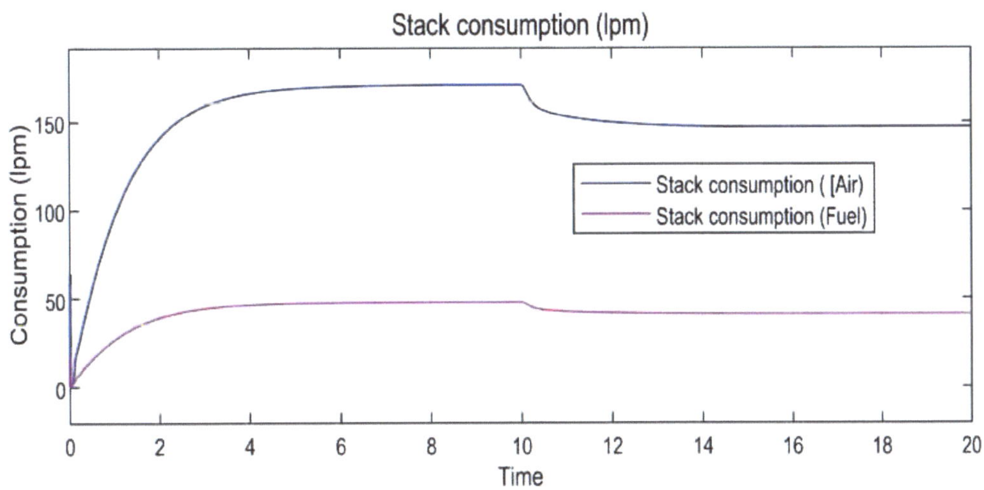

Fig. (17). Consumption and air.

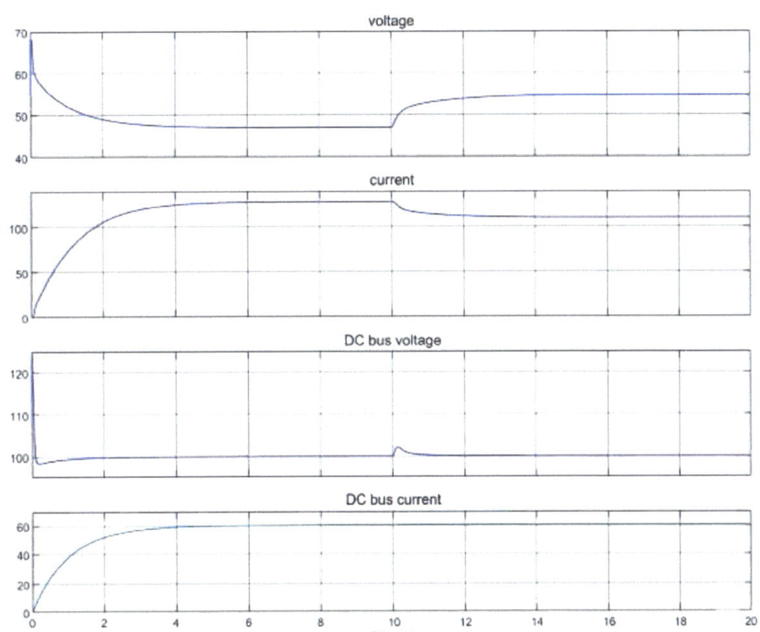

Fig. (18). Voltage and current control rate.

After performing simulations in MATLAB Simulink for the hydrogen-based drones, several key performance outputs were identified. Initially, the simulations aimed to determine optimal efficiency, resulting in a consistent fuel cell efficiency of 48% in Fig. (**19**). While the efficiency was higher at the start, it stabilised between 45% and 48% after reaching a saturation point. The second goal of the simulation was to control and measure the drone's speed. The results showed that the drone can achieve a maximum speed of 240 km per hour while carrying a payload. This capability highlights the drone's efficiency in transporting cargo over long distances at high speeds. In terms of payload capacity, the simulations indicated that the drone can carry up to 490 kg, making it suitable for substantial long-term deliveries. This capacity is crucial for intercity cargo transportation, allowing for the efficient handling of significant loads. Finally, the simulation results demonstrated an impressive flight duration. The drone can maintain continuous flight for up to 20 hours, providing extended operational time and reliability for extended delivery missions. Simulink simulations have provided valuable insights into the performance of hydrogen-based drones, confirming their high efficiency, speed, payload capacity, and long flight duration. These findings underscore the potential of hydrogen-powered drones as a viable solution for intercity cargo transportation.

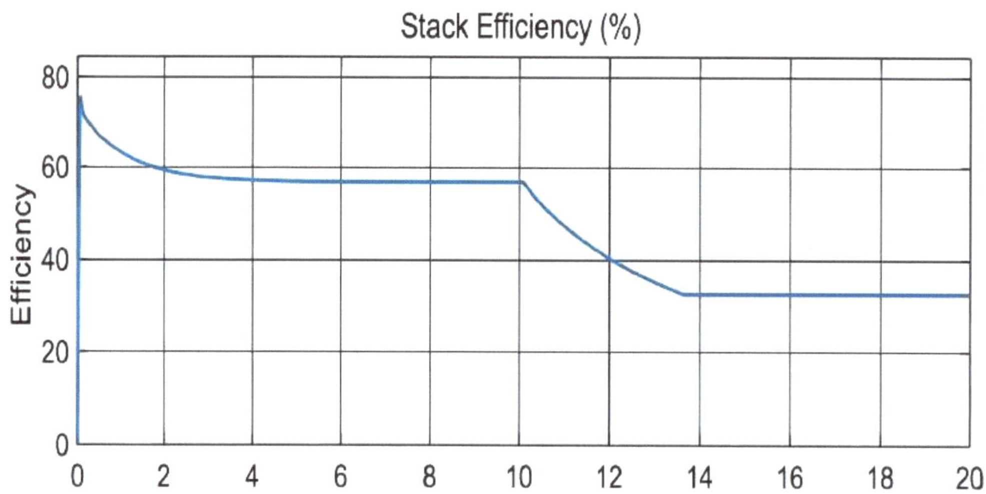

Fig. (19). Efficiency of fuel cell.

CONCLUSION AND FUTURE SCOPE

An important step toward more environmentally friendly and effective logistics solutions has been taken with the arrival of drones powered by hydrogen for intercity cargo transportation. Compared to traditional fossil fuels, hydrogen fuel cells are known for their excellent energy efficiency and low environmental impact. The drone system enables improved power management through the integration of hydrogen fuel cells with additional batteries, resulting in extended flight times and heightened operational dependability. MATLAB Simulink was used in the design and modeling of these drones, which brought to light a number of important performance indicators. While the drone's maximum speed, payload capacity, and flight length have been carefully adjusted to suit the demands of intercity cargo transport, continuous fuel cell efficiency has been enhanced using AI algorithms to assure maximum energy consumption. Having three propellers increases the aircraft's stability and maneuverability, which is necessary for navigating a variety of flight conditions and guaranteeing the safe and efficient delivery of goods. Drones powered by hydrogen offer a cleaner, lower-emission alternative to traditional freight transport, which could address the challenges associated with traditional freight systems. As the project moves further, validation of the design and performance metrics obtained in simulations will depend heavily on real-world testing and additional refinement. Development of advanced and efficient solutions for a range of technological uses is facilitated through the union of UAV systems and AI technology. Safe and effective transportation is one development that has been provided through the utilization of drones for cooperative transport. This collaborative approach also extends to last-mile delivery, where drones play a critical role in the logistics pipeline as they minimize transit times and optimize the delivery of products to their destinations. Drone design and hydrogen technology developments will probably continue to improve the system's dependability and efficiency, making hydrogen-powered drones a disruptive force in the logistics sector. The effective application of this technology may open doors for the wider adoption of environmentally friendly transportation options, resulting in an increasingly efficient and environmentally friendly future for intercity cargo transportation. Despite the fact that there are some major issues waiting ahead, the future for this technology is very promising. As a basis for building operations related to AI algorithms and drones, making sustainable and efficient batteries is an important issue.

REFERENCES

[1] M.N. Boukoberine, M.F. Zia, M. Benbouzid, Z. Zhou, and T. Donateo, "Hybrid fuel cell powered drones energy management strategy improvement and hydrogen saving using real flight test data", *Energy Convers. Manage.*, vol. 236, p. 113987, 2021. [http://dx.doi.org/10.1016/j.enconman.2021.113987]

[2] E. Ozbek, G. Yalin, M.U. Karaoglan, S. Ekici, C.O. Colpan, and T.H. Karakoc, "Architecture design and performance analysis of a hybrid hydrogen fuel cell system for unmanned aerial vehicle", *Int. J. Hydrogen Energy,* vol. 46, no. 30, pp. 16453-16464, 2021. [http://dx.doi.org/10.1016/j.ijhydene.2020.12.216]

[3] D. Hyun, J. Han, and S. Hong, "Power management strategy of hybrid fuel cell drones for flight performance improvement based on various algorithms", *Energies,* vol. 16, no. 24, p. 8001, 2023. [http://dx.doi.org/10.3390/en16248001]

[4] G.A.Q. Abdulrahman, N.A.A. Qasem, W.G. Abdelrahman, and A.M. Abdallah, "A review of powering unmanned aerial vehicles by clean and renewable energy technologies", *Sustain. Energy Technol. Assess.,* vol. 73, p. 104150, 2025. [http://dx.doi.org/10.1016/j.seta.2024.104150]

[5] R. Stroman, D. Edwards, P. Jenkins, S. Carter, D. Newton, and M. Kelly, "The hybrid tiger: A long endurance solar/fuel cell/soaring unmanned aerial vehicle", *Proc. 48th Power Sources Conf.,* pp. 317-320, 2018.

[6] R. Marqués, Á. Montero, C. Sánchez-Diaz, and I. Quintanilla, "Design methodology and simulation analysis of hybrid fuel cell and battery systems for powering unmanned aircraft systems", *Energy Convers. Manage.,* vol. 306, p. 118303, 2024. [http://dx.doi.org/10.1016/j.enconman.2024.118303]

[7] Z. Shen, S. Liu, W. Zhu, D. Ren, Q. Xu, and Y. Feng, "A review on key technologies and developments of hydrogen fuel cell multi-rotor drones", *Energies,* vol. 17, no. 16, p. 4193, 2024. [http://dx.doi.org/10.3390/en17164193]

[8] T. Hoff, F. Becker, A. Dadashi, K. Wicke, and G. Wende, "Implementation of Fuel Cells in Aviation from a Maintenance, Repair and Overhaul Perspective", *Aerospace (Basel),* vol. 10, no. 1, p. 23, 2022. [http://dx.doi.org/10.3390/aerospace10010023]

[9] S. Shaukat, and C-L. Wu, *"Impact of Hydrogen Fuel Cell Technology on Aircraft Maintenance: Reliability, Cost, and Safety," in *Challenges and Opportunities for Aviation Stakeholders in a Post-Pandemic World.* IGI Global, 2023, pp. 49-63. [http://dx.doi.org/10.4018/978-1-6684-6835-7.ch003]

[10] D. Hyun, J. Han, and S. Hong, "Power Management Strategy of Hybrid Fuel Cell Drones for Flight Performance Improvement Based on Various Algorithms", *Energies,* vol. 16, no. 24, p. 8001, 2023. [http://dx.doi.org/10.3390/en16248001]

[11] Z. Shen, S. Liu, W. Zhu, D. Ren, Q. Xu, and Y. Feng, "A Review on Key Technologies and Developments of Hydrogen Fuel Cell Multi-Rotor Drones", *Energies,* vol. 17, no. 16, p. 4193, 2024. [http://dx.doi.org/10.3390/en17164193]

[12] B. Sahoo, S.R. Samantaray, P.K. Rout, and G. Panda, "Dual Grid Energy Management Strategy for Electric Vehicles in Hybrid Microgrid Utilizing Matrix Pencil Method", *Int. J. Emerg. Electr. Power Syst.,* vol. 25, no. 3, pp. 1-15, 2024.

[13] M. Saadi, D. Djalel, B. Meghni, and D. Rekioua, "Intelligent Energy Management Strategy and Sizing Methodology for Hybrid Systems in Isolated Regions", *Chinese Journal of Electrical Engineering,* vol. 10, no. 3, pp. 50-62, 2024. [http://dx.doi.org/10.23919/CJEE.2024.000091]

[14] I. Marouani, T. Guesmi, B.M. Alshammari, K. Alqunun, A. Alzamil, M. Alturki, and H. Hadj Abdallah, "Integration of Renewable-Energy-Based Green Hydrogen into the Energy Future", *Processes (Basel),* vol. 11, no. 9, p. 2685, 2023. [http://dx.doi.org/10.3390/pr11092685]

[15] R.O. Stroman, D.J. Edwards, P. Jenkins, S. Carter, D. Newton, M. Kelly, S. Heinzen, T. Young, V. Dobrokhodov, J. Langelaan, J. Bird, and P.A. Reinecke, "The Hybrid Tiger: A long endurance solar/fuel cell/soaring unmanned aerial vehicle", *Proc. 48th Power Sources Conf.,* pp. 317-320, 2018.

[16] A.S. Mekonnin, K. Wacławiak, M. Humayun, S. Zhang, and H. Ullah, "Hydrogen storage technology, and its challenges: A review," *", *Catalysts,* vol. 15, no. 3, p. 260, 2025. [http://dx.doi.org/10.3390/catal15030260]

[17] S. Heinzen, "The Hybrid Tiger: A long endurance solar/fuel cell/soaring unmanned aerial vehicle", *Proc. 48th Power Sources Conf.,* pp. 317-320, 2018.

CHAPTER 6

A Study of Blockchain, IoT, and Cryptography in the Healthcare Sector: An Extensive Review

Priyanka Ghosh[1,*], **Paramita Sarkar**[1] and **Debdutta Pal**[2]

[1] *Department of Computer Science and Engineering, JIS University, Agarpara, Kolkata, India*

[2] *Department of Computer Science and Engineering, Adamas University, Kolkata, West Bengal, India*

Abstract: With a secure distributed ledger system, blockchain technology helps to shape the healthcare sector in terms of transparency and accountability. This research paper highlights the transformational impact that blockchain technology plays in the healthcare sector. It focuses on a variety of technologies, including patient data security, real-time monitoring enabled Internet of Things (IoTs). This paper also addresses the revolutionary impact that current technology, such as cryptography and Zero Knowledge Proofs (ZKPs), has played in shaping modern technology and improving privacy and security in the health care system. This study contrasts existing blockchain technologies with emergent developments that aid in the creation of a decentralized, safe ecosystem that promotes accountability. Blockchain provides a decentralized, immutable, and transparent ledger. It enhances security, privacy, and trust in data transactions without relying on centralized servers.

Keywords: Blockchain, Cryptography, Zero Knowledge Proofs (ZKPs), Internet of Things (IoT), Decentralized Ledger, Data Privacy, Smart Contracts, Electronic Health Record.

INTRODUCTION

Blockchain technology is a modern database mechanism that allows information sharing within a network with transparency [1]. A blockchain is a database that stores data in block format that is linked together within a chain. The data is chronologically consistent because it cannot be deleted or modified in the chain without consensus from the network. So, the blockchain can be used to create an unalterable ledger for tracking orders. It can also be used for tracking payments, accounts, and other transactions.

* **Corresponding author Priyanka Ghosh:** Department of Computer Science and Engineering, JIS University, Agarpara, Kolkata, India; E-mail: priyanka.ghosh@gnit.ac.in

Shilpa Gupta & Ritika Sharma (Eds.)

Blockchain is a digital system that executes and records transactions, which can be visualized as a building block, constructed from intelligent algorithms and secured by cryptography. In multiple fields like financial markets, military, or healthcare, private companies as well as governments are using blockchain technologies to design high-tech paradigms [2]. This is because trust is built into a model through immutable records on a distributed ledger. Many people consider blockchain technology as the most significant invention after the internet, and it is widely considered to resolve the trust issues of people using the internet using peer-to-peer networking and public key cryptography solutions [3]. It is commonly agreed that the technology currently needs time to mature, but we need to be ready for the adoption of this unprecedented archetype. There is a huge potential for Blockchain technology to radically transform interactions, raising critical questions for governments and society.

IMPLEMENTATION OF BLOCKCHAIN IN THE MEDICAL INDUSTRY

Blockchain can be applied in the healthcare sector due to its high-level security and patients' medical data exchange, which will lead to ultimate cost reduction and new ways to access patients' healthcare and maintain privacy [4]. The combination of the compounding nature of data and future-proofing technology can be applied to foster an era of innovation [5, 6]. Many companies are laying the foundations for a blockchain revolution. Discussing different types of blockchain with their advantages and disadvantages.

Table 1. Different types of blockchain.

SUBJECT	PUBLIC	PRIVATE	HYBRID	SECTORS
ADVANTAGES	• Independence • Transparency • Trust	• Access Control • Performance	• Access Control • Performance • Scalability	• Access Control • Scalability • Security
DISADVANTAGES	• Performance • Scalability • Security	• Trust • Audit ability	• Transparency • Upgrading	• Transparency
USE CASES	• Crypto currency • Document Validation	• Supply Chain • Asset Ownership	• Medical Sectors • Real Estate	• Banking • Research • Supply Chain

Public Blockchain: A public blockchain is a decentralized and open network where anyone can join, access, and participate without restrictions. All transactions and data are recorded on a transparent ledger visible to all participants. These blockchains rely on consensus mechanisms such as Proof of Work (PoW) or Proof of Stake (PoS) to validate transactions and maintain security. Public blockchains are highly secure and resistant to tampering due to their decentralized nature, though they may face issues related to scalability and energy consumption. Examples include Bitcoin and Ethereum, which are widely used for cryptocurrencies, decentralized applications, and smart contracts, as shown in Table **1**.

Private Blockchain: A private blockchain is a permissioned network where only authorized participants can access and contribute to the system. It is typically controlled by a single organization or a consortium of entities. Unlike public blockchains, private blockchains are more centralized and offer greater control over data access, privacy, and transaction speed. These features make private blockchains suitable for enterprise use cases such as supply chain management, internal auditing, banking, and healthcare systems. Hyperledger Fabric and R3 Corda are popular examples of private blockchain platforms.

Hybrid Blockchain: A hybrid blockchain combines elements of both public and private blockchains to provide a balanced solution. It allows certain data to be kept private while enabling other information to be shared on a public ledger. This structure is ideal for organizations that need both transparency and confidentiality. Hybrid blockchains offer flexibility, scalability, and controlled access while still benefiting from the security and immutability of blockchain technology. Use cases include government services, healthcare data sharing, and enterprise collaboration. Examples include Dragon Chain and XinFin (XDC).

DISTRIBUTED LEDGER TECHNOLOGY

A Blockchain is a system that records whatever is shared between participants. It records all the transactions carried out by any of the members, and all participants will have a copy of the ledger. This system is known as replication. Each transaction is enclosed in a block. A block may contain multiple transactions and is the basic unit to be verified by all the members. Each block contains a hash value of the previous block's header and thus forms a hash chain or blockchain. All the blocks are chained, so the order of the blocks is maintained. Each block serves as a timestamp of the enclosed transaction. Each member maintains a copy of the blockchain [6]. In a network, one could distinguish between permissioned and permissionless blockchain systems.

IMPORTANCE OF ZKPS (ZERO-KNOWLEDGE PROOFS) IN BLOCKCHAIN TECHNOLOGY

Zero-Knowledge Proofs (ZKPs) have received a lot of focus in blockchain research, acting as crucial instruments to improve privacy, scalability, and security. Zero-Knowledge Proofs (ZKPs) are advanced techniques that provide multiple ways for a prover to show a verifier that a statement is true without revealing any personal details [7]. Zero-Knowledge Proofs (ZKPs) allow for the creation of evidence while guaranteeing data confidentiality. In the modern world, Zero-Knowledge Proofs are becoming more beneficial for every sector (Table **2**).

Table 2. Advantages and disadvantages of blockchain in different papers.

References	Applications	Advantages	Limitations
Evaluating and Developing Internet of Things (IoT) in Healthcare [9]	IoT security for remote monitoring	Data migration Real-time surveillance	Limited storage and lack of regulatory guidance.
Blockchain Technology for Strategic Product Deletion Management and Supply Chain Information [10]	Supply chain transparency	Traceable transactions Enhances drug safety	Delays hinder precise demand forecasting.
Using Blockchain for Electronic Health Records [19]	Patient-centric electronic health records	Patient accessibility Graphical user interface for users	Learning curve for healthcare providers.
The Credentials Subcommittee at X / The District Hospital: Implementing Nursing Credentials and Re-credentials [20]	Medical staff credential verification	Patient safety Increased third-party reimbursement	Application review may take 90 days to 6 months.
The Smart Contracts and Supply Chain Management using Blockchain [21]	Smart contracts for insurance and supply chain settlements	Secure for insurance providers, enhanced transparency, and security	Smart contract processes are unchangeable.

With the coordination of Blockchain, ZKPs gain a crucial role in healthcare. The Zero-Knowledge Proofs are a solution for securely sharing patient information while maintaining privacy by protecting the patient's medical and healthcare data. The transactions are getting more transparent and more secure with the help of Blockchain and ZKPs. Thus, the implementation of ZKPs in Blockchain and cryptography will be conducive for all domains [8] (Fig. **1**).

IOT (INTERNET OF THINGS) TECHNOLOGIES IN HEALTHCARE

The optimal management of a vast amount of data generated by IOT devices by several technologies like artificial intelligence, machine learning, Blockchain, cloud and fog computing, and ML is essential for analyzing large datasets. It offers real-time insights into predictive analytics. It also offers anomaly detection [9]. It is also useful for trend prediction. This capability is vital for easy disease detection for preventive measures.

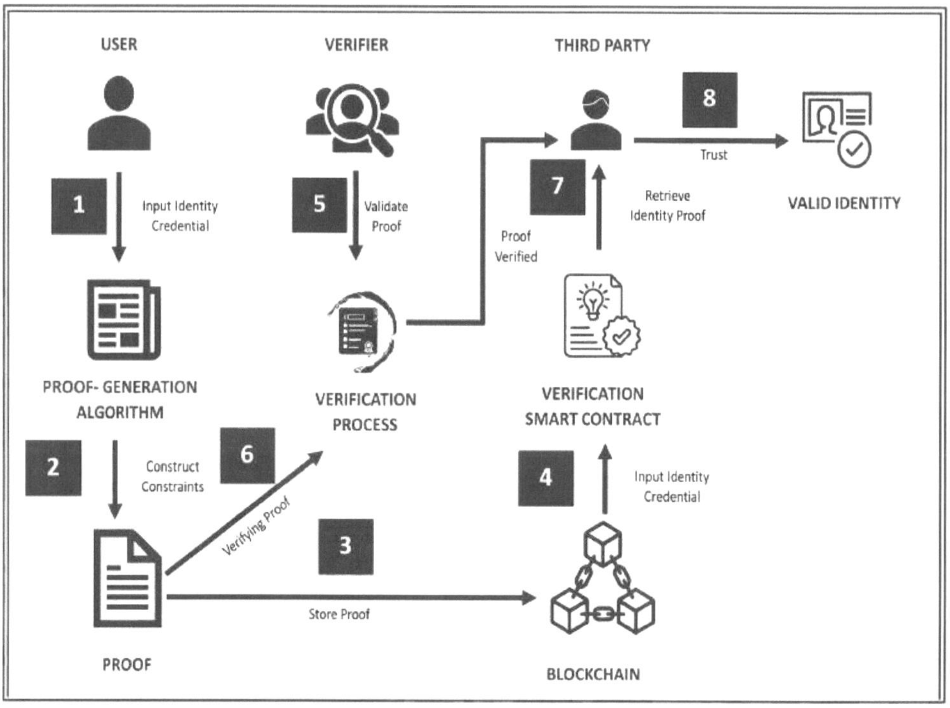

Fig. (1). ZKPs terminology with blockchain.

Restrictions on data access allow only authorized personnel [10]. This approach mitigates the risk of data bridges. It makes a robust solution for patient data confidentiality. Cloud and fog computing provide the necessary infrastructure that is required to manage this data. Cloud computing offers flexible storage and high processing power. On the other hand, fog computing extends processing capabilities, which are closer to the IOT devices. It reduces latency.

BLOCKCHAIN METHODOLOGY

Blockchain is an open digital ledger that securely stores data on a network of computers, ensuring transparency, unchangeability, and resistance to tampering. The Blockchain methodology consists of various technologies. Integrating Blockchain with other applications boosts its effectiveness and opens new opportunities, offering better scalability, privacy, and functionality in multiple sectors.

System and Working of Cryptography with Blockchain Technology

Cryptography is a method or technique used to attain message secrecy. Currently, the privacy of individuals is a major concern. Cryptography ensures a next level of security for organizations, ensuring that the data transmitted is protected in a manner that only the approved recipient has the ability to retrieve this data [11]. The cryptography technology maintains a system in which normal text is converted into ciphertext so that unauthorized individuals will not be able to understand what they are observing in a situation where they have obtained the data. In cryptography terminology, the given information, which is typically referred to as "plaintext," was typically masked. While the mimicking plaintext is called "encryption," the plaintext that has been encrypted is called "ciphertext. On the other hand, the process of ciphertext to plaintext is called decryption, where the ciphertext again becomes the plaintext. For both encryption and decryption, we need the key to compute the plaintext from the ciphertext and vice versa. The encryption and decryption support two types of encryption systems: symmetric encryption and asymmetric encryption. In symmetric encryption, the sender and the receiver both need the same security key to encrypt and decrypt. However, asymmetric encryption requires different keys (the sender needs a public key to encrypt and the receiver needs a private key to decrypt) (Fig. **2**).

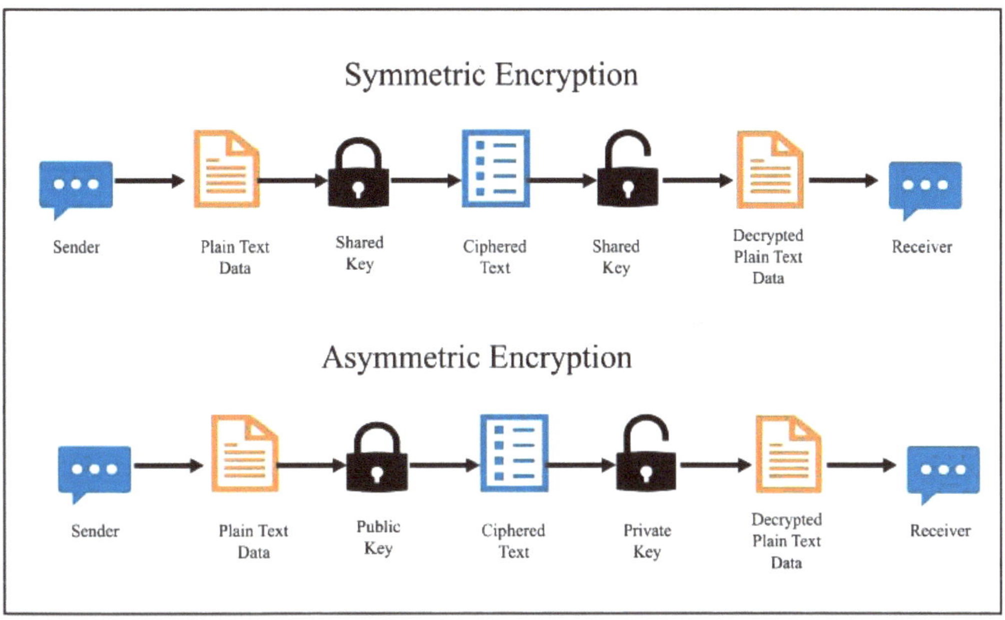

Fig. (2). Diagram of two types of encryption methods of cryptography.

The deployment of Blockchain technology utilizes cryptography to ensure security. It brings safety as well as transparency to transactions [12]. After the blockchain implementation, the security and privacy of any issued message always remain safe. With this, even in healthcare, the most important PHRs

(Patient Health Records) continuously remain in reliable hands, as doctors and individual patients will only have restricted access to specific data. The encrypted text, which is basically known as ciphertext, is established through various steps (Fig. **3**).

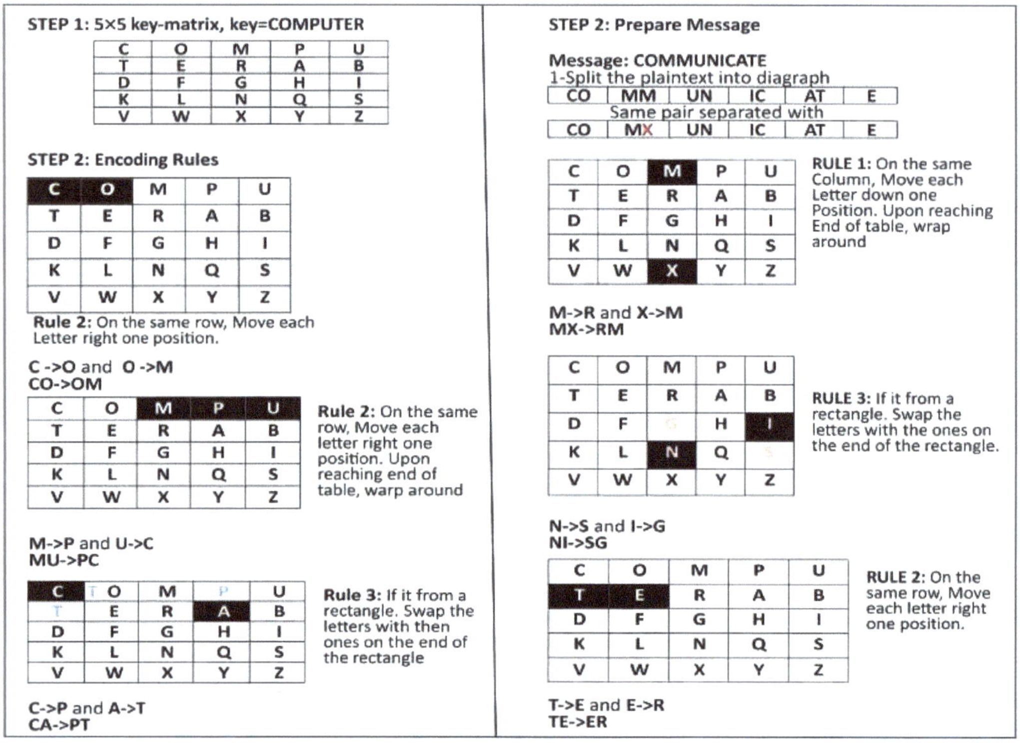

Fig. (3). Encryption process in cryptography with an example [12].

Strategic Product Deletion Management

Supply chains can be managed transparently, effectively, and with security (Fig. 4).

Blockchain is a decentralized digital record. When it comes to strategically deleting blocks, it works on a network of functions without a central database or authority. If the data is recorded, it cannot be changed because of cryptographic hashing, which improves data security [13]. Smart contracts are self-executing programs that, when certain circumstances are met, automatically make payments and minimize intermediaries and errors, cutting out the middleman [14].

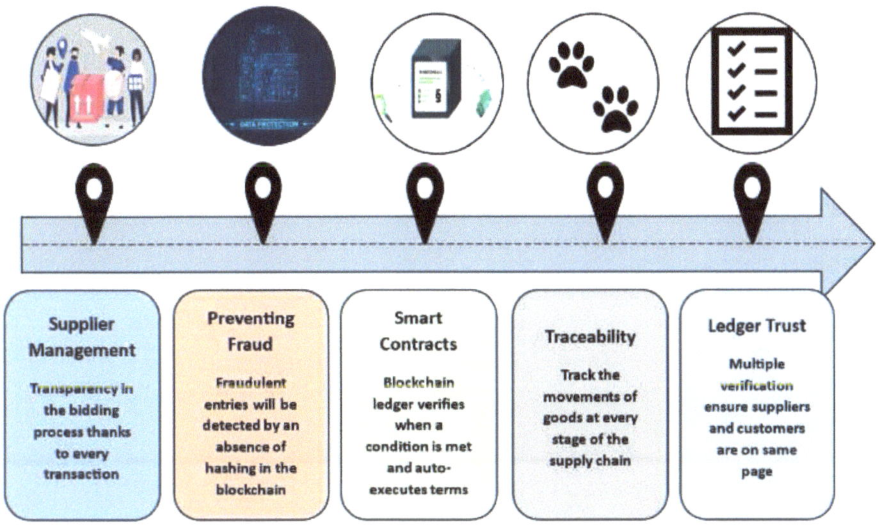

Fig. (4). Implementation of blockchain in supply chain.

Effects of Information Transparency on Supply Chain Quality Management

This research paper explains the context of supply chain quality management. Its focus is on the principal-agent model. This model addresses how sampling inspections and information transparency affect supplier behavior and thus product quality in a supply chain setting. This model explains key mathematical expressions, which include the demand function (Equation **1**).

$$D(p, \varepsilon) = a - bp + c\varepsilon \quad \textbf{(1)}$$

D is the quantity demanded of a product. P is the cost of the product. ε (epsilon) is the quality of the product. *a*, *b*, and *c* are parameters that control how sensitive demand is to changes in price and quality.

The function states that demand rises with better product quality (ε) and is affected by price (p). The parameters (a, b, c) help to define how gradual changes in price and quality will impact demand (D). Higher quality generally results in increased demand, and the sensitivity to price and quality varies based on these parameters.

Quality Cost Function:

$$v(\varepsilon) = \alpha s \varepsilon 2 + \beta s \quad \textbf{(2)}$$

The expression v(ε) denotes the cost related to achieving a specific level of product quality, denoted by ε (Equation **2**). The parameters α and β influence this cost, while s represents a scaling factor. The statement indicates that as the desired product quality ε gets closer to 1 (which likely signifies the highest quality), the additional cost required to improve quality—that is, the marginal cost—becomes higher. Achieving near-perfect quality is increasingly expensive [14].

Quality Management Combining Information Transparency and Punishment.

Here, we consider a combination of two control mechanisms: sampling inspection-based punishment and information transparency [15]. The supplier's expected properties (Equation **3**).

$$\Pi s3 = wD - (1 - \epsilon)Pm3(r + g)D - v \tag{3}$$

Π_{s3}: Profit of supplier s3 under certain quality and transparency conditions, c: Supplier charges to the next party in the supply chain, D: Represents em and, ε: Quality level of product, Pm3: Penalty or punishment rate, r: Base rate, g: Additional cost, v: Quality cost function depends on the quality level [16].

The manufacturer's expected profit is (Equation **4**):

$$\Pi_{m3} = (P - w) + (1 - \epsilon)P_{my}gD - (1 - P_{m3})\,(1 - \epsilon)\,Dh - I_3 \tag{4}$$

Π_{m3}: Profit or performance measure, p: Selling price of the product, c: Wholesale or unit cost, D: Demand, H: Quality related to inspection or penalty adjustment, ε: Quality related to inspection or penalty adjustment, Pm3:

Product level quality, g: Probability of penalty rate, h: Additional cost or penalty factor, I3: Holding or handling cost per unit [17].

By using the first-order condition, we can obtain the optimal quality level (Equation **5**):

$$\epsilon 3 *= P_{m3}(g + r)(a + bp - C_0) - \frac{wa}{2(a(r + g)P_{m3} - a_s)} \tag{5}$$

ϵ_3*: Target quality level for supplier s3, which maximizes their profit or minimizes their penalty, P: Punishment rate, g and r: Components of cost associated with product assurance, a, b, and c_0: Base demand level, Sensitivity of demand to price, Base demand offset, p: Price of the product, c: Wholesale rate. Then it can be proved that the optimal quality level under the combined mechanisms is higher than that obtained under information transparency. (The proof is omitted to save space.) [18].

Comparison with Previous and New Emerging Blockchain Technology in Healthcare

Permission Model

Previously, public blockchains like Bitcoin and Ethereum were used. This has shifted towards permissioned blockchains like Hyperledger Fabric for better privacy and access control.

Privacy Features

Basic features offered no advanced privacy controls. But with emerging technology, privacy-in-hand blockchains with zero-knowledge proofs enable confidential transactions (*e.g.*, Enigma, Zcash).

Transaction Speed

Beforehand, the transaction speed was low (Bitcoin: approximately 7 TPS; Ethereum: approximately 15 TPS). Nowadays, high-speed transaction networks have emerged (*e.g.*, Solana, Hedera Hashgraph) with over 10,000 TPS [19].

Healthcare Use Cases

previously, the focus was on general applications like cryptocurrencies or basic data sharing. But now, specialized platforms for healthcare are used (*e.g.*, BurstIQ, Pharma Ledger, Nebula Genomics, *etc.*), which enable precision medicine, drug traceability, and secure genomic data sharing [20].

CONCLUSION

Blockchain technology offers the potential to improve healthcare systems by providing a decentralized ledger. In this decentralized ledger, transactions are both immutable and traceable. This paper suggests that blockchain technology will enhance the public healthcare sector by promoting accountability and transparency in patient-focused services. Our approach employs zero-knowledge proofs for authentication and enables efficient and secure sharing of Electronic Health Records (EHRs) while preserving privacy. A hybrid encryption model that combines both symmetric and asymmetric encryption is included to address the limitations of proxy re-encryption. In this way, it serves as an access control mechanism for medical data. The implementation of blockchain with the Internet of Things (IoT) enables patients to share health-related data in real time with specific doctors and healthcare systems. Blockchain's best applications are rapidly emerging, and we plan to conduct further in-depth research on their potential applications in the healthcare sector in the future.

This paper also discusses the technologies used previously versus the technologies evolved now, using blockchain and cryptography mechanisms in the healthcare sector. It also includes the future scope for the development of such technologies.

REFERENCES

[1] A. Haleem, M. Javaid, R.P. Singh, R. Suman, and S. Rab, "Blockchain technology applications in healthcare: An overview", *International Journal of Intelligent Networks,* vol. 2, pp. 130-139, 2021. [http://dx.doi.org/10.1016/j.ijin.2021.09.005]

[2] A. Tandon, A. Dhir, A.K.M.N. Islam, and M. Mäntymäki, "Blockchain in healthcare: A systematic literature review, synthesizing framework and future research agenda", *Comput. Ind.,* vol. 122, p. 103290, 2020. [http://dx.doi.org/10.1016/j.compind.2020.103290]

[3] T. Justinia, "Blockchain technologies: Opportunities for solving real-world problems in healthcare and biomedical sciences", *Acta Inform. Med.,* vol. 27, no. 4, pp. 284-291, 2019. [http://dx.doi.org/10.5455/aim.2019.27.284-291] [PMID: 32055097]

[4] A. Kashyap, A. Yadav, V. Bajaj, Y. Khan, S. Arora, and L. Maini, "Blockchain technology in healthcare: The idea and what lies beyond", *MAMC Journal of Medical Sciences,* vol. 8, no. 3, pp. 187-192, 2022. [http://dx.doi.org/10.4103/mamcjms.mamcjms_26_22]

[5] A. K. Singh, and V. R. Kumar, "Smart contracts and supply chain management using blockchain", *J. Control Eng. Appl. Inf.,* vol. 24, no. 4, pp. 76-87, 2022. [http://dx.doi.org/10.36909/jer.ACMM.16307]

[6] E. Sud, S. Agarwal, and L.A.V. Upadhyay, "The Power I Know: Zero-knowledge proofs and their transformative role in the future of cryptography", pp. 147317–147329, 2025.

[7] H.R. Yugha, S. Chithra, N. Bhalaji, and S. Karthika, "Privacy protected IoT-Blockchain using ZKP for healthcare application", *J. Control Eng. Appl. Inf.,* vol. 24, no. 4, pp. 76-87, 2022.

[8] A. Rejeb, K. Rejeb, H. Treiblmaier, A. Appolloni, S. Alghamdi, Y. Alhasawi, and M. Iranmanesh, "The Internet of Things (IoT) in healthcare: Taking stock and moving forward", *Internet of Things,* vol. 22, p. 100721, 2023. [http://dx.doi.org/10.1016/j.iot.2023.100721]

[9] Q. Zhu, and M. Kouhizadeh, "Blockchain technology, supply chain information, and strategic product deletion management", *IEEE Eng. Manage. Rev.,* vol. 47, no. 1, pp. 36-44, 2019. [http://dx.doi.org/10.1109/EMR.2019.2898178]

[10] A.M. Qadir, and N. Varol, "A review paper on cryptography", *Symp. Digital Forensics and Security (ISDFS),* pp. 1-6, 2019.

[11] S. Ahmad, S.K. Arya, S. Gupta, P. Singh, and S.K. Dwivedi, "Study of cryptographic techniques adopted in blockchain", *in 2023 4th Int. Conf. Intell. Eng. Manag.,* (ICIEM), pp. 1-6, 2023. [http://dx.doi.org/10.1109/ICIEM59379.2023.10166591]

[12] Sugito, Luky Dwiantoro, Anggorowati, and Madya Sulisno, "Implementation of nursing credentials and recredentials by the credentials subcommittee at X District Hospital", *Jurnal Berita Ilmu Keperawatan,* vol. 16, no. 1, pp. 53-67, 2023. [http://dx.doi.org/10.23917/bik.v16i1.1375]

[13] C. Singh, R. Thakkar, and J. Warraich, "Blockchain in supply chain management", *European Journal of Engineering and Technology Research,* vol. 7, no. 5, pp. 60-69, 2022. [http://dx.doi.org/10.24018/ejeng.2022.7.5.2888]

[14] C.J.H. Xiao, Z.L. Cheng, C.W. Zhang, and K. Xie, "Effects of information transparency on supply chain quality management", *in 2012 IEEE Int. Conf. Ind. Eng. Eng. Manag.,* pp. 966-970, 2012. [http://dx.doi.org/10.1109/IEEM.2012.6837884]

[15] L.D.J.S.R. Dejan Vujičić, "Blockchain technology, bitcoin, and Ethereum: A brief overview, ResearchGate", Serbia, 2018.

[16] P.D. Vujičić, D. Jagodić, and S. Ranđić, "Blockchain technology, bitcoin, and Ethereum: A brief overview", *Symp. Infoteh-Jahorina (INFOTEH),* pp. 1-6, 2018. [http://dx.doi.org/10.1109/INFOTEH.2018.8345547]

[17] L.Z. Zheng, S. Xie, H. Dai, X. Chen, and H. Wang, "An overview of blockchain technology: Architecture, consensus, and future trends", *in 2017 IEEE Int. Congr. Big Data (BigData Congress),* pp. 557-564, 2017. [http://dx.doi.org/10.1109/BigDataCongress.2017.85]

[18] M.S. Al-kahtani, F. Khan, and W. Taekeun, "Application of internet of things and sensors in healthcare", *Sensors (Basel),* vol. 22, no. 15, p. 5738, 2022. [http://dx.doi.org/10.3390/s22155738] [PMID: 35957294]

[19] A. Shahnaz, U. Qamar, and A. Khalid, "Using blockchain for electronic health records", *IEEE Access,* vol. 7, pp. 147782-147795, 2019. [http://dx.doi.org/10.1109/ACCESS.2019.2946373]

[20] L. D. Sugito, A. M. H. Ardani, and M. Sulisno, "Implementation of nursing credentials and recredentials by the credentials subcommittee at X District Hospital", *J. Ber. Ilmu Keperawatan,* vol. 16, pp. 53-67, .

[21] A.K. Singh, and V.P. Kumar, ""Smart contracts and supply chain management using blockchain," J. Eng. Res", *ACM M,* no. Spec. Issue, pp. 1-11, 2022.

CHAPTER 7

Artificial Intelligence in Healthcare: A Guide to Strategic and Sustainable Integration

Sheetal[1], **Rajni Sharma**[2] and **Love Singla**[2,*]

[1] *Department of Zoology, Maharaja Agrasen University, Baddi, Himachal Pradesh, India*

[2] *Department of Biotechnology and Microbiology, Maharaja Agrasen University, Baddi, Himachal Pradesh, India*

Abstract: The advent of Artificial Intelligence (AI) is revolutionizing healthcare and reshaping diagnostics, treatment, and patient care. This chapter explores AI's transformative role in modern medicine, emphasizing its ability to enhance precision, streamline processes, and make healthcare more accessible. Through algorithms that analyze vast amounts of data, AI enables early detection of diseases, accurate diagnosis, and personalized treatment plans tailored to individual genetic profiles and health histories. It optimizes workflows, reducing the administrative burden on healthcare professionals and allowing them to focus more on patient care. AI-driven tools, such as predictive analytics, assist in identifying at-risk populations, aiding in preventative care and resource allocation. Robotics and AI-powered surgical systems enhance the accuracy and outcomes of complex procedures, reducing recovery times and complications.

Additionally, AI-driven telemedicine platforms increase access to healthcare in remote and underserved areas, breaking geographical barriers. However, the rapid integration of AI presents ethical and regulatory challenges, including concerns about data privacy, algorithmic biases, and the need for human oversight in critical decision-making. This chapter delves into these issues, discussing the evolving role of AI in clinical settings and research and the collaborative efforts required to ensure AI is used responsibly and effectively in healthcare. By examining case studies and current applications, the chapter aims to comprehensively understand how AI shapes a future where healthcare is more innovative, faster, and patient-centered.

Keywords: AI, Healthcare, Natural language processing, Robotics surgery.

INTRODUCTION

Artificial intelligence (AI) in the healthcare sector encompasses various applications, from image recognition technology that detects disease in images to

[*] **Corresponding author Love Singla:** Department of Biotechnology and Microbiology, Maharaja Agrasen University, Baddi, Himachal Pradesh, India; E-mail: Lsingla04@gmail.com

Shilpa Gupta & Ritika Sharma (Eds.)

predictive models that extrapolate patient outcomes. Key components of AI in this domain include Machine Learning (ML), Natural Language Processing (NLP), and robotics. Simply machine learning allows computers to learn from data, identify patterns, and improve accuracy without human intervention. Deep learning (a machine learning subtype based on artificial neural networks) is an essential player in complex tasks such as image and speech recognition, making it useful for medical image interpretation (*e.g.*, X-rays, MRIs) [1].

Natural Language Processing (NLP), the second pillar of AI, enables computers to understand human language and is used in many applications like Electronic Health Records (EHRs) and clinical documentation. NLP, which derives meaningful information from unstructured data like physician notes and medical literature, enhances the capacity to analyze medical records and research in real time. Although separate from AI, robotics includes automation and precision technologies driven by AI to improve surgical procedures, rehabilitation, and routine patient care tasks. Unlike humans, AI has the capability of processing and analysing data at speeds and scales that no human can handle, notably in healthcare, where the increasing amount of patient data exceeds our human ability to interpret it. Using genomic data, AI can predict disease risk, track vital signs in real time, and help clinicians identify the best treatment approach [2]. Therefore, AI serves as a partner for healthcare professionals, providing support to enhance human capabilities rather than being a replacement. We want to highlight the perfect blend of human intelligence and AI-driven insights with numerous untapped potential to improve healthcare outcomes.

AI in healthcare started with early research aimed at automating medical tasks and interpreting data in the mid-20th century. AI was first introduced into medicine in the 1960s when early experiments in clinical decision-making were carried out. For example, systems such as MYCIN and INTERNIST-I, which were developed in the 1970s, employed rule-based algorithms to help physicians diagnose infections and complex internal diseases. These systems showed that AI was possible, but at the time, their limited computing power and hard-coded rules made them impossible to apply widely anyway. The 1990s saw stumbling blocks in computing and data storage get knocked down, supporting more complex healthcare applications. While this happened, we were in the earlier stages of building AI-assisted tools to interpret medical images, including mammograms and CT scans. AI applications have also started in diagnostic labs, assisting pathologists with automated blood sample and cell image analysis [3]. Pioneering usage of artificial intelligence paved the way for considerations that would lead to modern AI: better computational capacity, more sophisticated algorithms, and datasets measured in petabytes. Widespread EHRs in the 2000s have facilitated access to clinical data, thus accelerating AI implementation." With the initiation of EHR systems, machine learning had a large new storehouse of patient data to operate on: digitized records that would enable algorithms to learn patterns, predict future outcomes, or make clinical recommendations. The proliferation of AI-based tools started managing patient records, reviewing medical literature, and helping physicians make evidence-based decisions [4]. AI applications have been proliferating over the last decade in almost every aspect of healthcare, from diagnostics and treatment planning to patient monitoring. Today, radiologists use AI to help them detect imaging anomalies, predict patient outcomes based on past data, and provide virtual care *via* telemedicine. Indeed, the COVID-19 pandemic served as an additional push for AI in healthcare, where AI models were used to forecast virus transmission, create vaccines, and detect vulnerable patients [5]. This undeniably emphasizes that technology may merely need a crisis to showcase its importance and potential adaptability.

AI's transformative role in healthcare is highlighted, with a particular emphasis on diagnostics, personalized medicine, Workflow optimization, Surgical precision, automation (assistance), Telemedicine, and Accessibility. Looking at all these aspects, this chapter aims to paint a holistic picture of the capabilities AI has adopted in transforming the healthcare space and bettering human lives.

AI-ENHANCED DIAGNOSTICS AND DISEASE DETECTION

AI has also changed diagnostics and disease detection, especially in the fields of radiology, pathology, and genomics, where it assists health professionals in early detection and the accuracy and operational efficiency of other types of upstream technology. AI has demonstrated its promise in the real world by supporting healthcare professionals in delivering high-quality, timely, and personalized patient care. By refining the basic frameworks of existing automated tools, AI plays a critical role in diagnostic pathways, offering accurate detection of some diseases, and through this process, alleviating the burden on healthcare services, ultimately allowing for more timely and accurate diagnostics in the future [6]. With the growth of AI, we could find it playing an even larger role in diagnostics, bringing incredible advancements to modern medicine that will further enhance global patient outcomes.

Identifying illnesses is vital for effective treatment and good results for patients. If a disease is diagnosed early, its spread can be reduced to some extent, survival rates can also increase, and the cost of treatment becomes lower. AI further ensures better early detection of diseases by examining medical images, lab results, and even patient history to spot potential indicators or patterns that are sometimes missed by human vision. Utilizing AI algorithms that identify deviations in data measurement, clinicians can be alerted to upcoming health problems early enough to take preventative measures. The most promising aspect of AI is how quickly it can analyze medical imaging data. Computer vision, a branch of AI that allows computers to interpret and understand visual data from the world around us, plays an essential role in many radiology applications where vast amounts of X-rays, CT scans, MRIs, and mammograms are generated daily. These images can then be scanned by an AI-powered algorithm in a matter of seconds, which will detect irregularities in the images such as tumors or lesions. Consider breast cancer screening; here, AI algorithms have shown a high sensitivity for scanning mammogram images and confirming the presence of early-stage cancers that are difficult to see in the actual lesion [7].

AI is also developing in areas outside imaging, such as biomarkers and genomic data analysis. AI algorithms, for example, in genomics, can identify combinations of mutations for a particular gene linked to the disease being studied, such as cancer or other hereditary disorders. For example, in predictive medicine, AI can identify mutations that suggest a higher risk of particular cancers, leading to early intervention and preventive measures before symptoms appear. AI-based models can determine the risk for cardiovascular disease, diabetes, and Alzheimer's when patient lifestyle, genetics, and lab data are evaluated as part of a screening process. Not only does AI increase detection accuracy, but it also makes the whole screening process efficient. Automated systems take a significant burden off the shoulders of healthcare workers so that they can direct their time, effort, and resources to where they are needed most. They help scan massive data sets and flag possible problem areas for medical professionals to check. Doing so hastens the diagnosis process while reducing the possibility of human error [8].

Benefits of AI in Improving Diagnostic Accuracy and Efficiency: Especially when it comes to accuracy and efficiency, we can find a variety of benefits from AI applications in diagnostics. Though popular among physicians due to their effectiveness, traditional diagnostic methods are still time-consuming and work with varied success based on clinicians' knowledge and implementation skill level. AI helps alleviate some of these restrictions by delivering transparency to the diagnostic process through evidence-based, data-driven insights. Fig. (**1**) illustrates the different applications of AI in diagnostic accuracy and efficiency.

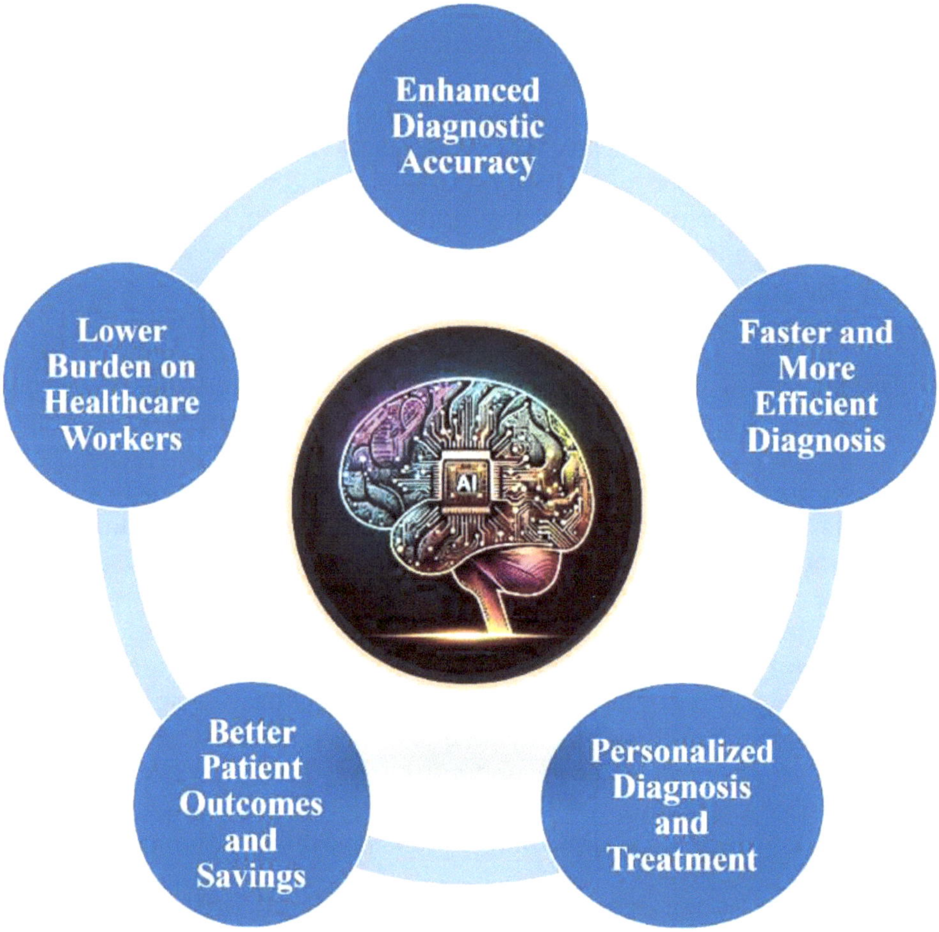

Fig. (1). Benefits of inculcating ai in improving diagnostic accuracy and efficiency.

1. **Enhanced Diagnostic Accuracy:** This helps boost the odds that a more accurate diagnosis will be received through AI pattern recognition capabilities, which allows AIs to detect disease markers with greater precision than what human imaging alone provides. This is particularly useful for detecting more subtle abnormalities, such as in medical images or genetic data that may easily be missed. In a breast cancer screening study, AI algorithms even reduced false negatives by 9.4% and false positives by 5.7%. Greater precision results in more accurate diagnoses, alleviating the emotional and financial toll associated with misdiagnosis, from which patients and families suffer [9].
2. **Faster and More Efficient Diagnosis:** AI rapidly speeds up the diagnosis process by handling routine tasks, freeing clinicians to work on more complex cases or direct care efforts. AI can quickly scan hundreds of images in seconds,

allowing for quicker diagnosis in emergencies, such as stroke or trauma cases, and has helped contribute to faster diagnostic success than is possible compared to a human being over time, such as in radiology. Likewise, when AI conducts initial assessments in pathology and genomics, not only do patient outcomes improve with expedient workflows, but so does pathologist and geneticist productivity as they can execute their work faster than ever before, knowing that these findings have been vetted by an intelligent algorithm [10].

3. **Lower Burden on the Healthcare Workers:** Lack of medical imaging and shortage of specialists have put an enormous workload on radiologists and pathologists. AI can help reduce this load by performing repetitive tasks, like initial scans or basic image comparisons, and flagging cases that need closer inspection. This decreases healthcare professionals' burnout chances while ensuring patients get diagnosed correctly and on time [11].
4. **Better Patient Outcomes and Savings:** AI can help detect diseases early, so the proper intervention can happen before it is too late. It prevents the onset of aggravation in chronic diseases and helps prevent complications by early detection *via* AI-based screening tools, thereby ensuring fewer intensive treatments are conducted. This also means fewer costs to healthcare providers and patients, as later treatment of disease is always more costly and complicated [12].
5. **Personalized Diagnosis and Treatment Planning:** AI takes care of diagnostics and assists with customized treatment planning. By combining patient history and genetic information data with diagnostic data, AI systems are able to offer personalized recommendations that match each patient. AI can be applied to oncology, which shows which template treatment will fit the patient after focusing on the tumor type and genetic markers, which makes for a more effective therapy [13].

Personalized Treatment and Precision Medicine: Artificial Intelligence (AI) has led to personalized treatment and precision medicine in the healthcare sector, which optimizes medical care based on patient-specific factors. In conjunction with the human ability to take genetic and health information from individuals, AI can allow for personalized medicine offered by healthcare providers to provide more effective and efficient treatments instead of mass-produced medications. This part discusses how AI provides personalized treatment by assessing genetic information and health data, with particular experience in oncology, pharmacology, and long-term illness management. It also shows how AI can help predict healthcare and preventive interventions, further revolutionizing patient care [14].

Role of AI in Personalized Medicine *via* Genetic and Health Data: Patients with identical symptoms are given a uniform treatment process in conventional medicine. Although this method seems to work, it does not consider how varied patients with the same disease are, as we are all genetically and environmentally different, thus having variations in our lifestyles, which also significantly impact responder/non-responder rates. Precision medicine aims to bridge this gap by tailoring treatments based on each individual's health and genetic history. AI is integral to the precision medicine paradigm, as it processes large datasets and searches for patterns and associations that guide treatment decisions. This is where AI systems, mainly the machine learning based ones, come to play, sifting through intricate genetic data and linking this up with health outcomes. Genomic analysis searches for genetic markers linked to particular diseases or drug responses. For instance, in cancer treatment, AI can analyze a person's genomic profile to identify which mutations drive tumor growth so that oncologists can treat patients with therapies against those specific mutations. As a result, the reliance on alternative general-purpose procedures such as chemotherapy, which typically inflict serious adverse consequences, can be minimized [13].

AI incorporates data through Electronic Health Records (EHRs), lifestyle, and real-time monitoring devices to provide a fuller picture than genetics alone. Using Natural Language Processing (NLP), AI systems can recognize hidden patterns in unstructured data within EHRs, like clinical notes, diagnostic reports, and prior treatments. This data, combined with genetic information, enables AI to produce a personalized treatment plan that considers the unique particulars of an individual patient. Such a high degree of personalization can be advantageous in chronic disease management, where adherence to treatment and lifestyle changes are key determinants of outcome. This capability allows healthcare providers to analyze vast data sets rapidly and precisely, employing data-driven decisions that enhance treatment efficiency while reducing potential adverse consequences. By paying less attention to the patient segment and instead emphasizing personalized treatment, AI-driven healthcare helps bolster a paradigm shift [15].

Applications in Oncology, Pharmacology, and Chronic Disease Management: The degree of AI's relevance to personalized treatment is especially striking in the contexts of oncology, pharmacology, and chronic disease management, where custom-made interventions can land significant blows against cancer or reduce the cost and health impact of comorbidities.

1. **Oncology - Artificial Intelligence for precision medicine in cancer treatment:** AI-powered precision medicine: One of the first best bets is cancer treatment. Every cancer differs from tumor to tumor, and individualized treatment provides a better outcome. For instance, AI algorithms can analyze tumor genomics to identify mutations responsible for cancer and recommend

targeted therapies based on these analyses. AI tools such as IBM Watson for Oncology help oncologists recommend personalized treatment plans by analyzing patient-specific genetic mutation data and comparing it to global cancer databases. The AI system can screen the drugs, determine how a patient may respond to the drug, and help clinicians make decisions regarding treatment options [16]. Immunotherapy, or a treatment that utilizes the patient's immune system to battle cancer, is another area of oncology where AI has found its place. Immunotherapy, one treatment modality that isn't effective for everyone, has its possibility of success foretold by AI algorithms analyzing patient genetic and proteomic data. This will help oncologists avoid preventable treatments and start with therapies with the most potential for success due to an AI-based algorithm. AI has effectively enabled more precise cancer treatments by predicting which patients will respond well to specific immunotherapies in clinical trials [17].

2. **Pharmacology - AI in Drug Development and Personalized Medication:** Pharmaceutical science Aids and simplifies the right way to manufacture customized medications. The process of developing traditional drugs takes a lot of time and money; it usually lasts for years before a new drug reaches the market. This process has been accelerated by AI's genetic and molecular data analysis to identify possible drug candidates and their potential efficacy quickly. AI-driven tools such as Atom-wise and *In-silico* Medicine apply deep learning algorithms to study molecular structure and forecast the species that will work against a given disease, dramatically shortening the time needed in preclinical testing [18]. Another aspect of AI strength is that personalized medication (drugs and drug doses) is targeted against individual patients. They metabolize drugs differently due to age, genetics, and health status. AI can analyse these factors and recommend optimal dosage amounts that maximise efficacy with minimal side effects. For example, AI-driven systems could examine patients' data to forecast the best doses for blood pressure medicines in hypertension cases, thus lowering trial-and-error pathways and ensuring better conformity with therapy. In pharmacology, AI improves patient outcomes by providing safer and more accurate use of medicines [19].
3. **Applications of AI in Diabetes, Cardiovascular Disease, and Other Chronic Conditions:** Chronic conditions, including diabetes and cardiovascular disease, necessitate continual management and monitoring; therefore, they are perfect targets for personalized AI care. AI tools take in continuous glucose monitor, insulin pump, and lifestyle record data to make customized recommendations on diet, insulin doses, and activity levels; all this is possible in diabetes management, as best illustrated by an IBM Watson Diabetes Care system. These real-time AI solutions enable the patient to manage their condition, ensuring they do not have any complications and live a

quality life [20]. AI also helps to handle cardiovascular disease problems by predicting heart attack/stroke events based on patient data. Using information such as cholesterol levels, blood pressure, lifestyle patterns, and possible genetic factors, predictive AI models compute an individual risk profile. Using this profile, healthcare providers can tailor a care plan, like suggesting specific lifestyle changes or modifying medications. Combining AI in chronic disease management can enhance patient engagement and help clinicians create customized treatment strategies that suit patients based on their needs and health risks [21].

Potential of AI in Predictive Healthcare and Preventive Interventions: The capability to predict health outcomes and proactively intervene has been one of AI's most touted prospects within precision medicine, transitioning healthcare from a model of reactive care to preventative care. Predictive healthcare aims to identify patients at risk for developing certain diseases before symptoms are present so that interventions can be undertaken to prevent or defer disease.

1. Predictive AI models assess genetic, lifestyle, and environmental risk factors to find the probability of diseases such as diabetes, cardiovascular disease, and Alzheimer's. For instance, Google Health and DeepMind have created AI algorithms predicting the likelihood of cardiovascular events from retinal scans. This will allow identifying patients who may benefit from lifestyle or medication changes earlier, to avoid heart attacks and strokes [22].
2. AI models are used to analyse genetic predisposition and family history, allowing the identification of individuals with a high risk of heritable cancers. AI systems identify carriers of genetic mutations that can lead to breast, ovarian, or colorectal cancer and suggest potential intervention options by directing them to preventive treatment protocols (regular screenings and prophylactic treatments); therefore, preventing a cancer from ever developing. In this manner, AI enables the patients to take preventive measures, leading to better long-term health results [23].
3. In mental health, predictive models that consider the likelihood of developing certain conditions (*e.g.*, depression and anxiety) are also emerging through AI. AI can analyze patient data, even behavioral and social indicators, to detect at-risk individuals and recommend preventative mental health interventions. This both lowers the severity of mental health conditions and allows for early intervention and care for individuals who may be at risk [24].
4. Predictive healthcare enables a personalised-managed approach to preventative care through individualised risk assessment and prediction, which aligns with the above vision for personalised medicine. The evolution of AI will further hone in on such predictive work, introducing a paradigm shift in healthcare as

we know it from a reactive to proactive stance, where the focus is towards preserving health rather than merely treating disease [25].

Optimizing Healthcare Workflows and Reducing Administrative Burden: AI is invaluable in streamlining healthcare workflows and helping to ease administrative burdens. Artificial intelligence is changing healthcare by improving clinical care and assisting with administrative tasks. AI streamlines data management, record-keeping, and billing processes to cut down the time spent on non-clinical tasks for health care providers; this helps them to spend more time with their patients. Clinical Decision Support Systems (CDSS) leveraging AI offer data-driven insights that assist in making fast and precise medical decisions. These AI-powered enhancements are combined to take away the burden from healthcare professionals, allowing them to focus on their choice of work, resulting in better outcomes for patients as well [26]. With the ongoing development of AI technology, this will likely be a big step toward transforming our healthcare system into one that is more efficient and patient-centered.

Simplifying Data Management and Record-Keeping Plus Billing

Access to accurate patient information and insight on treatment decisions can significantly improve patient care quality; thus, effective data management is paramount in healthcare-related delivery. Despite this, a lot of data is packed in Electronic Health Records (EHR) about patients (spanning their history, lab results, imaging reports, and various other details); managing it can be surreal. AI assists with data management by eliminating repetitive processes like data entry, sorting, or retrieval, allowing healthcare practitioners to access the information they need quickly and efficiently. AI data management systems utilize machine learning algorithms to categorize patient records and maintain the integrity of data [27]. NLP is significant because most of the patient data is found in unstructured text, such as physician notes or clinical reports, and it would not be feasible to store it until relevant information could be extracted. An AI-founded system, for one instance, could automatically flag things like allergies or previous surgeries to drastically reduce the chances of oversight in complicated cases [28].

Outside of Electronic Health Records (EHRs), AI can also help streamline billing processes through automated coding and billing, which previous administrative staff would perform. Medical billing is a complex area requiring specificity in coding to get necessary reimbursement from insurers. Using AI for automatic entry of codes, AI algorithms analyze patient records, identify the appropriate billing codes, and then automatically input them into the system, which reduces the chances of error. It saves you time and enhances revenue cycle management by cutting back on rejected claims, speeding up reimbursements, and lowering administrative costs. With these AI-powered advancements in data management, bookkeeping, and billing, healthcare professionals can take them away from doing paperwork and toward helping patients. They also minimize the chance of mistakes, enhance data availability, and guarantee that healthcare providers work with reliable, current information when making crucial choices, ultimately improving patient outcomes [29].

AI-Powered Clinical Decision Support Systems (CDSS)

Another resourceful AI tool, CDSS stands for Clinical Decision Support Systems, which organizes and analyzes clinical data available to the provider to give evidence-based treatment recommendations. Such systems leverage algorithms and machine learning models to analyze patient data, evaluate possible diagnoses, propose treatment plans, and notify providers of potential adverse interactions. CDSS improves the quality of clinical decision-making by providing data-driven recommendations that help practitioners provide accurate and timely care. CDSS platforms draw from patient records, medical literature, and clinical guidelines to provide a holistic patient case view [30]. For example, when a physician is contemplating a treatment plan for a patient with a complex medical history, the CDSS can surface similar cases, propose suitable medications, and alert to medication interactions based on the patient's other medications or known allergies. This instruction is particularly pertinent in emergency and desperate care settings where a few informed, fast choices can mean the difference between life and death. CDSS has one real-world application, *e.g.*, early signs of sepsis, when treatment can mean the difference between life and death in a few hours. CDSS systems based on AI analyze patient vital signs, lab results, and historical data to capture subtle trends indicative of impending sepsis even before clinical symptoms become apparent. CDSS can serve as warning signals to clinicians for possible cases of sepsis, allowing for rapid intervention that could ensure better outcomes and save lives [31].

In addition, in the sense of personalized medicine, CDSS can aid clinicians in choosing their treatment according to each patient. For instance, in oncology, CDSS systems assist oncologists in determining the optimum chemotherapy regimens based on current research and a patient's tumor characteristics. Despite the many new treatments and research, CDSS continues to provide healthcare providers with recent evidence-based information and to close the gap between research and clinical application. With CDSS, the burden on healthcare providers is alleviated, and they have an evidence-backed tool in their corner for complicated cases [32]. This ultimately increases patient safety, delivering more accurate treatment and guaranteeing that healthcare providers give the best care possible.

The Effects on Workload and Patient Outcomes for Healthcare Professionals

By enabling workflow optimizations and decision support systems driven by AI, the workload for health professionals and, thus, patient outcomes is profoundly impacted. Healthcare is a notoriously high-stress profession, with heavy administrative burdens and pressure to make fast, accurate clinical decisions, neatly aligning to produce central fatigue among providers. AMI eliminates these burdens by automating routine administrative tasks (*e.g.*, scheduling), assisting in data retrieval, and providing clinical decision support so that healthcare professionals can devote more time to care centered on the patient. The deployment of AI allows personnel to spend less time on tedious, repetitive tasks such as data entry and record management, giving them greater opportunities for face time with patients to understand their problems and cater to their needs [33]. The American Medical Association published a survey of physicians, which showed that the share of EHR documentation was substantially high in the hours spent on patient care. AI addresses this problem by simplifying EHRs, allowing physicians to spend more time on direct patient care, which ultimately translates into improved patient satisfaction and outcomes.

In addition, AI-powered tools minimize errors by offering healthcare workers accurate data and recommendations. For example, if clinicians are busy during the day or even at night and neglect to take a detailed look at a lab report because of all their other competing priorities, an AI system that identifies potential medication interactions or flags abnormal lab results ensures those important parameters will not be missed. That reduces the risks of adverse events based on human error or missed information, improving patient safety. The positive impact of AI on healthcare workflows also helps alleviate burnout, a rising problem in the sector. AI provides the necessary assistance in clinical decision-making and eases its administrative burden, enabling health care providers to practice more efficiently while having an improved work-life balance and reduced stress levels. That then adds up to an engaged, content, and happy workforce, which is an ingredient for providing high-quality patient care [34].

The overall outcome is that the incorporation and AI in healthcare processes helps create work efficiency, eventually affecting the efficacy of patient treatment. Less administrative burden allows those in the healthcare field to spend more time with patients, and AI does not replace human judgment in clinical decision-making but instead ensures providers can stay abreast of the newest, most accurate information when treating patients. Thus, here are some contributions made by AI that make healthcare a better thing for providers and patients, combining and connecting them into a patient-centric care system; all thanks to the power of artificial intelligence when it comes to automation [35].

THE APPLICATION OF ROBOTICS AND ARTIFICIAL INTELLIGENCE IN SURGICAL PROCEDURES

Robotics and Artificial Intelligence (AI) have transformed surgery, bringing a new level of accuracy, speed, and security to the theatre. AI robotic surgery has revolutionized the modern surgical procedure, allowing minimally invasive procedures with reduced human errors and improved patient outcomes. The introduction explains robotic surgery and AI-driven surgical instruments, discusses the benefits these technologies offer in accuracy, patient recovery times, and post-operative care, and touches upon ethical issues facing AI surgery, such as building trust with patients.

Improvements in Surgical Precision, Patient Recovery, and Post-Operative Care: Precision in surgery is enhanced by the integration of robotics and AI, leading to faster recovery times and improved post-operative care.

Increased Accuracy and Lower Chance of Mistakes

Robotic systems and AI algorithms can carry out surgical tasks consistently with high accuracy, minimizing the possibility of complications caused by human mistakes. Robotic arms, which can move more precisely than hands, help surgeons to work in tight spaces without disturbing the neighbouring tissues. It is conducive in sensitive surgeries, such as heart or spine surgery, where a small error can lead to disastrous results. AI algorithms also analyze data in real-time during surgeries and offer feedback by alerting the users whenever the system identifies any deviation from the planned surgery. By minimizing the potential for errors and assisting surgeons in making more precise movements, these safety features greatly enhance patient outcomes and lower the chance of revision surgery as patients heal [36].

Less Invasiveness and Quicker Recovery

Robotic and AI-enabled surgical tools make it easier for surgeons to work through small openings, thus enabling them to perform minimally invasive procedures. MIS is a surgical technique that benefits the patient with less trauma to the body, less blood loss, and a lower risk of infection, leading to faster recovery. Compared with traditional open surgery, robotic-assisted MIS typically results in less pain after surgery, a shorter stay in the hospital, and a quicker return to normal activities for patients. In some cases, robotic-assisted laparoscopic surgery means scarring is less visible and there are fewer complications because the precision of the robotic arms allows for smaller incisions. Patients also report less discomfort, decreasing the need for pain medication following surgery and promoting faster recovery [37].

Better Post-operative Management and Supervision

AI tools have also entered the post-operative phase, one of the most crucial parts of recovery. Advanced AI systems can be used to check a patient's vitals, identify potential complications arising, and make recommendations about post-operative analysis to parts of the medical staff. Wearable devices such as heart rate and oxygen saturation monitors use AI to monitor a patient's health after leaving the hospital, sending alerts if their readings are abnormal so that healthcare providers can take action as soon as possible. AI algorithms can also help analyze patient data, predict complications, and take action before such situations arise, thus helping minimize unplanned returns to clinics/ hospitals. AI-based post-operative systems help highlight and locate the patients who could be at risk, consequently making sure that patients receive customized attention for the best recovery results [38].

Ethical Considerations and Patient Trust in AI-Assisted Procedures: Robotics and AI open new gateways for surgeon intervention and recovery options. These technologies allow them to conduct procedures with pinpoint precision, decreased likelihood of human error, and improved opportunities for their patients' speedy recovery. In addition, using robotic tools and AI to navigate the patient's anatomy enhances the overall outcomes and quality of care, enabling minimally invasive surgery and providing real-time navigation. To fully integrate this high level of sophistication into the current medical system, specific ethical considerations and hurdles to patient confidence must be considered. The role and responsibility of the surgeon, as well as the transparency and consent of the patient, are critical to this process. Achieving a balance between the benefits of robotics and AI and ethical protections will help establish a conducive environment, patient-centered operating areas where superior expertise and cutting-edge robotics function interdependently to deliver unmatched health outcomes [39].

Informed consent is one of the pillars of medical ethics, and patients must be aware of AI and robotics in their procedures. Patients might not be as comfortable with robots or AI being so intimately involved in their surgeries if they perceive that these machines are impersonal and will make an error, which some patients may experience when realizing a humanoid-looking robot will perform surgery on them. Only when patients know what to expect regarding the capabilities and limits of AI-assisted surgery will they trust the process. Healthcare providers must clarify the operations of robotic and AI systems, stating that these are merely measuring tools to assist surgeons in the same way as their surgical experience. Openly communicating the safety, precision, and advantages of AI-enabled surgery can alleviate doubts from patients and encourage them to trust in AI-guided surgeries [40].

Surgical AI heavily depends on patient data, leading to privacy and security challenges. Sensitive surgical and health information is a part of patient data and must be protected from unauthorized access or breach. Strict data protection protocols and ensuring that AI systems abide by the data privacy regulations are essential for maintaining patient trust and protecting patient rights [41].

Telemedicine: A tool expanding healthcare access: AI-enabled telemedicine is revolutionizing healthcare delivery by ensuring people have wider access to quality medical services, especially in remote or underserved parts of a region. AI applications enabling virtual consultations and remote monitoring have greatly improved telemedicine, the practice of caring for patients remotely when the provider and patient are not physically present with each other. AI-powered telemedicine is essential in broadening healthcare access through virtual visits and remote surveillance. AI-based telemedicine breaks geographical and socioeconomic barriers, making healthcare services more all-inclusive than ever before, providing specific but affordable, timely, and effective care to one and all, regardless of space or economic status. AI-driven telemedicine also helps bridge the geographical and socioeconomic divide, allowing millions access to timely healthcare [42].

Role of AI in Virtual Consultations and Remote Monitoring

Virtual consultations have always had AI at their heart, allowing for fast and accurate remote assessments requiring zero in-person visits. AI tools like chatbots and virtual health assistants can walk patients through symptom-checking surveys, evaluate their responses, and give initial recommendations. By interpreting symptoms, these virtual assistants also prioritize the cases that require immediate medical attention, significantly cutting down on unnecessary consultations and further aiding the provider in focusing on critical cases. In these virtual consultations, data such as patient history and medical records are processed by AI algorithms that help physicians create the most likely diagnoses based on similar cases, thus optimizing the consultation protocol. Even AI helps people communicate with healthcare professionals who do not share the same language as you in real-time, breaking the communication barriers effectively [43].

The other game-changing feature of telemedicine using AI is remote monitoring. AI algorithms continuously analyse patient data on active vital signs received from any wearable, whether smartwatches or health monitors, such as heart rate, blood pressure, and glucose levels. AI systems can recognize early symptoms of potential medical problems in patients and notify them and healthcare professionals when something appears amiss. An example of this could be if an AI-powered wearable detects an irregular heartbeat and not-so-quickly sends out a notification to the patient's cardiologist, their data specialist can determine the urgency behind these results and act accordingly [44]. One can monitor a patient at all times, which is helpful in chronic diseases will reduce frequent visits.

Advantages of Overcoming Geographical and Socioeconomic Divides

The ability to convey healthcare remotely is probably the most essential purpose of introducing AI-driven technologies along with telemedicine, especially for patients in rural or isolated parts of the world without medical facilities and specialists. Patients no longer have to travel long distances for consultations when they can connect from home or anywhere! It minimizes travel expenses, loss of work time, and logistical difficulties, thus making health available and affordable [45].

It reduces the cost of healthcare delivery; thus, AI-based telemedicine also helps overcome socioeconomic barriers. Virtual consultations and remote monitoring can make medical services more affordable for providers and patients by minimizing physical infrastructure and reducing overhead expenses. This cost efficiency enables a healthcare system to reach more people and provide basic needs to the excluded in resource-limited parts of the globe [46]. Moreover, using Teledentistry powered by AI ensures healthcare accessibility in public health emergencies or natural disasters where physical hospital visits are limited. Telemedicine, for example, allowed for continual care while minimizing exposure risk during the COVID-19 pandemic. Telehealth powered by AI makes it possible to provide care despite the low conditions and ensures that healthcare delivery works for equity [47].

ETHICAL, LEGAL, AND REGULATORY CHALLENGES

The integration of AI into healthcare has undoubtedly proved revolutionary, but it also imposes ethical, legal, and regulatory challenges that need to be systematically explored to ensure responsible and equitable use as we advance. Medical AI models are built upon vast amounts of patient data, advanced algorithms, and intricate decision-making processes, making them prone to privacy issues, risk of overfitting, or biasing an existing medical model. By tackling these problems, we can build confidence, protect patient rights, and ensure equitable access to healthcare. The ethical and legal landscape of data privacy and patient consent, the impact of algorithmic biases on health care equity, and the shortcomings of current policy on AI in medicine are examined.

Problems with The Privacy of Data And Consent From Patients

A serious issue with artificial intelligence in healthcare is the risk of patient data privacy breaches. AI systems usually need to access detailed health records and other personal data, an issue of who has access to that data, for what purpose, and how well it is protected. In a conventional health engagement environment involving several healthcare activities like treatment, diagnosis, *etc*., the data generally resides within hospitals or clinics that play an active part during these procedures, but not anymore. AI systems often work with third-party developers who could be anywhere in the world and handle similar processes through any number of data processors and external cloud storage solutions, which only adds technicality to ownership [48]. Also, patients cannot always appropriately provide informed consent for using an AI, as there can be low levels of understanding about how data will be used after surgery involving complex AI algorithms. Patients need to clearly understand what is being done with their data; whether it will be used for research purposes, commercial use, or even with third parties. Transparency of patient data collection, storage, and analysis is essential to build confidence in patients [49]. To overcome these privacy concerns, healthcare providers and AI developers must implement the highest protective measures and protocols, such as encryption, access controls, and anonymization tools. It is also imperative to ensure that AI systems comply with data privacy laws such as the U.S. Health Insurance Portability and Accountability Act (HIPAA) and the General Data Protection Regulation (GDPR) in the EU. Moreover, ensuring explicit, informed consent from patients before utilizing their data for AI systems is imperative for honoring patient autonomy while protecting their rights [50].

Harms of Algorithmic Biases in an Equitable Health Care System

Another crucial consideration in the ethical use of AI in health care is algorithmic bias. The training process of AI systems is data-dominated, and the data can often reflect societal biases or the under-representation of certain groups (for example, racial or ethnic minorities, lower-income populations, and other vulnerable communities). When left unchecked, these biases can lead to erroneous or biased results from AI algorithms that amplify inequities in health care. An AI trained on data primarily consisting of a certain demographic may perform poorly regarding patients from minority backgrounds. For example, an AI model that was used to predict health outcomes assigned lower risk scores for Black patients compared with white patients who were equally sick, leading to inequities in care access. Such bias results in disparity in treatment recommendations, wrong diagnosis, and eventually poor health outcomes for the marginalised groups [51].

To avoid algorithmic bias, AI developers must train algorithms with diverse population datasets because preparing a mini dataset of various massive forms by the AI model will provide diversity and inclusivity. By regularly updating and testing AI systems, it is possible to detect underlying biases that may develop over time. Furthermore, regulation and healthcare providers should ensure the transparency and interpretability of AI algorithms so that clinicians can understand how decisions are reached or intervene when needed. To establish an ethical and inclusive system, the need for suiting fairness and equity in AI-driven healthcare is indispensable [52]. With bias appropriately addressed, AI can enhance access to care and improve health outcomes across all patient populations, irrespective of demographics or socioeconomic status.

Need for Policies and Frameworks

With the fast-paced advancements of AI technologies in healthcare and their complexities, there is an impending call for policy-level frameworks that govern their usage. Such frameworks are essential to guarantee that AI systems are designed, deployed, and regulated in a manner that prioritises public safety, data security, and fairness, in the absence of Unified Standards. Inadequate standardization can bring about differences in how AI technologies are performed and controlled, confusing care providers and patients. If some hospitals or clinics implement less oversight over their AI systems than others, this could cause a disparate standard of care. Clear guidelines for AI usage will help align practices across healthcare institutions in a trusted and transparent manner [53].

Regulatory agencies/authorities like the U.S. Food and Drug Administration (FDA) are starting to create frameworks for responding to medical AI challenges. Nevertheless, these regulations are usually unable to catch up with rapidly evolving AI. Emerging technologies can be major drivers of healthcare change in the coming years, and safety frameworks must adapt to meet these new potential impacts [54].

It is all the more important for these policies to address key issues such as transparency in AI algorithms, accountability for outcomes, and a process by which impacted patients can seek recourse if an error occurs. A regulatory framework, for example, may require the developers of AI models to disclose how their algorithms work so that they can be independently audited for correctness and fairness [55]. We also need to set out some guidelines around patient consent and data protection, and inform them how they can or cannot use patient data in any AI applications. In addition, AI ethics in healthcare should also stress that the 'human-centred' nature of care must continue to be preserved. AI may assist but cannot replace a doctor's decision-making, and since healthcare is inherently human-centered, clinicians must remain in control over patient care. Regulatory frameworks that balance the advantages of AI against ethical principles can create a circumstance where technology is employed to augment, and not supplant, human experience.

CONCLUSION

The healthcare industry is deeply influenced by AI, which improves diagnostic precision, tailors treatments to individual patients, streamlines clinical workflows, and extends access to medical services. From AI-enhanced diagnostics, surgical robots, and telemedicine, healthcare is becoming far more efficient by being tailored to the individual patient. The potential of AI to unlock predictive health and personalized therapies through the analysis of larger datasets facilitates early disease detection, resulting in a better quality of life and outcomes for patients. A critical aspect of the impact of AI is its contribution to a more patient-centered healthcare system. AI often changes treatment plans' status quo from generic to much more personalised care based on each patient's unique health profile, lifestyle, and genetics. Moreover, AI-powered technology minimizes administrative work and assists clinicians with diagnostic and treatment-related decisions, increasing patient face time.

Yet, we can only fully harness its remarkable potential through responsible, ethical, and collaborative integration of AI into medicine. There is an urgent need to combat this by mitigating data privacy and algorithmic bias, necessitating regulatory frameworks so that AI may engender trust whilst delivering equitable benefits to all patients. However, even as AI advances, the solution still requires continual partnership between healthcare providers, technology developers, and policymakers. AI can lead us towards a future of advanced, compassionate, and inclusive healthcare through prioritising ethics and putting patient welfare first.

REFERENCES

[1] L. Pinto-Coelho, "How Artificial Intelligence Is Shaping Medical Imaging Technology: A Survey of Innovations and Applications", *Bioengineering (Basel),* vol. 10, no. 12, p. 1435, 2023. [http://dx.doi.org/10.3390/bioengineering10121435] [PMID: 38136026]

[2] E. Hossain, R. Rana, N. Higgins, J. Soar, P.D. Barua, A.R. Pisani, and K. Turner, "Natural Language Processing in Electronic Health Records in relation to healthcare decision-making: A systematic review", *Comput. Biol. Med.,* vol. 155, p. 106649, 2023. [http://dx.doi.org/10.1016/j.compbiomed.2023.106649] [PMID: 36805219]

[3] R. Hirani, K. Noruzi, H. Khuram, A.S. Hussaini, E.I. Aifuwa, K.E. Ely, J.M. Lewis, A.E. Gabr, A. Smiley, R.K. Tiwari, and M. Etienne, "Artificial Intelligence and Healthcare: A Journey through History, Present Innovations, and Future Possibilities", *Life (Basel),* vol. 14, no. 5, p. 557, 2024. [http://dx.doi.org/10.3390/life14050557] [PMID: 38792579]

[4] V.D. Karalis, "The Integration of Artificial Intelligence into Clinical Practice", *Applied Biosciences,* vol. 3, no. 1, pp. 14-44, 2024.

[http://dx.doi.org/10.3390/applbiosci3010002]

[5] S.A. Alowais, S.S. Alghamdi, N. Alsuhebany, T. Alqahtani, A.I. Alshaya, S.N. Almohareb, A. Aldairem, M. Alrashed, K. Bin Saleh, H.A. Badreldin, M.S. Al Yami, S. Al Harbi, and A.M. Albekairy, "Revolutionizing healthcare: the role of artificial intelligence in clinical practice", *BMC Med. Educ.,* vol. 23, no. 1, p. 689, 2023.
[http://dx.doi.org/10.1186/s12909-023-04698-z] [PMID: 37740191]

[6] F. Gou, J. Liu, C. Xiao, and J. Wu, "Research on Artificial-Intelligence-Assisted Medicine: A Survey on Medical Artificial Intelligence", *Diagnostics (Basel),* vol. 14, no. 14, p. 1472, 2024.
[http://dx.doi.org/10.3390/diagnostics14141472] [PMID: 39061610]

[7] V.R. Umapathy, S. Rajinikanth B, R.D. Samuel Raj, S. Yadav, S.A. Munavarah, P.A. Anandapandian, A.V. Mary, K. Padmavathy, and A. R, "Perspective of Artificial Intelligence in Disease Diagnosis: A Review of Current and Future Endeavours in the Medical Field", *Cureus,* vol. 15, no. 9, p. e45684, 2023.
[http://dx.doi.org/10.7759/cureus.45684] [PMID: 37868519]

[8] M. Frasca, D. La Torre, M. Repetto, V. De Nicolò, G. Pravettoni, and I. Cutica, "Artificial intelligence applications to genomic data in cancer research: a review of recent trends and emerging areas", *Discover Analytics,* vol. 2, no. 1, p. 10, 2024.
[http://dx.doi.org/10.1007/s44257-024-00017-y]

[9] O. Ali, W. Abdelbaki, A. Shrestha, E. Elbasi, M.A.A. Alryalat, and Y.K. Dwivedi, "A systematic literature review of artificial intelligence in the healthcare sector: Benefits, challenges, methodologies, and functionalities", *Journal of Innovation & Knowledge,* vol. 8, no. 1, p. 100333, 2023.
[http://dx.doi.org/10.1016/j.jik.2023.100333]

[10] M. Javaid, A. Haleem, R.P. Singh, and M. Ahmed, "Computer vision to enhance healthcare domain: An overview of features, implementation, and opportunities", *Intelligent Pharmacy,* vol. 2, no. 6, pp. 792-803, 2024.
[http://dx.doi.org/10.1016/j.ipha.2024.05.007]

[11] C. Mello-Thoms, and C.A.B. Mello, "Clinical applications of artificial intelligence in radiology", *Br. J. Radiol.,* vol. 96, no. 1150, p. 20221031, 2023.
[http://dx.doi.org/10.1259/bjr.20221031] [PMID: 37099398]

[12] D. Dixon, H. Sattar, N. Moros, S.R. Kesireddy, H. Ahsan, M. Lakkimsetti, M. Fatima, D. Doshi, K. Sadhu, and M. Junaid Hassan, "Unveiling the Influence of AI Predictive Analytics on Patient Outcomes: A Comprehensive Narrative Review", *Cureus,* vol. 16, no. 5, p. e59954, 2024.
[http://dx.doi.org/10.7759/cureus.59954] [PMID: 38854327]

[13] A.D.E. Parekh, O.A. Shaikh, S. Simran, S. Manan, and M.A. Hasibuzzaman, "Artificial intelligence (AI) in personalized medicine: AI-generated personalized therapy regimens based on genetic and medical history: short communication", *Ann. Med. Surg. (Lond.),* vol. 85, no. 11, pp. 5831-5833, 2023.
[http://dx.doi.org/10.1097/MS9.0000000000001320] [PMID: 37915639]

[14] K.B. Johnson, W.Q. Wei, D. Weeraratne, M.E. Frisse, K. Misulis, K. Rhee, J. Zhao, and J.L. Snowdon, "Precision Medicine, AI, and the Future of Personalized Health Care", *Clin. Transl. Sci.,* vol. 14, no. 1, pp. 86-93, 2021.
[http://dx.doi.org/10.1111/cts.12884] [PMID: 32961010]

[15] J. Ye, J. Hai, J. Song, and Z. Wang, "The role of artificial intelligence in the application of the integrated electronic health records and patient-generated health data", *medRxiv,* p. 2024.05.01.24306690.
[http://dx.doi.org/10.1101/2024.05.01.24306690]

[16] J. Liao, X. Li, Y. Gan, S. Han, P. Rong, W. Wang, W. Li, and L. Zhou, "Artificial intelligence assists precision medicine in cancer treatment", *Front. Oncol.,* vol. 12, p. 998222, 2023.
[http://dx.doi.org/10.3389/fonc.2022.998222] [PMID: 36686757]

[17] R. Sharma and V. Mehan, "Skin Disease Detection using Image Processing and Soft Computing," in

ECS Transactions, 2022.
[http://dx.doi.org/10.1149/10701.17051ecst]

[18] D.R. Serrano, F.C. Luciano, B.J. Anaya, B. Ongoren, A. Kara, G. Molina, B.I. Ramirez, S.A. Sánchez-Guirales, J.A. Simon, G. Tomietto, C. Rapti, H.K. Ruiz, S. Rawat, D. Kumar, and A. Lalatsa, "Artificial Intelligence (AI) Applications in Drug Discovery and Drug Delivery: Revolutionizing Personalized Medicine", *Pharmaceutics,* vol. 16, no. 10, p. 1328, 2024.
[http://dx.doi.org/10.3390/pharmaceutics16101328] [PMID: 39458657]

[19] L.K. Vora, A.D. Gholap, K. Jetha, R.R.S. Thakur, H.K. Solanki, and V.P. Chavda, "Artificial Intelligence in Pharmaceutical Technology and Drug Delivery Design", *Pharmaceutics,* vol. 15, no. 7, p. 1916, 2023.
[http://dx.doi.org/10.3390/pharmaceutics15071916] [PMID: 37514102]

[20] M. Khalifa, and M. Albadawy, "Artificial intelligence for diabetes: Enhancing prevention, diagnosis, and effective management", *Comput. Methods Programs Biomed. Update,* vol. 5, p. 100141, 2024.
[http://dx.doi.org/10.1016/j.cmpbup.2024.100141]

[21] I. Rojek, P. Kotlarz, M. Kozielski, M. Jagodziński, and Z. Królikowski, "Development of AI-Based Prediction of Heart Attack Risk as an Element of Preventive Medicine", *Electronics (Basel),* vol. 13, no. 2, p. 272, 2024.
[http://dx.doi.org/10.3390/electronics13020272]

[22] M. Singh, A. Kumar, N.N. Khanna, J.R. Laird, A. Nicolaides, G. Faa, A.M. Johri, L.E. Mantella, J.F.E. Fernandes, J.S. Teji, N. Singh, M.M. Fouda, R. Singh, A. Sharma, G. Kitas, V. Rathore, I.M. Singh, K. Tadepalli, M. Al-Maini, E.R. Isenovic, S. Chaturvedi, D. Garg, K.I. Paraskevas, D.P. Mikhailidis, V. Viswanathan, M.K. Kalra, Z. Ruzsa, L. Saba, A.F. Laine, D.L. Bhatt, and J.S. Suri, "Artificial intelligence for cardiovascular disease risk assessment in personalised framework: a scoping review", *EClinicalMedicine,* vol. 73, p. 102660, 2024.
[http://dx.doi.org/10.1016/j.eclinm.2024.102660] [PMID: 38846068]

[23] Z. Guan, G. Parmigiani, D. Braun, and L. Trippa, "Prediction of hereditary cancers using neural networks", *Ann. Appl. Stat.,* vol. 16, no. 1, pp. 495-520, 2022.
[http://dx.doi.org/10.1214/21-AOAS1510] [PMID: 37873507]

[24] E.E. Lee, J. Torous, M. De Choudhury, C.A. Depp, S.A. Graham, H.C. Kim, M.P. Paulus, J.H. Krystal, and D.V. Jeste, "Artificial Intelligence for Mental Health Care: Clinical Applications, Barriers, Facilitators, and Artificial Wisdom", *Biol. Psychiatry Cogn. Neurosci. Neuroimaging,* vol. 6, no. 9, pp. 856-864, 2021.
[http://dx.doi.org/10.1016/j.bpsc.2021.02.001] [PMID: 33571718]

[25] M. Barrett, J. Boyne, J. Brandts, H.P. Brunner-La Rocca, L. De Maesschalck, K. De Wit, L. Dixon, C. Eurlings, D. Fitzsimons, O. Golubnitschaja, A. Hageman, F. Heemskerk, A. Hintzen, T.M. Helms, L. Hill, T. Hoedemakers, N. Marx, K. McDonald, M. Mertens, D. Müller-Wieland, A. Palant, J. Piesk, A. Pomazanskyi, J. Ramaekers, P. Ruff, K. Schütt, Y. Shekhawat, C.F. Ski, D.R. Thompson, A. Tsirkin, K. van der Mierden, C. Watson, and B. Zippel-Schultz, "Artificial intelligence supported patient self-care in chronic heart failure: a paradigm shift from reactive to predictive, preventive and personalised care", *EPMA J.,* vol. 10, no. 4, pp. 445-464, 2019.
[http://dx.doi.org/10.1007/s13167-019-00188-9] [PMID: 31832118]

[26] T. Zayas-Cabán, T.H. Okubo, and S. Posnack, "Priorities to accelerate workflow automation in health care", *J. Am. Med. Inform. Assoc.,* vol. 30, no. 1, pp. 195-201, 2022.
[http://dx.doi.org/10.1093/jamia/ocac197] [PMID: 36259967]

[27] K. Adane, M. Gizachew, and S. Kendie, "The role of medical data in efficient patient care delivery: a review", *Risk Manag. Healthc. Policy,* vol. 12, pp. 67-73, 2019.
[http://dx.doi.org/10.2147/RMHP.S179259] [PMID: 31114410]

[28] E. Sezgin, S.A. Hussain, S. Rust, and Y. Huang, "Extracting Medical Information From Free-Text and Unstructured Patient-Generated Health Data Using Natural Language Processing Methods: Feasibility Study With Real-world Data", *JMIR Form. Res.,* vol. 7, no. 1, p. e43014, 2023.

[http://dx.doi.org/10.2196/43014] [PMID: 36881467]

[29] V. Kilanko, "The Transformative Potential of Artificial Intelligence in Medical Billing: A Global Perspective," academia.edu, Accessed: Jan. 10, 2025. [Online]. Available from: https://www.academia.edu/download/105533784/Volume4-Issue3-May-Jun-No.438-345-353.pdf 10.51542/ijscia.v4i3.8

[30] E.B. Sloane, and R.J. Silva, "Artificial intelligence in medical devices and clinical decision support systems", In: *Clinical Engineering Handbook*. 2nd ed. Academic Press, 2020, pp. 556-568. [http://dx.doi.org/10.1016/B978-0-12-813467-2.00084-5]

[31] K. Ackermann, J. Baker, M. Green, M. Fullick, H. Varinli, J. Westbrook, and L. Li, "Computerized Clinical Decision Support Systems for the Early Detection of Sepsis Among Adult Inpatients: Scoping Review", *J. Med. Internet Res.*, vol. 24, no. 2, p. e31083, 2022. [http://dx.doi.org/10.2196/31083] [PMID: 35195528]

[32] S.E. Klarenbeek, H.H.A. Weekenstroo, J.P.M. Sedelaar, J.J. Fütterer, M. Prokop, and M. Tummers, "The Effect of Higher Level Computerized Clinical Decision Support Systems on Oncology Care: A Systematic Review", *Cancers (Basel),* vol. 12, no. 4, p. 1032, 2020. [http://dx.doi.org/10.3390/cancers12041032] [PMID: 32331449]

[33] L.C. Rink, T.O. Oyesanya, K.C. Adair, J.C. Humphreys, S.G. Silva, and J.B. Sexton, "Stressors Among Healthcare Workers: A Summative Content Analysis", *Glob. Qual. Nurs. Res.,* vol. 10, p. 23333936231161127, 2023. [http://dx.doi.org/10.1177/23333936231161127] [PMID: 37020708]

[34] M. Bala, and R. Sharma. Artificial Intelligence: Unleashing the Future. Bentham Science Publishers, 2025.

[35] J. Bajwa, U. Munir, A. Nori, and B. Williams, "Artificial intelligence in healthcare: transforming the practice of medicine", *Future Healthc. J.,* vol. 8, no. 2, pp. e188-e194, 2021. [http://dx.doi.org/10.7861/fhj.2021-0095] [PMID: 34286183]

[36] K. Reddy, P. Gharde, H. Tayade, M. Patil, L.S. Reddy, and D. Surya, "Advancements in Robotic Surgery: A Comprehensive Overview of Current Utilizations and Upcoming Frontiers", *Cureus,* vol. 15, no. 12, p. e50415, 2023. [http://dx.doi.org/10.7759/cureus.50415] [PMID: 38222213]

[37] P. Biswas, S. Sikander, and P. Kulkarni, "Recent advances in robot-assisted surgical systems", *Biomed. Eng. Adv.,* vol. 6, p. 100109, 2023. [http://dx.doi.org/10.1016/j.bea.2023.100109]

[38] S.L. Solanki, S. Pandrowala, A. Nayak, M. Bhandare, R.P. Ambulkar, and S.V. Shrikhande, "Artificial intelligence in perioperative management of major gastrointestinal surgeries", *World J. Gastroenterol.,* vol. 27, no. 21, pp. 2758-2770, 2021. [http://dx.doi.org/10.3748/wjg.v27.i21.2758] [PMID: 34135552]

[39] D.A. Hashimoto, G. Rosman, D. Rus, and O.R. Meireles, "Artificial Intelligence in Surgery: Promises and Perils", *Ann. Surg.,* vol. 268, no. 1, pp. 70-76, 2018. [http://dx.doi.org/10.1097/SLA.0000000000002693] [PMID: 29389679]

[40] D.D. Farhud, and S. Zokaei, "Ethical Issues of Artificial Intelligence in Medicine and Healthcare", *Iran. J. Public Health,* vol. 50, no. 11, pp. i-v, 2021. [http://dx.doi.org/10.18502/ijph.v50i11.7600] [PMID: 35223619]

[41] B. Murdoch, "Privacy and artificial intelligence: challenges for protecting health information in a new era", *BMC Med. Ethics,* vol. 22, no. 1, p. 122, 2021. [http://dx.doi.org/10.1186/s12910-021-00687-3] [PMID: 34525993]

[42] A. Haleem, M. Javaid, R.P. Singh, and R. Suman, "Telemedicine for healthcare: Capabilities, features, barriers, and applications", *Sens. Int.,* vol. 2, p. 100117, 2021. [http://dx.doi.org/10.1016/j.sintl.2021.100117] [PMID: 34806053]

[43] Z. Jeddi, and A. Bohr, "Remote patient monitoring using artificial intelligence", In: *Artificial Intelligence in Healthcare.* Academic Press, 2020, pp. 203-234. [http://dx.doi.org/10.1016/B978-0-12-818438-7.00009-5]

[44] S. Shajari, K. Kuruvinashetti, A. Komeili, and U. Sundararaj, "The Emergence of AI-Based Wearable Sensors for Digital Health Technology: A Review", *Sensors (Basel),* vol. 23, no. 23, p. 9498, 2023. [http://dx.doi.org/10.3390/s23239498] [PMID: 38067871]

[45] "Revolutionizing medical practice: the impact of artificial intelligence (AI) on healthcare," *OA J Applied Sci Technol*, vol. 2, no. 1, pp. 1–16, 2024. [http://dx.doi.org/10.33140/OAJAST.02.01.07]

[46] B.S. Rintyarna, Sasmiyanto, O.D. Insantuan, I. Widiawati, R.Y. Purwoko, and P. Haekto-Dinas Kesehatan Kabupaten Timor Tengah Utara, "Telehealth in Remote Areas: A New Artificial Intelligence-Based Model", *Int. J. Sci. Soc.,* vol. 5, no. 4, pp. 243-254, 2023. [http://dx.doi.org/10.54783/ijsoc.v5i4.782]

[47] L. Al-Muzian, D. Farsi, S. Hiremath, D. Farsi, and S. Hiremath, "Global Scenario of Teledentistry during COVID-19 Pandemic: An Insight", *Int. J. Clin. Pediatr. Dent.,* vol. 14, no. 3, pp. 426-429, 2021. [http://dx.doi.org/10.5005/jp-journals-10005-1952] [PMID: 34720519]

[48] K.-H. Yu, A. L. Beam, and I. S. Kohane, "Artificial intelligence in healthcare," Nat. Biomed. Eng., vol. 2, no. 10, pp. 719–731, 2018. [http://dx.doi.org/10.1038/s41551-018-0305-z]

[49] M.R. MacIntyre, R.G. Cockerill, O.F. Mirza, and J.M. Appel, "Ethical considerations for the use of artificial intelligence in medical decision-making capacity assessments", *Psychiatry Res.,* vol. 328, p. 115466, 2023. [http://dx.doi.org/10.1016/j.psychres.2023.115466] [PMID: 37717548]

[50] N. Khalid, A. Qayyum, M. Bilal, A. Al-Fuqaha, and J. Qadir, "Privacy-preserving artificial intelligence in healthcare: Techniques and applications", *Comput. Biol. Med.,* vol. 158, p. 106848, 2023. [http://dx.doi.org/10.1016/j.compbiomed.2023.106848] [PMID: 37044052]

[51] R. Walker, J. Dillard-Wright, and F. Iradukunda, "Algorithmic bias in artificial intelligence is a problem—And the root issue is power", *Nurs. Outlook,* vol. 71, no. 5, p. 102023, 2023. [http://dx.doi.org/10.1016/j.outlook.2023.102023] [PMID: 37579574]

[52] R.A. Shams, "· Didar Zowghi, and · Muneera Bano, "AI and the quest for diversity and inclusion: a systematic literature review,"", *AI Ethics,* no. Nov, pp. 1-28, 2023. [http://dx.doi.org/10.1007/s43681-023-00362-w]

[53] H. Siala, and Y. Wang, "SHIFTing artificial intelligence to be responsible in healthcare: A systematic review", *Soc. Sci. Med.,* vol. 296, p. 114782, 2022. [http://dx.doi.org/10.1016/j.socscimed.2022.114782] [PMID: 35152047]

[54] L. Pantanowitz, M. Hanna, J. Pantanowitz, J. Lennerz, W.H. Henricks, P. Shen, B. Quinn, S. Bennet, and H.H. Rashidi, "Regulatory Aspects of Artificial Intelligence and Machine Learning", *Mod. Pathol.,* vol. 37, no. 12, p. 100609, 2024. [http://dx.doi.org/10.1016/j.modpat.2024.100609] [PMID: 39260776]

[55] B. Kaplan, "Seeing through health information technology: the need for transparency in software, algorithms, data privacy, and regulation", *J. Law Biosci.,* vol. 7, no. 1, p. lsaa062, 2020. [http://dx.doi.org/10.1093/jlb/lsaa062] [PMID: 34350004]

CHAPTER 8

Histogram Based Quantitative Analysis for Steganographic Detection

Ayush Yadav[1], **Digant Raj**[1] and **Garima Thakur**[2,*]

[1] *Department of UIE-Computer Science, Chandigarh University, Gharuan, Mohali, Punjab, India*

[2] *Department of Electronic and Communication Engineering, Chandigarh University, Gharuan, Mohali, Punjab, India*

Abstract: This chapter provides an overview of histogram-based steganography detection techniques, one of the earliest methods in contemporary steganalysis. Despite its early development, this technique did not receive the recognition it deserved, with more focus on methods like LSB, DWT, and DCT. To address this, the histogram model is revisited to enhance its performance and efficiency. Using small datasets, we demonstrated that this approach is versatile, faster, and capable of detecting hidden information with minimal data. Additionally, the histogram technique offers potential for further technical improvements, such as integration into widely used platforms like Google Gmail, Microsoft Outlook, and Google Messages. This would enhance security in media-sharing applications by preventing the transmission of harmful hidden information. Our research confirms the efficiency of the histogram technique, particularly in comparison to other steganography detection methods, making it a clear and easily implementable solution for current digital security challenges.

Keywords: Algorithm, Contemporary steganalysis, DWT (Discrete Wavelet Transform), DCT (Discrete Cosine Transform), Histogram steganography detection, LSB (Least Significant Bit), Steganographic detection.

INTRODUCTION

In past centuries, steganography was commonly used to transmit sensitive information in concealed formats, such as invisible ink on letters or messages embedded in wax tablets [1]. In the digital age, steganography has evolved into a critical technique for ensuring secure communication and protecting digital rights. Modern digital media—including images, audio, and video—can potentially harbor hidden data. Various techniques have emerged for embedding information,

* **Corresponding author Garima Thakur:** Department of Electronic and Communication Engineering, Chandigarh University, Gharuan, Mohali, Punjab, India; E-mail: garimathakur1994@gmail.com

Shilpa Gupta & Ritika Sharma (Eds.)

such as adaptive steganography, transform domain methods, LSB (Least Significant Bit) substitution [2], spread spectrum techniques, patchwork methods, and masking or filtering approaches.

As the importance of data security grows, steganalysis—the process of detecting concealed information—has become increasingly vital. Advanced steganalysis leverages statistical analysis, machine learning, and deep learning techniques to uncover hidden content [3]. These technological advancements have simultaneously increased the complexity of both steganographic techniques and their detection.

Emerging innovations such as quantum computing and artificial intelligence further expand the scope of steganography. These developments promise new applications in Digital Rights Management (DRM), privacy, and secure communication by enhancing the capacity, stealth, and robustness of data embedding techniques [4]. According to Pevný, Bas, and Fridrich, future steganographic systems will integrate advanced detection mechanisms capable of identifying even highly complex data hiding strategies [5].

As technology progresses, steganography and steganalysis will play a key role in areas such as law enforcement, digital forensics, and cybersecurity. The continuous advancement of steganographic tools necessitates robust detection mechanisms to prevent misuse. Thus, ongoing research exploring the relationship between steganography and steganalysis is essential to maintaining secure communication systems.

This study focuses on histogram-based steganalysis as a technique for detecting hidden information in digital images. Histogram steganalysis identifies anomalies in the statistical distribution of pixel values that may result from data embedding. Our work enhances traditional histogram analysis by integrating a pretrained machine learning model, further fine-tuned with a curated dataset to improve domain-specific detection. By leveraging the pretrained model's feature extraction capabilities and adapting it to our dataset, the model's sensitivity to subtle pixel distribution changes is improved, which is indicative of steganographic content. Our results show a marked improvement in detection accuracy over conventional histogram methods. Performance was evaluated using standard metrics such as accuracy, precision, recall, and F1-score, confirming the effectiveness of our approach.

The covert nature of steganographic content poses significant challenges to security analysts. Because the modifications made to carrier media (*e.g.*, images) are often imperceptible, conventional detection methods may fail. This highlights the need for innovative steganalysis techniques tailored to expose hidden patterns.

Our proposed approach addresses this gap by offering a reliable, efficient method for detecting steganography in images.

RELATED WORK

Classical Spatial-Domain Approaches: Edge Detection with LBP

Early spatial domain methods embed data in the Least Significant Bits (LSBs) of pixel intensities; however, LSB schemes are easily detected or manipulated. Recent work, therefore, combines edge detection (Canny, Sobel, Prewitt) with Local Binary Pattern (LBP) codes to raise both capacity and imperceptibility. By watermarking only edge pixels and exploiting local texture information, these hybrid methods achieve higher payloads without visible artefacts and remain resilient to common image processing attacks [6]. These methods restrict embedding to high-frequency regions (edges) and leverage local texture features to resist distortion and attacks. Logical OR operations and morphological dilation are often used to refine edge maps and embedding zones.

Despite these advancements, spatial techniques remain vulnerable to geometric transformations, noise, and filtering attacks [7]. Additionally, methods based on LBP may struggle with image textures that lack contrast, reducing embedding opportunities and making the payload detection-prone in smooth regions.

Frequency-Domain Techniques: Histogram Shifting and DCT Integration

Bandyopadhyay *et al.* integrate histogram shifting with the Discrete Cosine Transform (DCT) to hide text in greyscale images while preserving perceptual quality [8, 9]. Quantitative evaluation with PSNR and BER shows high fidelity (PSNR > 40 dB) and low extraction error for payloads up to 60 characters. Despite these strengths, PSNR drops steadily as payload grows and robustness declines under aggressive compression. Subsequent studies combine spatial histogram adjustment with DCT domain embedding to balance capacity and invisibility, but they still inherit the transform domain's computational overhead and are less effective against deep learning steganalysers.

Learning-Based Detection Models: Neural Networks for Steganalysis

Recent steganalytic models learn histogram anomalies directly from data. Symmetric histogram neural networks outperform hand-crafted detectors on LSB and histogram shifting payloads by exploiting deep features from both spatial and transform domains [10, 11]. However, detection accuracy degrades as payload size grows, and models remain sensitive to adversarial image perturbations.

Moreover, training such networks demands large annotated datasets, limiting practical deployment.

Multi-Stage Hybrid Systems: RIWT, Laplacian Pyramid, and Deep Learning

A robust medical image system combines Redundant Integer Wavelet Transform (RIWT), Laplacian Pyramid decomposition, Arnold scrambling, and adaptive histogram shifting [12, 13]. Noise residual computation, feature extraction, and SVM/ensemble classification iteratively adjust embedding parameters until stego images pass a learned detector. The scheme achieves high NCC and PSNR, yet its multi-stage pipeline increases complexity and requires significant computational resources for real-time use.

Comparative Analysis and Research Gaps

The literature reveals a clear trend from simple spatial LSB techniques toward hybrid spatial–frequency and learning based systems that trade complexity for robustness. Current methods still face three open challenges:

- *Scalability* – payload growth and high-resolution images reduce PSNR or raise BER.
- *Generalisation* – deep detectors trained on specific datasets exhibit accuracy drops on unseen cover sources.
- *Computational Cost* – sophisticated pipelines (RIWT, deep CNNs) hinder real-time or low-power deployment.

Our work addresses these gaps by combining lightweight histogram analysis with transfer learned models to improve detection accuracy while retaining computational efficiency. A concise comparison of prior drawbacks and our targeted improvements is provided in Table **1**.

EXPERIMENTAL

Table **2** provides a detailed comparison of image histograms to examine variations between the original, steganographic, and comparison images. It displays histogram data for the original image, the steganographic image (which has embedded hidden information), and a separate comparison image. Furthermore, it highlights the differences between the histograms of the original and steganographic images, as well as the original and comparison images. This analysis, performed using VS Code and Colab environment, helps assess how steganographic embedding affects an image's characteristics.

Table 1. Drawbacks and improvements.

References	Drawbacks	Improvement
[14]	i. lack of training data: inference to generalisability and stability. ii. overfitting risk: fine-tuning with specific datasets can decrease the effectiveness of the algorithm in diversified or even unseen data. iii. lack of metrics: not fully capturing the true applicability in practice, including time to compute and the ability to adapt to new techniques. iv. high computation requirements: not suitable for low-resource environments or real-time applications. v. susceptibility to malicious methods: it needs constant evolution and a learning mechanism.	• increase dataset diversity and size • apply regularization techniques and cross-validation • include comprehensive metrics and conduct real-world testing • optimize algorithms and use hardware acceleration • employ adversarial training and continuous learning
[15]	i. low embedding capacity: it uses edge pixels for embedding only. ii. low quality of visual content. the embedding process affects the visual quality of images, and more so for those with high-density levels of edges. iii. lack of robustness: vulnerable to strong steganalysis attacks on methods that follow an edge-based approach. iv. complex computation: it has more edge detectors and logical operations, thus increasing the demand for computational power.	• increase embedding capacity: use non-edge pixels or improve the efficiency of data encoding. • apply perceptual masking: minimize visible changes in the image using advanced techniques. • integrate cryptographic techniques: enhance security with cryptographic methods or more advanced steganographic techniques. • optimize algorithm: improve computational efficiency or use hardware acceleration.
[16]	i. decreased detection accuracy: increases with the number of embedded bits. ii. high randomness impact: affects detection accuracy for specific networks. iii. scalability issues: time consumption and memory requirements scale quadratically with input sample size. iv. variable detection accuracy: varies across different neural networks and datasets.	• train with diverse datasets: include varying levels of embedded bits to improve generalization. • enhance feature extraction: minimize randomness in output vectors with more robust techniques. • optimize data processing: improve memory management and handling of large datasets. • implement adaptive algorithms: adjust to different network and dataset characteristics.
[17]	i. lack of accurate reversibility: in dwt-based embedding. ii. low robustness and embedding capacity: in iwt-based approaches. iii. high complexity: in achieving high embedding capacity and robustness. iv. security vulnerabilities: in conventional scrambling algorithms.	• implement the integer wavelet transform (iwt) for better reversibility and data fidelity. • use redundant discrete wavelet transform (rdwt) to enhance robustness and increase embedding capacity. • introduce redundant integer wavelet transform (riwt) to combine the benefits of rdwt and iwt for improved performance.

Table 2. Histogram analysis.

Constraints	Image 1	Image 2
Image data		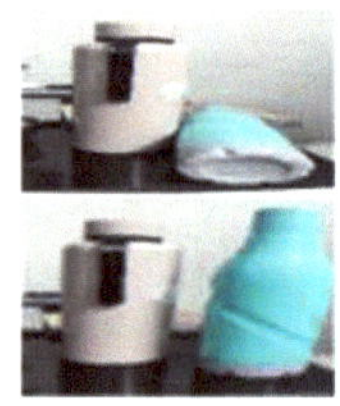
Original image histogram		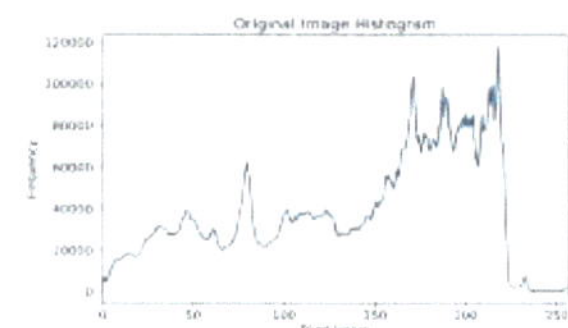
Steganographic image histogram	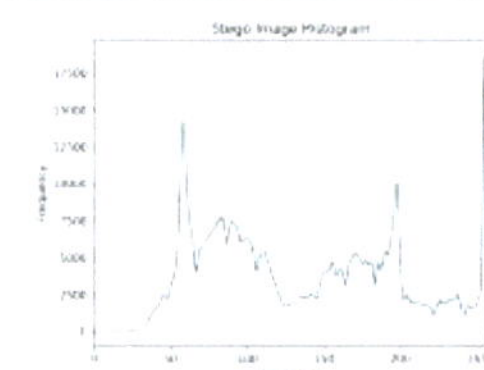	
Comparison image histogram		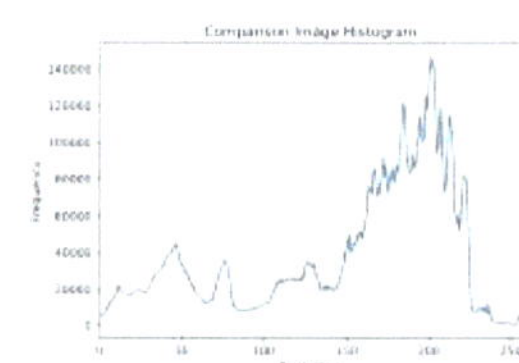
Original vs stego Image histogram	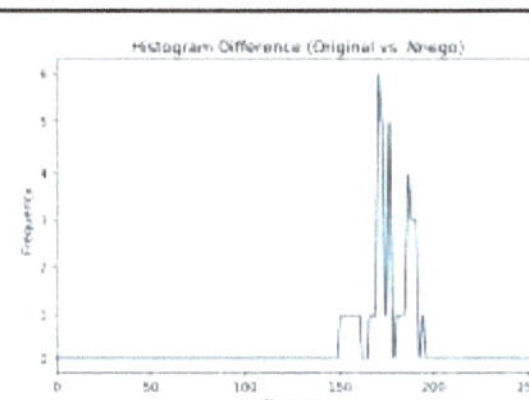	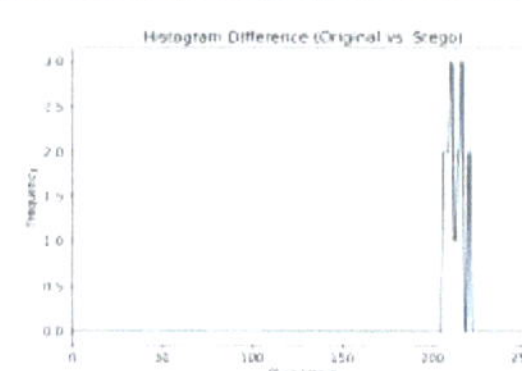
Original vs Comparison image histogram	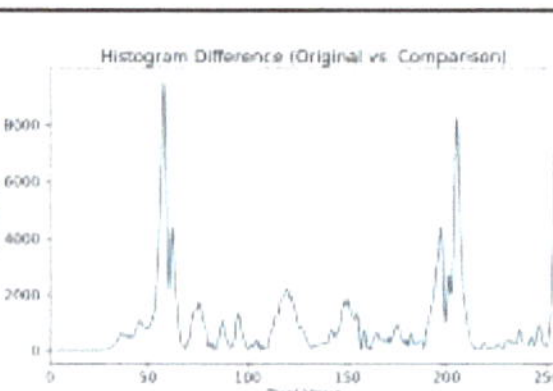	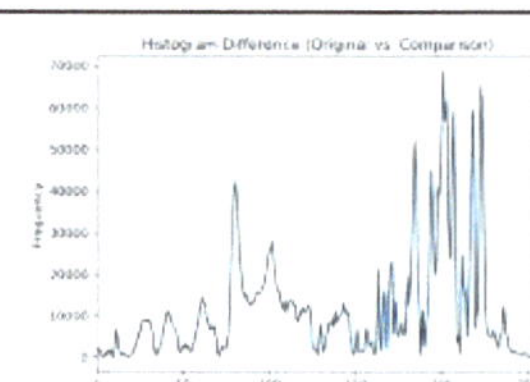

The histogram difference sum is calculated by taking the absolute difference between the corresponding bin values of the histograms of two images and summing these differences. This method allows us to quantify how much the histograms of two images differ from each other. Here's the step-by-step process:

1. Calculate histograms: for each image, calculate the histogram that counts the frequency of each pixel value (0-255).
2. Compute absolute differences: for each bin (0-255) of the histograms, compute the absolute difference between the bin values of the two histograms being compared.
3. Sum the differences: sum up all the absolute differences obtained in the previous step to get the total histogram difference.

The formula for the histogram difference sum can be represented by Equation (1):

$$\text{Difference sum}=\sum i=0255|h1(i)-h2(i) \quad \textbf{(1)}$$

Where:

- h1(i) is the value of the i-th bin in the histogram of the first image.
- h2(i) is the value of the i-th bin in the histogram of the second image.

RESULTS

Steganography refers to the practice of concealing information—such as text, audio, or images—within another file format to make the presence of that data undetectable. Unlike cryptography, which encrypts content, steganography aims to hide the existence of the message itself. Image steganography employs several embedding techniques, the most common being Least Significant Bit (LSB) insertion, where the LSBs of pixel values are modified slightly, ensuring minimal perceptual distortion. Other approaches include palette-based techniques, which alter color indices in indexed images, and transform-domain techniques that modify frequency components via the Discrete Wavelet Transform (DWT) or Discrete Cosine Transform (DCT).

In our study, histogram analysis was used to quantitatively measure the impact of steganographic embedding. Tables **3** and **4** show the Histogram Difference Sum (HDS) values between original images, steganographic images, and control (comparison) images. A lower HDS indicates minimal deviation from the original image, implying better imperceptibility and greater difficulty in detection.

Table 3. Result of image 1.

Comparison	Histogram Difference Sum
original vs stego	78.0
original vs. comparison	235456.0
message	hidden message

Table 4. Result of image 2.

Comparison	Histogram Difference Sum
original vs stego	30.0
original vs. comparison	2961806.0
message	hidden message

These results demonstrate that histogram-based detection is effective in quantifying pixel-level alterations introduced by steganographic embedding. In both cases, the difference between the original and stego images is minimal compared to the difference with unrelated comparison images. This affirms the imperceptibility of the embedding process. Histograms serve as a valuable tool for detecting hidden data because they reflect the statistical distribution of pixel intensities, revealing variations in contrast, brightness, and texture [18, 19]. Techniques such as histogram comparison, anomaly detection, and differencing are used to identify unusual patterns introduced by data embedding.

Despite its effectiveness, histogram-based steganalysis has certain limitations. It is sensitive to image processing operations—like compression, filtering, or enhancement—which can distort the histogram and impact detection accuracy. Nevertheless, due to its non-intrusive, lightweight, and quantitative nature, it remains a widely adopted technique in the field of digital image forensics.

PROPOSED APPROACH

Algorithm: Image steganography and histogram analysis

1. Load and preprocess image: load the original image from the file path. If image loading fails, print an error message. Load comparison image from file path.
2. Embed message in image: input: original image, message to hide. Append delimiter '#####' to message. Convert the message to binary. For each pixel in the image: modify the least significant bit (lsb) with the message bit. Save the modified image as a stego image.

3. Calculate histograms: calculate a histogram for the original image. Calculate the histogram for the stego image. Calculate the histogram for the comparison image.
4. Visualize histograms: plot a histogram of the original image. Plot a histogram of the stego image. Plot a histogram of the comparison image.
5. Compare histograms: compute the difference between the histograms of the original and stego images. Compute the difference between the histograms of the original and comparison images. Plot differences in histograms.
6. Extract hidden message: input: stego image. Extract binary data from lsb of each pixel. Convert binary data to characters until the delimiter is found. Output: extracted message.
7. Display results: print extracted message. Summarize and display histogram differences.
8. Main function: load images. Embed the message and create a stego image. Calculate and plot histograms. Compare histograms and extract the message. Display results in tabular format. End algorithm.

CONCLUDING REMARKS

Throughout the paper discussing image steganography techniques, several improvements are studied that enhance both security and capacity of images as data-hiding carriers. The novel approaches mainly concentrate on keeping the data hidden and increasing the volume of data to be embedded in one image. An important set of innovations involves spatial domain techniques like edge detection, Local Binary Patterns (LBP), and histogram shifting. These have been designed with the objective of making the steganography process subtler and more robust. The use of frequency domain approaches, such as the DCT, is being more widely applied, providing more flexibility in embedding data without compromising the quality of an image.

Indeed, machine learning has improved steganalysis, which is the detection of hidden data, most remarkably with the help of neural networks. The techniques it uses are more accurate, particularly in big data and complex patterns, which offer higher accuracy in the detection of concealed information, making steganography more resistant to unauthorized detection. For example, wavelet transformations and the design of encryption schemes increase the layers of protection and, hence, make these methods for data or image storage appropriately apply even to critical applications as storing sensitive medical images.

Consequently, this development in steganographic systems seems more like progress from traditional, primarily spatial methods towards a merging of frequency-domain techniques with artificial intelligence. This combination is likely to augment the safety, stability, and efficiency in protecting sensitive data, hence extremely relevant in today's information-driven world.

REFERENCES

[1] F.A.P. Petitcolas, R.J. Anderson, and M.G. Kuhn, "Information hiding-a survey", *Proc. IEEE,* vol. 87, no. 7, pp. 1062-1078, 1999.
[http://dx.doi.org/10.1109/5.771065]

[2] N.F. Johnson, and S. Katzenbeisser, "A survey of steganographic techniques", In: *Information Hiding Techniques for Steganography and Digital Watermarking.,* S. Katzenbeisser, F. Petitcolas, Eds., Artech House, 2000, pp. 43-78.

[3] J. Fridrich, *Steganography in Digital Media: Principles, Algorithms, and Applications.* Cambridge Univ. Press: Cambridge, U.K., 2009.
[http://dx.doi.org/10.1017/CBO9781139192903]

[4] I. Cox, M. Miller, J. Bloom, J. Fridrich, and T. Kalker, *Digital Watermarking and Steganography.* 2nd ed. Morgan Kaufmann: San Francisco, CA, USA, 2007.

[5] T. Pevný, P. Bas, and J. Fridrich, "Steganalysis by subtractive pixel adjacency matrix", *Proc. 11th ACM Workshop Multimedia Security,* pp. 75-84, 2009.
[http://dx.doi.org/10.1145/1597817.1597831]

[6] D-L. Li, Z. Yang, and C-H. Cheng, "Face recognition using nonparametric-weighted Fisherfaces", *EURASIP J. Adv. Signal Process.,* vol. 2012, no. 1, pp. 1-11, 2012.

[7] N. Thomas, M. Thomas, and K. Chandrasekaran, "Multimedia streaming using cloud-based P2P systems", *Procedia Comput. Sci.,* vol. 57, pp. 25-32, 2015.
[http://dx.doi.org/10.1016/j.procs.2015.07.359]

[8] N. Provos, and P. Honeyman, "Hide and seek: an introduction to steganography", *IEEE Secur. Priv.,* vol. 1, no. 3, pp. 32-44, 2003.
[http://dx.doi.org/10.1109/MSECP.2003.1203220]

[9] S. Katzenbeisser, and F.A.P. Petitcolas, *Information Hiding Techniques for Steganography and Digital Watermarking.* Artech House: Norwood, MA, USA, 2000.

[10] X.Y. Luo, D.S. Wang, P. Wang, and F-L. Liu, "A review on blind detection for image steganography", *Signal Processing,* vol. 88, no. 9, pp. 2138-2157, 2008.
[http://dx.doi.org/10.1016/j.sigpro.2008.03.016]

[11] Y. Qian, Z. Peng, and X. Zhang, "Image steganalysis based on convolutional neural networks using spatial and histogram features", *J. Vis. Commun. Image Represent.,* vol. 64, p. 102632, 2019.
[http://dx.doi.org/10.1016/j.jvcir.2019.102632]

[12] K.U. Singh, "A survey on image steganography techniques", *Int. J. Comput. Appl.,* vol. 97, no. 18, pp. 1-5, 2014.

[13] S. Bhattacharyya, P. Das, and A. Pal, "A robust image steganography method using PMM in bit plane domain", *Int. J. Comput. Inf. Eng.,* vol. 8, no. 9, pp. 1712-1726, 2015.

[14] A.A.H. Khan, R. Khan, M.A. Zia, I.U. Din, and J.J.P.C. Rodrigues, "A survey of steganography techniques for secure data hiding in IoT and edge devices", *Future Internet,* vol. 15, no. 3, pp. 1-27, 2023.
[http://dx.doi.org/10.3390/fi15030108]

[15] R.S. Mane, "Image steganography using LSB and histogram analysis", *Int. J. Res. Appl. Sci. Eng. Technol.,* vol. 7, no. 4, pp. 1619-1623, 2019.
[http://dx.doi.org/10.22214/ijraset.2019.4063]

[16] I.U. Khan, F. Akram, Z. Wang, A. Mushtaq, and S. Ullah, "A hybrid method for image steganography

using LSB and Arnold map", *Symmetry (Basel),* vol. 15, no. 5, pp. 1-17, 2023. [http://dx.doi.org/10.3390/sym15051079]

[17] A. Kumar, P. Kumar, and H. Kim, "A secure image steganography based on RSA and hash-LSB techniques using hybrid optimization algorithm", *Multimedia Syst.,* vol. 28, no. 2, pp. 383-397, 2022. [http://dx.doi.org/10.1007/s00530-020-00665-6]

[18] A. Aljarf, H. Zamzami, and A. Gutub, "Integrating machine learning and features extraction for practical reliable color images steganalysis classification", *Soft Comput.,* vol. 27, no. 19, pp. 13877-13888, 2023. [http://dx.doi.org/10.1007/s00500-023-09042-7]

[19] D. Megías, and D. Lerch-Hostalot, "Subsequent embedding in targeted image steganalysis: Theoretical framework and practical applications", *IEEE Trans. Depend. Secure Comput.,* vol. 20, no. 2, pp. 1403-1421, 2023. [http://dx.doi.org/10.1109/TDSC.2022.3154967]

CHAPTER 9

Empowering Green Futures: The Role of AI in Renewable Energy Transformation

Om Prakash Yadav[1,*], **Anurag Verma**[2] and **Abhishek Nigam**[3]

[1] *Department of Electrical Engineering, Sandip Institute of Technology and Research Centre, Nashik, Maharashtra, India*

[2] *Electrical Engineering Department, IET Engineering College, Lucknow, Uttar Pradesh, India*

[3] *Electronics Engineering Department, IET Engineering College, Lucknow, Uttar Pradesh, India*

Abstract: Artificial Intelligence (AI) is revolutionizing the renewable energy sector by providing innovative solutions to challenges related to energy production, storage, and distribution. Due to increasing demand and the need for an uninterrupted supply to consumers, AI applications have become essential for optimizing Renewable Energy Systems (RES). Renewable energy sources like solar energy, wind power, hydro, geothermal, and biomass generate clean energy without emitting greenhouse gases, hence reducing global warming. AI technologies, including Machine Learning (ML), Deep Learning (DL), and robotics, enable better forecasting of weather conditions, energy production, and distribution while optimizing energy storage systems to address intermittency issues. AI algorithms enhance grid management by dynamically balancing supply and demand, ensuring efficient energy distribution, and reducing environmental impact. In addition to this, AI plays a crucial role in predictive fault diagnosis and maintenance, maximizing the lifespan of RES and minimizing repair and operational costs. Despite these benefits, challenges, such as qualitative data availability, the high cost of AI implementation, and the difficulty of replacing existing energy infrastructure remain. However, by improving decision-making through advanced AI algorithms such as reinforcement learning, generative AI, and edge computing, efficient energy generation, grid stability, and energy distribution can be achieved, and environmental harassment can be avoided. In this context, this chapter provides a comprehensive roadmap to incorporate AI benefits in renewable energy systems for efficient and sustained green energy production and its distribution.

Keywords: AI technology, Energy storage management system, Grid management, Predictive maintenance, Renewable energy system.

* **Corresponding author Om Prakash Yadav:** Department of Electrical Engineering, Sandip Institute of Technology and Research Centre, Nashik, Maharashtra, India; E-mail: opnit05@gmail.com

Shilpa Gupta & Ritika Sharma (Eds.)

INTRODUCTION

The world is currently seeking innovative solutions to reduce its dependency on fossil fuels and embrace clean, sustainable energy sources [1]. It is now essential to transition into renewable energy systems due to the escalating impacts of climate change and escalating worldwide energy usage [2, 3]. Renewable energy, including solar, wind, hydropower, and geothermal, offers the potential to not only prevent climate change but also provide secure and sustainable energy for future generations [4]. Infrastructure efficiency and resource variability are the primary challenges facing Renewable Energy Systems (RES). The aging grid systems designed for traditional energy systems need to be modified to accommodate the dispersed and variable character of RES. AI, when incorporated with renewable energy, opens up new possibilities for resolving issues with grid connection and variability. By enhancing data analysis, prediction, and optimization, Artificial Intelligence (AI) helps address these problems and promises more seamless integration and reliability of renewable energy [5, 6].

For instance, in solar energy, AI is applied to optimize photovoltaic panel placement, predict solar irradiance, and optimize maintenance schedules for better energy integration and operational efficiency [7, 8]. Similarly, in wind energy, AI-powered predictive models allow for more accurate forecasts of wind speeds, optimization of turbine performance, and effective layout design to maximize energy capture [6, 7, 9]. Hydropower, being an old renewable energy source, is not left behind by AI innovations. AI in hydropower systems helps improve the management of the reservoir, optimal turbine operation, and predictive maintenance based on the analysis of hydrological data [7, 10, 11]. On the other hand, in geothermal energy, AI-driven models help streamline the exploration process through the analysis of geophysical and geochemical data, thereby improving resource identification and optimizing energy extraction [12].

Through analysing huge amounts of data collected from resources including solar radiation, weather patterns, and wind speeds, AI plays a critical role in the renewable energy industry by enhancing predictions of energy output [13]. AI helps to predict variations in supply and demand by utilizing machine learning, which makes grid management and energy distribution more efficient [14]. Furthermore, by capturing energy trends that improve energy production, storage, and overall efficiency, AI-driven data analysis optimizes RES [15, 16]. By providing accurate estimates, sophisticated prediction models using AI can further boost energy management by empowering grid operators to make effective decisions that ensure a robust and reliable energy infrastructure [17]. This further strengthens the potential of AI when brought together with emerging technologies such as Blockchain and smart grids. AI can enhance the transparency and security of energy transactions, support demand-response systems, and improve energy storage capabilities to ensure a reliable and sustainable source of energy [17, 18]. In the future, AI will be expected to play a greater role in renewable energy. The future innovations will be based on reinforcement learning, hybrid energy systems, and advanced energy storage solutions [19 - 21]. Therefore, AI is poised to play a central role in the global transition to a clean, sustainable energy future, driving efficiency and resilience across renewable energy systems.

This chapter describes the comprehensive application of AI in renewable energy sectors, providing insights into how AI has emerged as a transforming agent to answer global energy demands. Finally, the challenges, opportunities, and possibilities of AI innovations in the renewable energy sector are summarised.

GLOBAL AND INDIA'S RENEWABLE ENERGY GENERATION CAPACITY

The percentage share of different renewable energy sources: According to the report by the International Renewable Energy Agency, at the end of 2023, RE capacity globally witnessed an increase of a whopping 473 GW, with an increase of 13.9% [22]. In leading this expansion, solar energy achieved a tremendous surge of 346 GW, amounting to 32.2% growth and approaching 1419 GW; wind energy amounted to 116 GW with 12.9% growth and approaches 1017.2GW; in contrast, the growth in hydropower, bioenergy, and geothermal energy is moderate. Hydropower generation approaches 1,267.9 GW, thus second to renewable sources, and the generation of biomass, waste, and geothermal energy together approaches 165.3 GW. Fig. (**1**) depicts the share of each source of renewable energy. It is presented that solar power production has the maximum share, *i.e.*, it produces 37% of global renewable energy output.

According to the statistics until October 2024, India has a total of 452.69 GW in electricity generation, out of which renewable energy generation has reached up to 203.18 GW, which forms more than 46.3% of total electricity generation in the country. Solar power leads with 92.12 GW, harnessing abundant sunlight, followed by wind energy at 47.72 GW, utilizing coastal and inland wind corridors. Hydropower contributes 52 GW, combining large (46.93 GW) and small (5.07 GW) hydro projects. Bio power, derived from biomass and biogas, and geothermal, adds 11.34 GW, further enhancing the renewable mix [23]. Fig. (**2**) showcases the installed renewable energy capacity in India, with solar power generation accounting for 45% of the total renewable energy installations. Table **1** shows the installed renewable energy capacity for both the global and India. These efforts highlight India's commitment to sustainable and diverse energy solutions. This capacity is expected to grow significantly in India and globally to reduce CO_2 emissions, enhance energy security, and provide environmental and economic benefits associated with clean energy adoption.

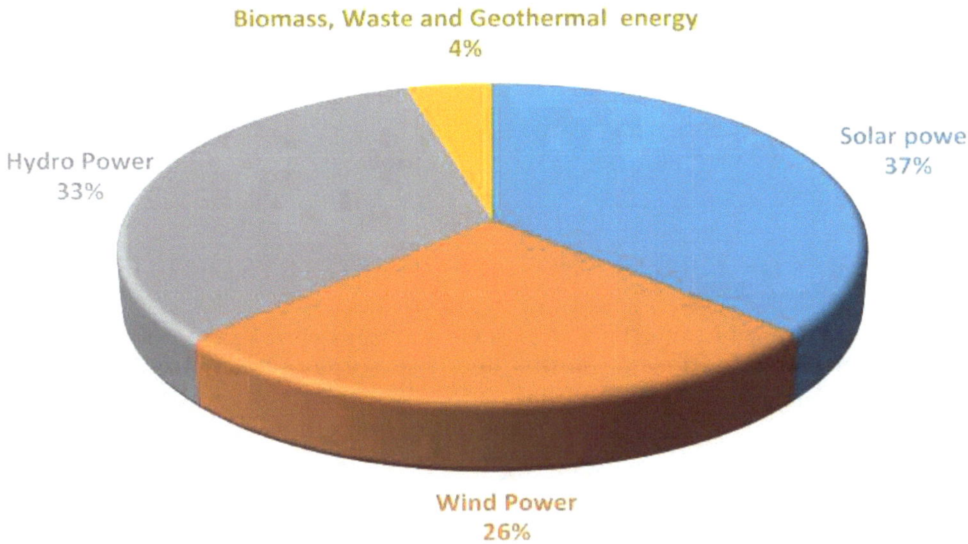

Fig. (1). Sector-wise distribution of installed renewable energy capacity at the global level [22].

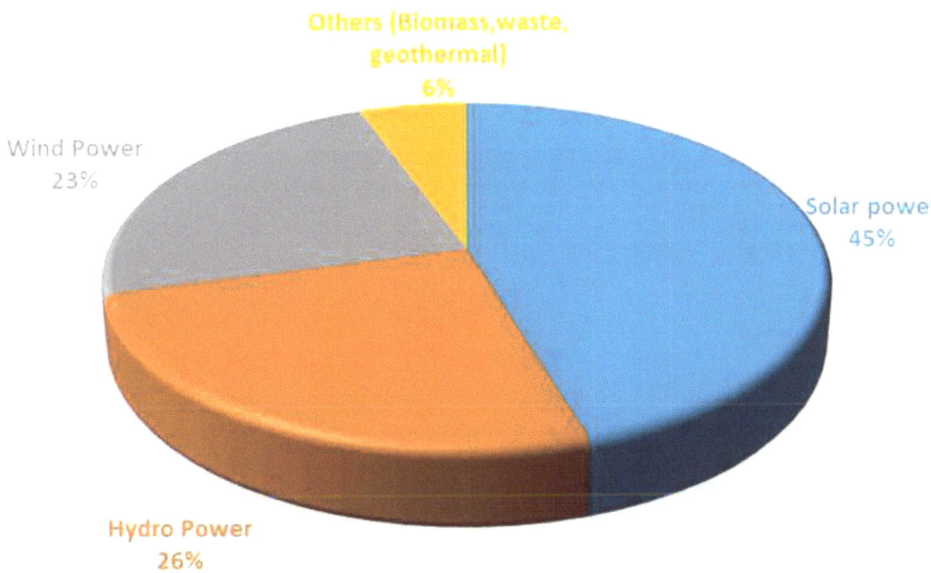

Fig. (2). Percentage share of installed renewable energy capacity across different sectors in india [23].

Table 1. Global and india's installed renewable energy capacity.

Different Sectors of RE	World RE Installed Capacity at the end of 2023 (GW)	RE Installed Capacity in India by October 2024 (GW)
Solar power	1419.0	92.12
Wind Power	1017.2	47.72
Hydro Power	1,267.9	52
Biomass, Waste, and Geothermal Energy	165.3	11.34

APPLICATION OF AI IN RENEWABLE ENERGY SYSTEM

The field of renewable energy is seeing an upsurge, as AI is solving the major issues related to production variability, energy storage, and its distribution. AI ensures maximum energy output under different circumstances by optimizing the efficiency of RES utilizing sophisticated algorithms. Fig. (**3**) depicts an optimized application of AI in various domains of renewable energy. The next part of this book chapter elaborates deeply on the application of AI in the search for solar, hydro, wind, and geothermal energies.

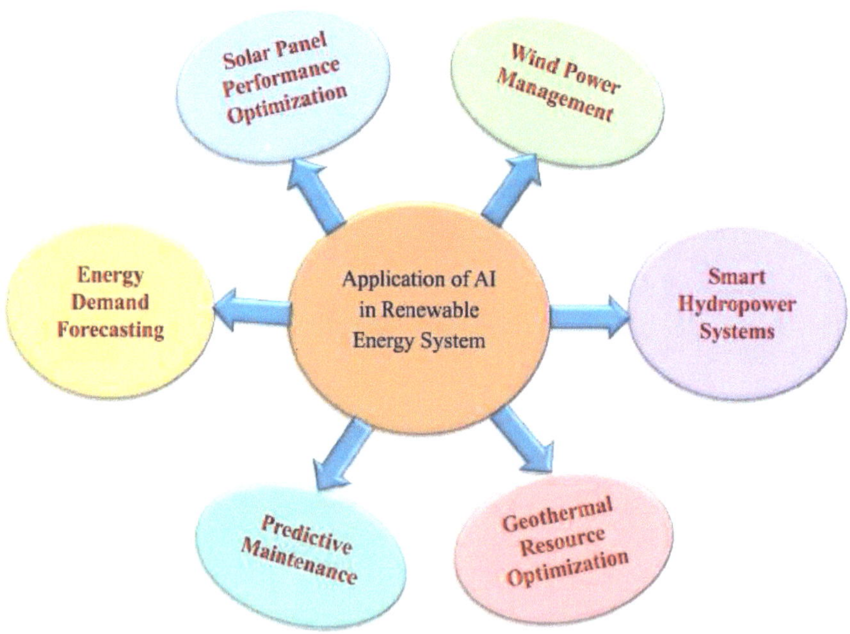

Fig. (3). AI applications in diverse sectors of renewable energy.

AI-DRIVEN SOLAR ENERGY OPTIMIZATION

By providing cutting-edge solutions for optimizing efficiency, sustainability, and cost-effectiveness, the incorporation of AI into solar energy systems is revolutionizing the renewable energy industry. By boosting grid integration, optimizing system performance, and improving energy management, the AI technologies are transforming the generation and distribution of solar energy [8]. Through two primary applications as improving energy management for grid stability and maximizing solar panel performance, this chapter examines how artificial intelligence is transforming solar energy.

Optimizing Solar Panel Performance and Predictive Maintenance with AI

The AI is restructuring the performance of solar panels by enhancing solar irradiation monitoring, output power optimization, and predictive maintenance. One of the leading innovations is the AI-powered solar tracking systems, which dynamically adjust the tilt and direction of the solar panels to track the daily movement of the sun. Unlike traditional fixed panels, these AI-based systems ensure maximum sunlight exposure by analysing real-time data such as weather conditions, solar irradiance, and sun positioning, boosting energy production, especially in large solar farms where sunlight variability is more pronounced [19]. Data processing using an AI algorithm also addresses environmental factors affecting panel performance, such as shading, cloud cover, and dust accumulation. AI algorithms monitor these elements continuously and adjust panel orientation to ensure peak efficiency and minimize energy losses even when weather conditions change.

Besides optimizing panel placement, AI plays a pivotal role in fault detection and predictive maintenance. It processes real-time data collected from previous history to predict incipient faults before they cause failure to shut down the system [19, 20]. Monitoring parameters such as voltage, temperature, and power output, AI can detect anomalies that may indicate issues like failing inverters or damaged photovoltaic (PV) cells. Early detection enables timely repairs, reducing costly downtime [21, 24]. AI also improves maintenance schedules, analyzing the amassing of dust, debris, and pollution in panels. As it determines at what times these panels can best be cleaned, AI ensures efficient cleaning without additional, potentially harmful maintenance that damages panels. Its predictive approach adds years to the lifespan of equipment and reduces operational expenses while improving solar energy systems' efficiency.

Enhancing Grid Integration and Energy Management with AI

The intermittence of solar energy challenges the mainstream integration of its production into electricity grids because it varies with weather and seasons, as well as by time of day. AI technologies give optimum solutions through improved forecasting and optimized management of energy. By analyzing historical data, conditions of the weather, and solar irradiance, AI algorithms have been proven to predict solar energy output correctly in both short-term (minutes to hours) and long-term (days) predictions [5]. These predictions enable grid operators to anticipate system fluctuations while maintaining grid stability to balance supply and demand, minimize fossil fuel dependence [13]. The solar farm operators can also use these predictions to optimize energy dispatch by either storing the excess in batteries or feeding it into the grid at peak demand.

AI further enhances energy storage systems by scheduling efficient charging and discharging cycles. It ensures surplus solar energy is stored during high production periods and used when demand peaks, thus reducing the strain on fossil fuel-based power sources and improving the sustainability of the grid [18]. In addition, AI supports Virtual Power Plants (VPPs) by aggregating energy from decentralized sources like residential solar systems and storage units [25, 26]. These AI-managed networks ensure the flexibility and resiliency of the grid with decreased energy transmission loss. AI plays a critical role in Smart Grids through optimizing energy flow with real-time data, forecasting demand, fault detection, and enhancement of reliability. In trading, AI will predict price changes using market trends, weather, and grid conditions so that excess energy can be sold profitably by the solar producer [25]. Through these breakthroughs, AI is accelerating solar energy adoption as well as innovation in renewable power systems.

AI holds immense potential to revolutionize solar energy by improving efficiency, reducing costs, and enhancing sustainability. However, challenges include managing vast and inconsistent data, the complexity and resource-intensive nature of AI algorithms, and limited datasets in regions with underdeveloped solar infrastructure. Technical issues in integrating AI with existing systems and regulatory concerns, such as data privacy laws, further complicate adoption. Despite these hurdles, AI presents significant opportunities when combined with IoT, enhancing solar energy forecasting, optimizing energy production, predicting faults and maintaining panels, and improving grid dynamics for efficient power transmission and distribution.

AI-BASED PERFORMANCE OPTIMIZATION OF WIND POWER SYSTEM

Wind energy is also an important renewable energy source to converts wind's kinetic energy to electricity using wind turbines. However, its variability and unpredictability present significant challenges for both energy producers and grid operators. Wind power generation is subject to fluctuations in wind speed, direction, and atmospheric conditions, leading to operational inefficiencies and reduced energy yield [27]. Wake effects, which occur in the downstream regions of turbines and lead to lower wind speeds and increased turbulence, further complicate the management of wind farms. Optimizing turbine placement, operational strategies, and maintenance schedules is critical to maximizing wind energy production. Artificial Intelligence (AI) is revolutionizing the wind energy sector by offering data-driven solutions to overcome these challenges [9].

Wind Power Forecasting

Accurate forecasting of wind power is important to ensure efficient integration of the grid and optimal energy use. Because the wind speed and direction are variable, the more precise prediction of power output calls for AI-based technologies in the field of forecasting. Traditional techniques of forecasting include Persistence and Physical Models, but they are quite inadequate because these methods cannot effectively capture the intricate and dynamic character of wind. AI-driven models, especially Artificial Neural Networks (ANNs), have become very effective tools in improving the accuracy of wind power predictions. Two of the most popular AI approaches used in wind power forecasting are Multilayer Perceptrons (MLP) and Long Short-Term Memory (LSTM) networks. MLP is good for recognizing patterns within historical meteorological data, and LSTM is good at temporal dependencies in general, and is therefore especially useful for time-series forecasting. They are generally well-suited for short-term prediction (below 30 minutes) where there is real-time availability of data and model complexity is lower. Long-term predictions are enhanced with hybrid models that integrate AI with statistical methods, such as SVM and ARIMA, to incorporate nonlinear relations between input features and the corresponding wind power output. AI-based forecasting techniques not only make predictions more accurate but also facilitate real-time integration of data from various sources [26].

Performance Optimization of Windmill

Performance optimization in wind energy systems aims to maximize energy production and enhance turbine efficiency. AI plays a critical role in the process, examining real-time data from the turbine's operation and adjusting parameters like blade pitch, yaw, and rotor speed in response to wind conditions. Thus, it will ensure that the turbines operate at their optimal efficiencies even when weather conditions are unstable. The most crucial area to which AI has proven to make improvements is in the positioning and coordination of wind turbines within a farm to optimize the layout. Wake effects come about whenever wind flows behind turbines. The flow of wind becomes weaker for downstream turbines and reduces their ability to capture energy. AI models use real-time wind data to enhance positioning and adjust operational strategies, hence minimizing wake losses. This coordination ensures that every turbine is operating at its peak, thus achieving a higher energy yield for the entire wind farm.

Further, digital twin technology employs AI for making virtual replicas of wind turbines that integrate both real-time physical data and predictive analytics. By simulating various operational scenarios, AI may predict performance outcomes, which aid in optimizing maintenance schedules and operational settings [8]. The leading companies in the wind energy sector, such as General Electric (GE) and Vestas, have implemented AI-driven solutions to optimize wind turbine performance. GE's Digital Wind Farm platform and Vestas' Performance Diagnostics Center use machine learning algorithms to assess turbine conditions and predict potential issues, enabling operators to make data-driven decisions that improve turbine reliability and performance.

Predictive Maintenance of Wind Turbine

Traditionally, reactive methods address faults only after they have already occurred. It caused unplanned shutdowns, raised repair costs, and reduced the reliability of the turbine. AI transformed this approach to predictive maintenance with the help of data insights used to predict failure before it actually happens. The machine learning technique analyzes vast amounts of operational data collected from sensors embedded in components of the turbines. These sensors monitor parameters like vibration, temperature, and rotor speed, continuously providing data streams for AI models to assess component health in real time. For instance, unusual vibrations or temperature fluctuations can be flagged for investigation before they cause catastrophic breakdowns. This proactive approach reduces unplanned downtime, cuts maintenance costs, and extends component lifespans. Predictive maintenance, powered by AI, can reduce surprise turbine shutdowns by as much as 40%, optimize maintenance schedules, and improve turbine uptime [6]. Integration with SCADA systems further enhances these capabilities. By analyzing real-time SCADA data, AI models provide continuous performance tracking, delivering actionable insights and enabling operators to refine maintenance strategies based on actual turbine conditions.

The use of predictive maintenance not only ensures better turbine reliability and efficiency but also meets the wider needs of sustainability and optimizing renewable energy.

HYDROPOWER INNOVATIONS DRIVEN BY AI

Hydropower, a central pillar of renewable energy, offers steady and clean electricity but is still beset by inefficiencies, aging infrastructure, and vagaries in water inflows brought on by climate change, and the energy and ecological sustainability nexus. Its operational problems necessitate advanced technologies for optimization and sustainability enhancement. AI is the revolutionary solution that harnesses the potential of big data analysis for transforming hydropower. The amount of data that AI processes leads to predictive analytics, optimization, and real-time monitoring [10, 11]. A very critical application is in the prediction of water inflows, crucial for energy production, using meteorological and hydrological data for forecasting patterns that are affected by rainfall, snowmelt, and climate conditions. These insights allow real-time adjustments to turbine operations and reservoir levels, optimizing output while mitigating risks like flooding and water shortages. AI also aligns power generation with grid demands, improving flexibility and system responsiveness to fluctuations in energy consumption and environmental conditions.

Advanced techniques like Reinforcement Learning (RL) and Online Machine Learning (OML) enable dynamic management, adjusting to changing weather patterns and water inflows. Optimisation algorithms, such as Genetic Algorithms (GA) and Particle Swarm Optimization (PSO), handle multi-objective problems by optimizing energy production, water conservation, and environmental sustainability. This method minimizes the cost of operations as well as ecological impacts by taking into consideration seasonal inflows and energy demands in addition to the capacity of reservoir storage. IoT-enabled sensors provide real-time data on water levels, flow rates, and reservoir capacities, facilitating precise control and planning. Additionally, Blockchain will ensure safe and transparent data sharing, and digital twins will simulate water systems for predictive maintenance and operational optimization. Thus, by enhancing efficiency, adaptability, and sustainability, AI is transforming hydropower operations. It addresses traditional inefficiencies, supports sustainable energy production, and ensures resilience in the face of growing energy demands and environmental challenges. As these pressures intensify, AI's role in hydropower will become increasingly critical for a sustainable energy future.

PREDICTIVE MAINTENANCE OF HYDRO PLANTS

Predictive fault diagnosis of hydropower systems can significantly reduce the cost of maintenance of machinery by incipient fault detection. Sensors give operators useful information by continuously monitoring temperature, vibrations, and turbine performance. This reduces downtime, minimizes repair costs, and extends the lifespan of critical components. Additionally, AI-based analytics streamline energy dispatch strategies by forecasting load demand and optimizing turbine output. Hydropower plants can then efficiently allocate resources, ensuring a consistent energy supply while maintaining grid stability, through the analysis of factual data.

AI-powered digital twins simulate plant operations, offering a virtual replica for testing and optimizing processes. These simulations allow operators to explore different scenarios, evaluate the impact of changes, and implement improvements without disrupting actual operations. Furthermore, robotics and autonomous systems enhance safety and precision in maintenance tasks, reducing risks for human workers and ensuring consistent operational performance. The integration of IoT with AI enables seamless communication between devices, creating a smart hydropower ecosystem capable of self-monitoring and self-optimization.

The challenges of implementing AI in hydropower include modernizing legacy systems, assuring high-quality, comprehensive datasets, and upgrading expensive hardware and software. The implementation is further hampered by costs associated with sensor installation, data collection, and maintenance. But AI has a lot of potential, and new developments are opening it up to smaller plants. Efficiency, flexibility, and sustainability are improved by combining AI with IoT and Blockchain [17, 19]. By transforming hydropower into resilient systems, these technologies can lessen their negative effects on the environment while fulfilling future energy demands. Unlocking AI's full potential to transform hydropower systems would require investments in infrastructure, research, and supportive policies.

ARTIFICIAL INTELLIGENCE IN GEOTHERMAL EXPLORATION

Geothermal energy, which is generated from the Earth's internal heat, is a renewable and sustainable source of energy in place of fossil fuels such as petroleum. The major geothermal exploration fields include Wairakei in New Zealand, Darajat Site in Indonesia, Larderello in Italy, Poga Valley in India, and the Geysers in California, which show that geothermal energy can be produced for long periods. Exploration of geothermal sources is challenging because of high costs, uncertain subsurface conditions, and the requirement of advanced technology to access deep reservoirs. Improving exploration efficiency and accuracy calls for innovative methods for overcoming these barriers [7].

Advanced AI techniques can handle extremely complex datasets, encompassing geological, geophysical, geochemical, and thermal information, to determine significant subsurface attributes. The NNs will consequently be able to identify critical subsurface features, such as the reservoir temperature, fluid properties, and flow rates, thus aiding decision-making in geothermal exploration and management. AI also reduces the uncertainties associated with exploration in geothermal energy development and helps interpret data better [12]. Open efforts, such as the OpenEI Geothermal Data Repository sponsored by the U.S. Department of Energy, provide easy access to critical datasets that allow researchers to implement AI-driven solutions more effectively. GOOML, for instance, is a great example of how AI can optimize resource use, predict when maintenance is needed, and increase overall performance. As AI develops these types of partnerships, along with incorporating vast amounts of data into algorithms, geothermal energy is thus transformed from becoming costlier and unsustainable to remaining competitive in a global market of energy.

CHALLENGES AND OPPORTUNITIES RELATED TO INCORPORATION OF AI IN ADVANCING RENEWABLE ENERGY SYSTEMS

The AI technique has a vast potential for revolutionizing the renewable energy sector, offering significant opportunities for optimization and sustainability. However, its implementation faces several challenges that need to be resolved for its maximum impact. The different challenges related to the application of AI in advancing the RES sector are shown in Fig. (**4**). The major challenges and opportunities are explained below.

Major Challenges Related to the Incorporation of AI with RES

Data Quality, Protection, and Processing: The collection of high-quality information in RES is difficult because of the far-off locations of the plants, adverse geophysical patterns, usability constraints, sensor implantation, and infrequent data transmission. As a result, RES data may be incomplete, inconsistent, and less reliable. The expensive technique of gathering, storing, guarding against cyber-attacks, and processing massive datasets may potentially impede AI adoption, particularly for smaller businesses and developing countries.

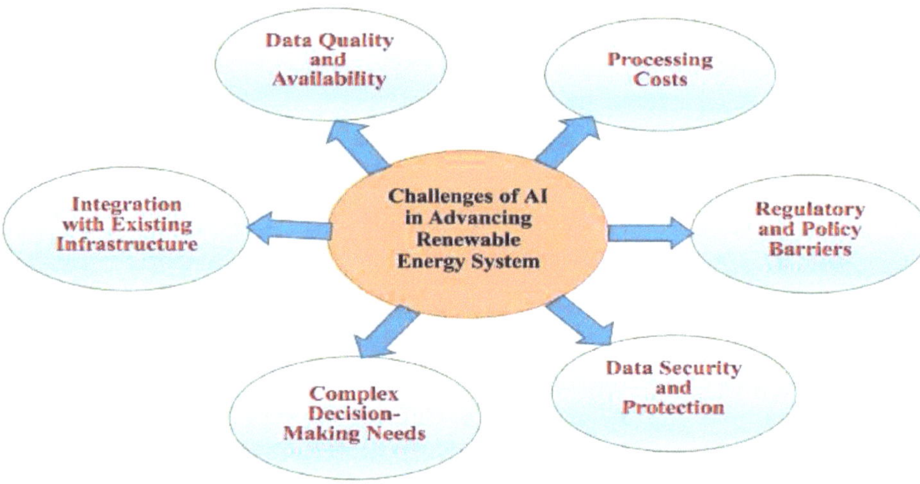

Fig. (4). Different challenges of AI in advancing renewable energy systems.

Incorporation with Existing Infrastructure: Due to the inconsistent nature of renewable energy sources, it highly demands an innovative AI-driven robust infrastructure to integrate it with the existing grid management system. The policies and regulatory of the government are also leading to vague information to broadly adopt the AI technology.

Opportunities to Adopt AI Technology in RES

Optimization of Energy Production and Consumption: The AI technology can significantly enhance the efficiency of RES by predicting energy generation based on weather patterns, climate conditions, and seasonal variability. This helps improve energy storage, distribution, and grid stability, ensuring a better match between supply and demand.

Energy Storage Optimization: The AI technology provides an effective energy distribution by predicting variations in demand and supply of electricity. It helps in managing and optimizing battery storage infrastructure.

Cost Reduction: AI-driven predictive maintenance and operational efficiency improvements can minimize downtime in renewable energy plants, streamlining maintenance schedules and reducing costs.

Policy and Strategy Development: AI can support decision-making by providing statistical information on renewable energy and modelling various circumstances, aiding the development of long-term energy strategies and policies.

CONCLUSION

Artificial Intelligence integration in the RES is, in fact, a change of dimension to more sustainable, efficient, and optimized energy systems. In an era where solar and wind sources are being integrated into daily lives, the contribution of AI to energy production, distribution, and consumption has been pivotal. AI can better improve energy forecasting through predictive analytics, optimize grid management, and allow for more effective energy storage solutions that eliminate the intermittency problems of the renewable sources. However, exploring the AI adoption in RES is not without challenges. Data scarcity, high costs, and the complexity of incorporating AI into the current framework are some of the significant challenges. The lack of robust regulatory frameworks and standardized policies also creates challenges for the smooth deployment of AI solutions. These obstacles underscore the need for continued investment in data collection, technological advancements, and policy development. With these challenges, there is no question about the opportunities presented by AI. AI could make renewable energy more operationally efficient, decrease its costs, and increase reliability overall. Beyond this, AI-enabled tools will support policymakers in the design of much more informed and data-driven energy strategies, creating much more sustainable and equitable systems of energy production. As AI technology accelerates, the transition into a more sustainable and resilient future for energy resources it's well on its way to facilitating the global aim of reducing carbon emissions and working to combat climate change.

REFERENCES

[1] S.C. Necula, "Assessing the Potential of Artificial Intelligence in Advancing Clean Energy Technologies in Europe: A Systematic Review", *Energies,* vol. 16, no. 22, p. 7633, 2023. [http://dx.doi.org/10.3390/en16227633]

[2] T. Ahmad, H. Zhu, D. Zhang, R. Tariq, A. Bassam, F. Ullah, A.S. AlGhamdi, and S.S. Alshamrani, "Energetics Systems and artificial intelligence: Applications of industry 4.0", *Energy Rep.,* vol. 8, pp. 334-361, 2022.
[http://dx.doi.org/10.1016/j.egyr.2021.11.256]

[3] L. Cheng, and T. Yu, "A new generation of AI: A review and perspective on machine learning technologies applied to smart energy and electric power systems", *Int. J. Energy Res.,* vol. 43, no. 6, pp. 1928-1973, 2019.
[http://dx.doi.org/10.1002/er.4333]

[4] M. Khalid, "Energy 4.0: AI-enabled digital transformation for sustainable power networks", *Comput. Ind. Eng.,* vol. 193, p. 110253, 2024.
[http://dx.doi.org/10.1016/j.cie.2024.110253]

[5] X. Wen, Q. Shen, W. Zheng, and H. Zhang, "AI-driven solar energy generation and smart grid integration: A holistic approach to enhancing renewable energy efficiency", *International Journal of Innovative Research in Engineering and Management,* vol. 11, no. 4, pp. 55-66, 2024.
[http://dx.doi.org/10.55524/ijirem.2024.11.4.8]

[6] W.S. Udo, J.M. Kwakye, D.E. Ekechukwu, and O.B. Ogundipe, "Optimizing wind energy systems using machine learning for predictive maintenance and efficiency enhancement", *Journal of*

Renewable Energy Technology, vol. 28, no. 3, pp. 312-330, 2024.

[7] J. Widén, N. Carpman, V. Castellucci, D. Lingfors, J. Olauson, F. Remouit, M. Bergkvist, M. Grabbe, and R. Waters, "Variability assessment and forecasting of renewables: A review for solar, wind, wave and tidal resources", *Renew. Sustain. Energy Rev.,* vol. 44, pp. 356-375, 2015. [http://dx.doi.org/10.1016/j.rser.2014.12.019]

[8] A. Mohammad, and F. Mahjabeen, "Revolutionizing solar energy with AI-driven enhancements in photovoltaic technology", *BULLET: Journal Multidisiplin Ilmu,* vol. 2, no. 4, pp. 1174-1187, 2023.

[9] F.P. García Márquez, and A. Peinado Gonzalo, "A comprehensive review of artificial intelligence and wind energy", *Arch. Comput. Methods Eng.,* vol. 29, no. 5, pp. 2935-2958, 2022. [http://dx.doi.org/10.1007/s11831-021-09678-4]

[10] Y. Villeneuve, S. Séguin, and A. Chehri, "AI-based scheduling models, optimization, and prediction for hydropower generation: Opportunities, issues, and future directions", *Energies,* vol. 16, no. 8, p. 3335, 2023. [http://dx.doi.org/10.3390/en16083335]

[11] F.C. Jong, M.M. Ahmed, W.K. Lau, and H.A. Denis Lee, "A new hybrid Artificial Intelligence (AI) approach for hydro energy sites selection and integration", *Heliyon,* vol. 8, no. 9, p. e10638, 2022. [http://dx.doi.org/10.1016/j.heliyon.2022.e10638] [PMID: 36164526]

[12] M. Al Gaiar, M. Hossain, A. Petrovski, A. Lashin, and N. Faisal, "Applications of artificial intelligence in geothermal resource exploration: A review," Geothermal Energy, vol. 3, no. 3, Special Issue, pp. 269–285, Sept. 2024.

[13] P. Arévalo, and F. Jurado, "Impact of artificial intelligence on the planning and operation of distributed energy systems in smart grids", *Energies,* vol. 17, no. 17, p. 4501, 2024. [http://dx.doi.org/10.3390/en17174501]

[14] A.N.F. Ali, M.F. Sulaima, I.A.W.A. Razak, A.F.A. Kadir, and H. Mokhlis, "Artificial intelligence application in demand response: advantages, issues, status, and challenges", *IEEE Access,* vol. 11, pp. 16907-16922, 2023. [http://dx.doi.org/10.1109/ACCESS.2023.3237737]

[15] A.N. Abdalla, M.S. Nazir, H. Tao, S. Cao, R. Ji, M. Jiang, and L. Yao, "Integration of energy storage system and renewable energy sources based on artificial intelligence: An overview", *J. Energy Storage,* vol. 40, p. 102811, 2021. [http://dx.doi.org/10.1016/j.est.2021.102811]

[16] M.S.H. Lipu, M.S. Miah, T. Jamal, T. Rahman, S. Ansari, M.S. Rahman, R.H. Ashique, A.S.M. Shihavuddin, and M.N. Shakib, "Artificial Intelligence Approaches for Advanced Battery Management System in Electric Vehicle Applications: A Statistical Analysis towards Future Research Opportunities", *Vehicles,* vol. 6, no. 1, pp. 22-70, 2023. [http://dx.doi.org/10.3390/vehicles6010002]

[17] N.M. Kumar, A.A. Chand, M. Malvoni, K.A. Prasad, K.A. Mamun, F.R. Islam, and S.S. Chopra, "Distributed energy resources and the application of AI, IoT, and blockchain in smart grids", *Energies,* vol. 13, no. 21, p. 5739, 2020. [http://dx.doi.org/10.3390/en13215739]

[18] W. Hua, Y. Chen, M. Qadrdan, J. Jiang, H. Sun, and J. Wu, "Applications of blockchain and artificial intelligence technologies for enabling prosumers in smart grids: A review", *Renew. Sustain. Energy Rev.,* vol. 161, p. 112308, 2022. [http://dx.doi.org/10.1016/j.rser.2022.112308]

[19] A. Sayal, *N. C., J. Jha, and N. Allagari, "AI-Based Predictive Maintenance Strategies for Improving the Reliability of Green Power Systems," in Digital Technologies to Implement the UN Sustainable Development Goals.* Springer Nature: Cham, Switzerland, 2024, pp. 19-46.

[20] M. Islam, M.R. Rashel, M.T. Ahmed, A.K.M.K. Islam, and M. Tlemçani, "Artificial Intelligence in

Photovoltaic Fault Identification and Diagnosis: A Systematic Review", *Energies,* vol. 16, no. 21, p. 7417, 2023.
[http://dx.doi.org/10.3390/en16217417]

[21] A. Abubakar, C.F.M. Almeida, and M. Gemignani, "Review of Artificial Intelligence-Based Failure Detection and Diagnosis Methods for Solar Photovoltaic Systems", *Machines,* vol. 9, no. 12, p. 328, 2021.
[http://dx.doi.org/10.3390/machines9120328]

[22] Available from: https://www.irena.org/-/media/Files/IRENA

[23] Available from: https://pib.gov.in/PressReleaseIframePage.aspx

[24] A. Thakfan, and Y. Bin Salamah, "Artificial-Intelligence-Based Detection of Defects and Faults in Photovoltaic Systems: A Survey", *Energies,* vol. 17, no. 19, p. 4807, 2024.
[http://dx.doi.org/10.3390/en17194807]

[25] M. Kiasari, M. Ghaffari, and H. Aly, "A comprehensive review of the current status of smart grid technologies for renewable energies integration and future trends: The role of machine learning and energy storage systems", *Energies,* vol. 17, no. 16, p. 4128, 2024.
[http://dx.doi.org/10.3390/en17164128]

[26] K. Ukoba, K. O. Olatunji, E. Adeoye, T. C. Jen, and D. M. Madyira, "Optimizing renewable energy systems through artificial intelligence: Review and future prospects," Energy & Environment, vol. 0958305X241256293, 2024.

[27] K. Kumar, P. Prabhakar, A. Verma, S. Saroha, and K. Singh, "Advancements in wind power forecasting: A comprehensive review of artificial intelligence-based approaches", *Multimedia Tools Appl.,* vol. 84, no. 10, pp. 8331-8360, 2024.
[http://dx.doi.org/10.1007/s11042-024-18916-3]

CHAPTER 10

Secure Monitoring of an IoT Smart Office Using Wire Guard VPN Protocol

Deepti Chaudhary[1,*], **Priyanka Jangra**[1] and **Kuldeep**[1]

[1] *University Institute of Engineering and Technology, Kurukshetra University, Kurukshetra, Haryana, India*

Abstract: The Internet of Things (IoT) is not a new thing today. The networks used in offices, homes, shopping complex, railways, etc., can be made smart by using IoT technologies. Once a smart network is designed, the network admin and the owner may access the smart network from a far location. For example, the tech admin on a business tour or the owner at their home. The proposed network is designed to deal with these security issues of the network. The proposed network is about the secure remote monitoring of an IoT-enabled smart office using VPN (Virtual Private Network) technology. The network makes use of the Wire Guard protocol framework to secure the data of the IoT network on the internet.

Keyword: IOT, Remote access, Smart office, Virtual private network.

INTRODUCTION

IoT makes the ordinary devices 'smart'. Normal wrist watches are now smart watches, speakers are now smart speakers, and cars are self-driving smart cars, illustrating the technology's widespread application. The evolution of the IoT has enabled the automatic control of previously manually controlled electronic devices, giving rise to automated devices. Many places, such as homes, campuses, offices, and shopping malls, are made IoT-enabled smart by using smart nodes and IoT technologies [1].

The smart network chosen for the proposed network is an IoT-enabled smart-connected office network [2, 3]. Users can operate different appliances locally within the campus or a closed area by using a smart network. This network doesn't make use of the internet. It mainly focuses on the control and automation of basic services such as light, doors, security devices, and other electronic and electrical devices within the campus. On the other hand, the proposed smart

* **Corresponding author Deepti Chaudhary:** University Institute of Engineering and Technology, Kurukshetra University, Kurukshetra, Haryana, India; E-mail: deeptic2015@gmail.com

Shilpa Gupta & Ritika Sharma (Eds.)

connected network allows for remote control and management of appliances, typically over IP-based networks (*e.g.*, the Internet). This type of network provides services promoting and supporting security, energy management, and healthcare. Additionally, it includes a central hub (gateway) from which the system can be controlled, together with a graphical user interface that can be operated through a smartphone. Hence, a smart connected network merges the functionality of both the smart network and the connected network. The proposed network is shown in Fig. (**1**). Smart devices have different types of sensors equipped in them and have been given computing capabilities. These devices sense and collect data from the environment, like temperature and pressure, from human behaviour, like walking and speaking, user inputs, or usage patterns. This collected data can then be used to monitor and control nodes remotely.

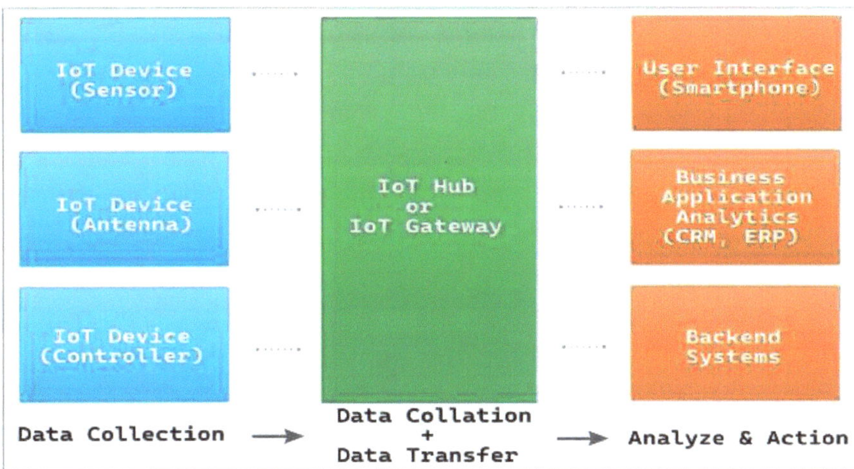

Fig. (1). Proposed network system.

A gateway device interconnects all the smart nodes together and makes them part of a single infrastructure. There are many options available to be used as an IoT gateway, for example, MCU (Microcontroller Unit, like Arduino Uno), SBC (Single Board Computer, like Raspberry Pi), and Wi-Fi routers. The choice of IoT gateway for this network is a Wi-Fi router with VPN capabilities.

The IoT registration server has the application and services enabled, so that it can be used to register all the IoT devices with it. It acts as a channel between the remote controlling device and the IoT end devices for smart functions. An IoT infrastructure may have the IoT server at the company's premises itself, or the company may rely on cloud solutions like AWS, Azure, Cisco, or some other similar IoT cloud service provider. An-house registration server is used in the given network design. The role of these remote monitoring devices will be to get the data over the internet, which was collected by the IoT smart nodes and was sent to the gateway, and then internet.

Introduction to VPN

Security is the major issue when monitoring IoT nodes *via* the Internet from a distant place [4]. Communication between two internal networks of an organization used to be a costly method in the past, a frame-relay and MPLS WAN connection [5].

VPN is an alternative technology that may be used to connect one private network with another private network over the public Internet. VPN make use of a variety of security protocols, like SSL and IPSec etc., to provide secure data transmission at lower costs than dedicated, private links. VPN is a private network as represented in Fig. (**2**) [6] created over a public network for safe & secure communication [7].

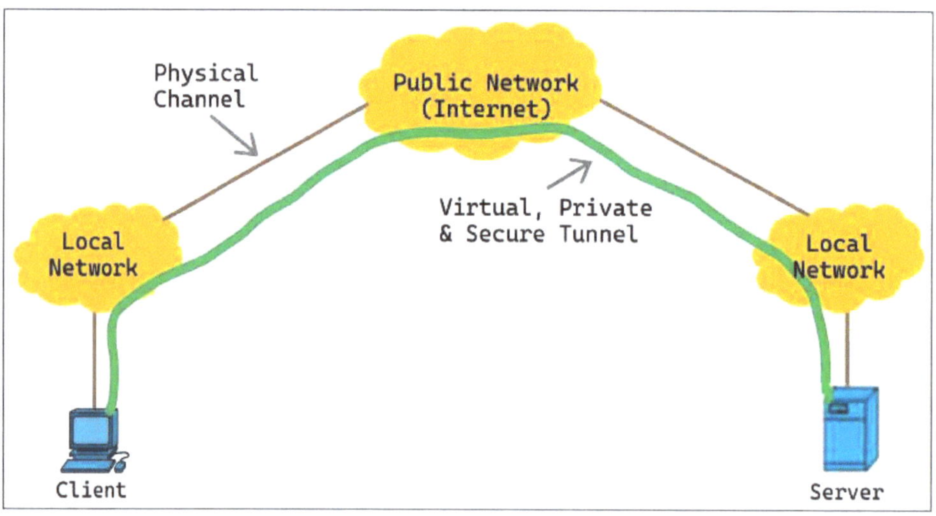

Fig. (2). Virtual private network [6].

VPN technology relies on the concept of tunnelling. Tunnelling involves establishing and maintaining a logical network association. So, a VPN is a private tunnel over an insecure path that allows users/systems to connect securely, a tunnel to allow remote users to access the organization's private network [8]. VPN uses network security protocols like IPSec and WireGuard [9] to provide privacy and data integrity.

Introduction to the Proposed Network

The proposed network has the following components:

- Smart end devices
- IoT gateway/internet edge
- Registration server
- Monitoring devices

The IoT applications wouldn't exist without sensors. They are the building blocks of IoT ecosystems. Smart devices have different types of sensors equipped in them and have been given computing capabilities, as represented in Fig. (**3**) [10, 11]. These devices sense and collect data from the environment like temperature, pressure, from human behaviour like walking and speaking, user inputs, or usage patterns. This collected data can then be used to remotely monitor and control IoT nodes.

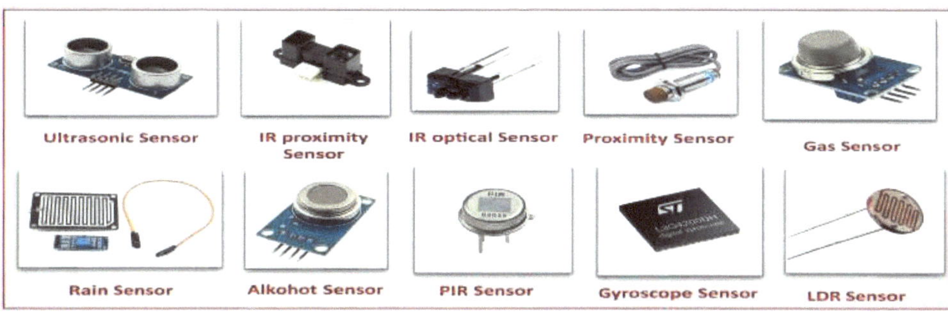

Fig. (3). Different sensor types used in IoT [11].

Gateway device interconnects all the smart nodes together and makes them part of a single IoT infrastructure [12, 13]. There are many options available to be used as an IoT gateway, for example, MCU (Microcontroller Unit, like Arduino Uno), SBC (Single Board Computer, like Raspberry Pi), and Wi-Fi routers. The choice of IoT gateway for this network is a Wi-Fi router with VPN capabilities, as represented in Fig. (**4**) [14].

The IoT registration server has the application and services enabled, so that it can be used to register all the IoT devices with it. An in-house registration server is used in the given network design [15]. The abundance of smartphones all over the world has made it a great choice for the same. A laptop is also used just to show the possibilities and availability as an added option [16].

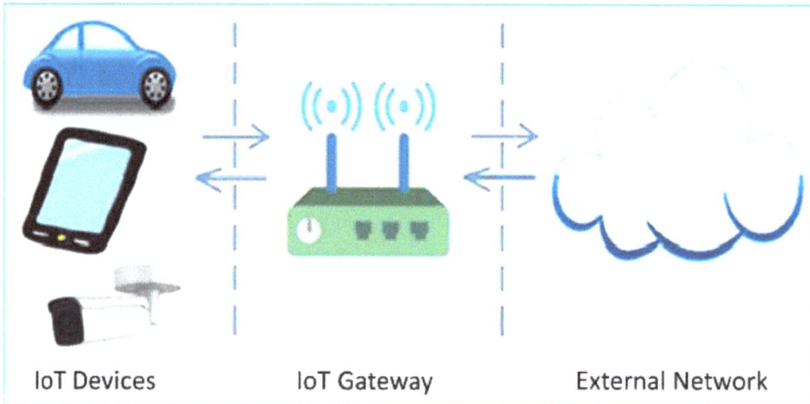

Fig. (4). IoT gateway [14].

INTRODUCTION TO WIREGUARD

WireGuard is an open-source 'Noise' protocol framework [17, 18] based on a communication protocol used to secure data transmission and maintain data confidentiality by setting up VPNs. It operates at the network layer, which protects the data by encapsulating it inside an encrypted tunnel. Through data encryption, authentication, and integrity check technologies, it ensures the integrity, reliability, privacy, and confidentiality of data transmission.

LITERATURE REVIEW

The concept of IoT-based smart networks is gaining pace in India. A considerable amount of work has been carried out so far in other countries and in India, where such smart networks are already in place. Much research is happening in the home, campus, hospital, and office automation systems. This section presents the literature review related to the work.

Nivedita M and Sharnil P [1]. investigated various security issues present at the IoT level. The perceptual layer, network layer, support layer, and application layer focused on DDOS attacks. The authors compared intrusion detection and preventive models to reduce DDOS attacks and focused on intrusion marking models. Additionally, the authors discussed the classification of intrusion detection systems, various anomaly detection techniques, different intrusion detection system models of datasets, and various machine learning and deep learning techniques for data preprocessing and malware detection. Ultimately, a broader perspective was planned, but discussions on research challenges, proposed solutions, and future visions were held. Khanam S, Ahmedy I [4] *et al.* provide an overview of IoT, its well-known system architecture, and enablement technologies, and discuss security challenges and goals. Their study also analyzes the security gaps and provides a state-of-the-art security taxonomy. The most relevant current taxonomy of IoT security attacks is presented for applications, networks, and physical layers. Furthermore, authors discover the safety challenges that the research community can provide in relation to security in a non-uniform IoT environment. Jabbar W and Kian T [10] *et al.* present a portable, inexpensive, hybrid (local and remote) IoT-based home automation system. This is a cheap and reliable system with a user-friendly interface for smartphones and laptops. A prototype called IoT Home has been developed with algorithms to enable monitoring of home conditions and automate control of home appliances over the Internet.

Abdul Aziz N, Anak Revhie R, Mohd Bakry B, *et al.* presented a security analysis in a smart home environment. The Cisco Package Tracer simulation software set up a testbed for a basic smart home set consisting of electronic devices, devices, and monitoring systems. Possible weakness issues were simulated at the network and application layers. The weaknesses and possible attacks in smart home network environments have been successfully identified. Abdur Razzaq M, Sajid Habib G *et al.* [19] provided a comprehensive study on security and data protection issues in IoT networks. The main focus of this research was to highlight the key security issues of the Internet of Things and to concentrate on security attacks and their countermeasures. Huh Wu, Chunkai Qiu *et al.* [20] presented a child-based hybrid network system architecture for applications that are not suitable for transferring data from any type of sensor in a network using a single gateway and further processing towards the cloud. Several gateways need to be used to support a variety of IoT protocols. The proposed system consists of a hybrid driver and an IoT gateway. Desmukh D and Iyer B [21] register the design of an IP Secure VPN for remote access using the Cisco Packer Traces platform for simulation, analysis, and review purposes. Budiyanto S and Gunawan D [22] compared QoS and analysed several security system mechanisms, including delays, jitter, throughput, and packet loss for several tunnel protocols. Hasebullah J and Amir M [23] evaluated the potential of WireGuard S as an efficient VPN solution for IOT device resources. The authors compared the performance of WireGuard and IoT in a simulated IoT environment using standard protocols OpenVPN and IPSEC. Measured metrics include throughput, latency, and jitter during file transmission. K. Sasikumar & Sivakumar N [24] investigated and analyzed a variety of encryption methods, including deoxyribonucleic acid (DNA), elliptic curves, homomorphic, hybrids, writers, and new methods. Shaikh Z *et al.* [25] systematically review the security of protection processes and data protection to provide compliance with official compliance and implement industry 5.0 cryptographic information security as a comprehensive solution that is a guideline in addition to industrial goals.

The proposed work is inspired by the introduction of WireGuard, a new VPN protocol, and compares the differences between cutting-edge VPNs under normal, unreliable network conditions on various operating systems (OSs). This study was achieved by examining previous comparisons of VPN solutions to determine which metrics to analyse and which VPN solutions were recommended. A testbench was then created in the laboratory network, and it controlled the network during testing. Many researchers carry out a variety of tasks in the field of intelligent and secure IOT systems.

RESEARCH GAPS

One of the problems with existing IoT monitoring solutions is the need for separate hardware to be used as an IoT gateway, such as an MCU (Arduino Uno, for example) and an SBC (Raspberry Pi). They are dependent on external internet gateways to be connected to the internet and the outside world. It adds cost and complexity to the design of the IoT infrastructure. Another considerable gap found is the use of cloud for data storage and access. For the networks not allowing the use of cloud services due to security protocols or reliance on private, in-house cloud infrastructure, this creates unnecessary compliance, cost, and security concerns. Finally, there is not much work found to integrate the use of VPN technologies with the IoT and smart networks. Adding security to the IoT and smart networking domain is still considered a difficult and costly affair.

MOTIVATION

It is not required to have full-fledged IoT solutions like separate multi-feature gateways, complex AI and ML algorithms, and cloud services for the managers and owners of small, smart offices. Because all they want is the secure remote access of the smart network they have built. The proposed network is motivated by this simple need. Such a smart, remotely accessible network is desired by those who also have their own in-house private cloud.

Another important aspect that has driven the design and development of the proposed network is the availability of the Internet for both mobile and PC/laptop users and for static and roaming users. The use of fibre in the WAN has made the internet cheap and easily available for most home users. So, the use of a Wi-Fi router as the gateway and internet edge makes the implementation cheaper and the overall network more available.

In addition, the 4G cellular network is already in use and is heading towards 5 G. The Internet is not a problem at all in most parts of the world. It makes remote accessing, monitoring, and management of smart networks possible at all times by all sorts of users. The proposed network is also motivated by the fact that the rich and powerful VPN technologies have not been used that much in the IoT domain, as they could have been, as found from the literature review so far.

OBJECTIVES

The main objective of the proposed network is to build a simple, smart, and secure connected small-scale office using Wi-Fi and WireGuard VPN technologies.

Wi-Fi routers are commonly used at the edge of a company's sites, to get Internet services, and because this is the device that will be used as the gateway itself in the proposed network, to interconnect smart devices of IoT infrastructure, there is no extra cost involved and any of the sites. The same device is supposed to be used as both the Internet edge and the IoT gateway.

This makes the design and implementation of the smart office network easier and cost-effective from the perspective of configuration and monitoring. The reason is that technical people already have hands-on experience with these same tools, as per the requirements of their job profile, most of the time.

RESEARCH METHODOLOGY

In the IoT smart networks, confidential data of users and organizations travels through the Internet, which makes it vulnerable to security attacks like sniffing and man-in-the-middle attacks. The given fig. (**5**) depicts the entire process of protecting the data traveling over the internet. This procedure is executed in four stages:

i. Small office network topology design where subnets and IP addresses will be decided to be used on the chosen IoT nodes.
ii. Local remote access configuration of the smart office network, where the devices will be registered on the registration server/IoT controller.
iii. WireGuard VPN configuration between the smart office router and home router where peers will be configured to create a secure and encrypted VPN tunnel for the demonstration of encrypted traffic analysis between both sides.
iv. Result verification of secure data transfer between both sites, where encrypted packets will be opened and analysed to confirm the creation and maintenance of secure data transfer over the VPN tunnel.

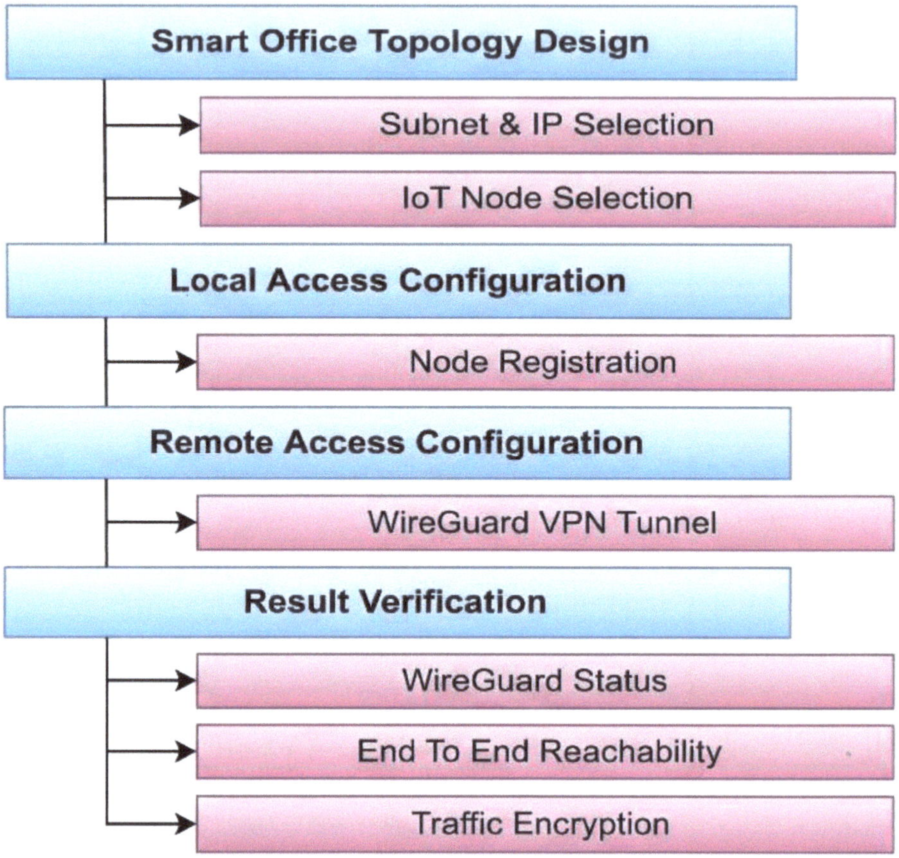

Fig. (5). Flow chart of methodology used.

Smart Office Network Topology Design

The first part is about selecting the subnet and required IoT/smart office nodes for the topology design. The IP network scheme used in the topology will be 192.168.0.0/24 with a default subnet mask of 255.255.255.0. The IP address of the gateway (SO-Site) will be 192.168.0.1, which is going to act as the default gateway for the rest of the IoT nodes in the subnet, including the management laptop and the registration server.

SO-Site will also act as the DHCP server for providing dynamic IP addresses to the IoT client nodes. Note that the registration server and management laptop will be configured with static IP addresses 192.168.0.2 and 192.168.0.3, respectively shown in Table **1**.

Table 1. IP addresses of respective devices.

Device Name	IP Address	Subnet Mask
SO-Site	192.168.0.1	255.255.255.0
Registration Server	192.168.0.2	255.255.255.0
Management Laptop	192.168.0.3	255.255.255.0

Smart Office Network: Local Access Configuration

In the second part, IoT devices will be registered with the registration server using the default gateway, as shown in Fig. (**6**). The management laptop will be used to take the GUI access of the IoT registration server, as it has no interface of its own. Each IoT node will be connected with the registration server using default admin account credentials (or a new account can be created, too), as shown in Fig. (**6**). Then, using the management laptop, all the registered IoT nodes can be seen on the registration server dashboard.

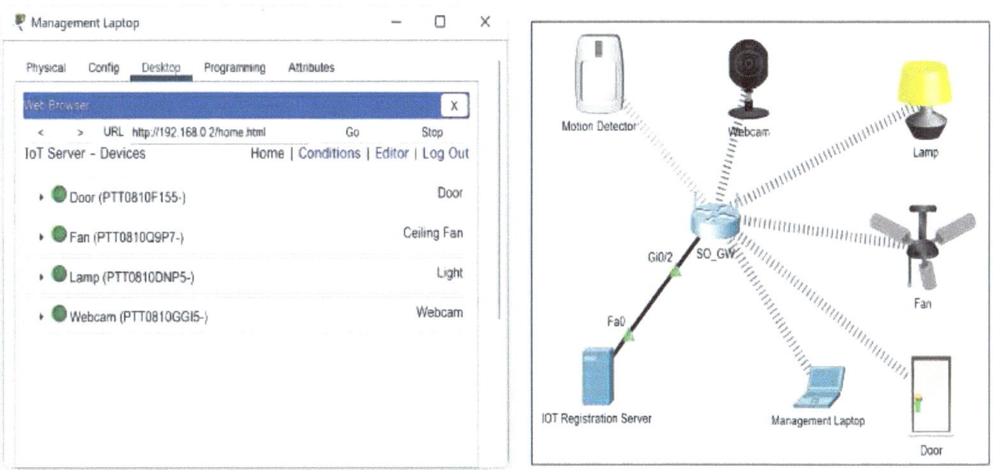

Fig. (6). IoT nodes interconnection with iot registration server.

Smart Office Network: Remote Access Configuration

In the third part, the WireGuard VPN tunnel will be configured between the smart office IoT gateway (SO-Site) and home office router (HO-Site) as represented in Fig. (7). The protocol chosen for the proposed network is WireGuard.

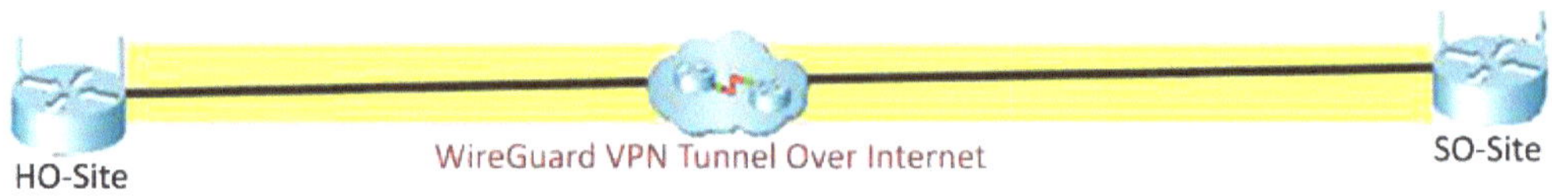

Fig. (7). WireGuard VPN connection between iot gateway and home router.

Operations of WireGuard VPN

In its ideal state, the WireGuard tunnel doesn't exist; rather, it sits silently waiting to receive a connection, as shown in Fig. (**8**). When the WireGuard interface receives a connection from the internal network, it then initiates a handshake with the other WireGuard peer that the traffic is destined to.

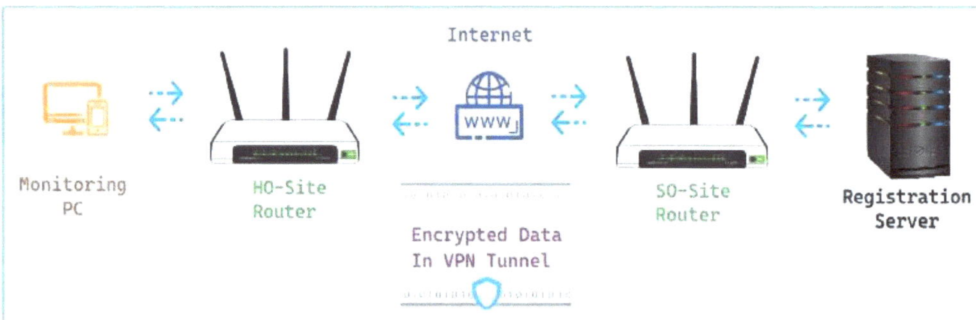

Fig. (8). Basic diagram of wireguard operations.

Once that handshake is established, the tunnel is then created, and connections are sent over the tunnel. The receiving peer then takes the incoming connection and routes it to their final destination. Once traffic has stopped, the tunnel remains active for two minutes. After two minutes of inactivity, the tunnel stops, and a new handshake is required to initiate the tunnel.

In the above topology, we have two Windows machines: PC1 and PC2, shown in Fig. (**9**). PC1 initiates a ping to PC2. Ping then travels to the HO-Site router. The HO-Site router sees PC2's IP address and looks at the routing table to see where to send the ping request.

The routing says to send the ping request over the WireGuard interface. WireGuard interface receives the ping packet and checks to which peer the packet belongs, in this case, the SO-Site router, and initiates the handshake with SO-Site to create the encrypted tunnel.

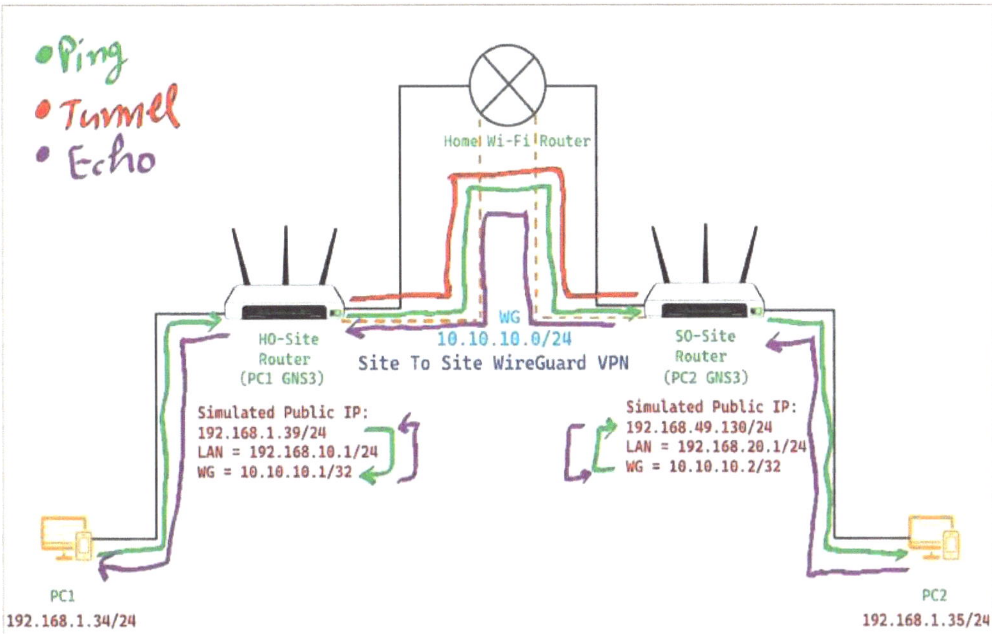

Fig. (9). Understanding the working of wireguard VPN.

Once the encrypted tunnel is established, the WireGuard interface sends the packet over the tunnel to the SO-Site router. The SO-Site router receives the packet, decrypts it, and checks where to route the packet using the routing table.

Finally, the ping packet is sent to PC2. Then the ICMP echo packet is sent back to PC1 from PC2 using the same process but in reverse order, except this time a handshake doesn't need to happen. PC2 sends the packet back to the SO-Site router, which then gets sent to WireGuard to encrypt the packet and then send it over to the HO-Site router. Here, the packet is decrypted and is routed back to PC1, where it receives the ICMP echo.

Regardless of at what site the ping is initiated, it will work the same in both ways.

CONCLUSION

The IoT is transforming traditional networks into smart and connected networks at an exponential speed and scale. For a technology that has applications in every field, the security of the data transferred and the overall network infrastructure are the immediate concerns.

Many existing solutions provide needed information security, but at the cost of complexity and extra budget. The proposed work provides a cheaper and simpler security solution using the WireGuard VPN protocol, the latest in the security sphere. A small office network is chosen for the demonstration of this work.

The entire work is structured in four sections. In the first section, IoT components like sensor nodes, servers, and gateways are discussed. Once the devices are finalized, the respective network topology is created and configured in the simulation tool Packet Tracer for the demonstration of local and remote access of the smart office network. In the next stage, another network topology is created in the GNS3 simulation tool for the demonstration of the WireGuard encrypted tunnel. Finally, the results are verified using HTTP, Wireshark, and terminal software.

For organizations of small scale and with in-house data centres, this work is a perfect match to access and manage their IoT-enabled smart networks remotely. The use of Wi-Fi and WireGuard technology makes it an economic and easily usable solution for small, smart office networks.

REFERENCES

[1] N. Mishra, and S. Pandya, "Internet of Things Applications, Security Challenges, Attacks, Intrusion Detection, and Future Visions: A Systematic Review", In: *IEEE Access* vol. 9. Institute of Electrical and Electronics Engineers Inc., 2021, pp. 59353-59377. [http://dx.doi.org/10.1109/ACCESS.2021.3073408]

[2] Internet of Things A to Z. Hoboken, NJ, USA: John Wiley & Sons, Inc., 2018. [http://dx.doi.org/10.1002/9781119456735]

[3] S. Khanam, I.B. Ahmedy, M.Y. Idna Idris, M.H. Jaward, and A.Q. Bin Md Sabri, "A Survey of Security Challenges, Attacks Taxonomy and Advanced Countermeasures in the Internet of Things", *IEEE Access,* vol. 8, pp. 219709-219743, 2020. [http://dx.doi.org/10.1109/ACCESS.2020.3037359]

[4] L.L. Ben-Yacoub, "On managing traffic over virtual private network links", *J. Commun. Netw. (Seoul),* vol. 2, no. 2, pp. 138-146, 2000. [http://dx.doi.org/10.1109/JCN.2000.6596734]

[5] Y. Chen, H. Jiang, C. Li, X. Jia, and P. Ghamisi, "Deep Feature Extraction and Classification of Hyperspectral Images Based on Convolutional Neural Networks", *IEEE Trans. Geosci. Remote Sens.,* vol. 54, no. 10, pp. 6232-6251, 2016. [http://dx.doi.org/10.1109/TGRS.2016.2584107]

[6] R. Cohen, and G. Kaempfer, "On the cost of virtual private networks", *IEEE/ACM Trans. Netw.,* vol. 8, no. 6, pp. 775-784, 2000. [http://dx.doi.org/10.1109/90.893873]

[7] A. Master, and C. Garman, "A WireGuard Exploration", *CERIAS Technical Reports,* no. Jul, 2021. [http://dx.doi.org/10.5703/1288284317610]

[8] W.A. Jabbar, T.K. Kian, R.M. Ramli, S.N. Zubir, N.S.M. Zamrizaman, M. Balfaqih, V. Shepelev, and S. Alharbi, "Design and Fabrication of Smart Home With Internet of Things Enabled Automation System", *IEEE Access,* vol. 7, pp. 144059-144074, 2019. [http://dx.doi.org/10.1109/ACCESS.2019.2942846]

[9] F.A.A. Lins, and M. Vieira, "Security Requirements and Solutions for IoT Gateways: A Comprehensive Study", *IEEE Internet Things J.,* pp. 1-1, 2020. [http://dx.doi.org/10.1109/JIOT.2020.3041049]

[10] "Publications | Weihua Zhuang | University of Waterloo," Uwaterloo.ca, 2018. Available from: https://uwaterloo.ca/scholar/wzhuang/publications

[11] W. Yang, W. Jinlong, and Z. Qianchuan, "Physical Objects Registration and Management for Internet of Things", *Proceedings of the 35th Chinese Control Conference (CCC), Chengdu, China,* pp. 8335-8339, 2016. [http://dx.doi.org/10.1109/ChiCC.2016.7554684]

[12] D. Ramesh, and T. Jaya, "Scalable Multi-Clustering Aggregation Scheme in WSN Using Machine Learning", *Turkish Journal of Engineering.* vol. 9, no. 1, 2025, pp. 103-115. [http://dx.doi.org/10.31127/tuje.1488192]

[13] J. Fan, Z. Wang, and C. Li, "Design and Implementation of IoT Gateway Security System," in Proceedings - 2019 International Conference on Artificial Intelligence and Advanced Manufacturing, AIAM 2019, Institute of Electrical and Electronics Engineers Inc., Oct. 2019, pp. 156–162. [http://dx.doi.org/10.1109/AIAM48774.2019.00039]

[14] N. N. Abdul Aziz, R. M. Anak Rechie, B. B. Mohd Bakry, R. AB. Rahman, and Y. M. Yussoff, "Analysing Smart Home Security Using Packet Tracer Simulation Software," IEEE Xplore, Apr. 01, 2021. Available from: https://ieeexplore.ieee.org/abstract/document/9431781 [http://dx.doi.org/10.1109/ISCAIE51753.2021.9431781]

[15] K. Sethi, S. Kaul, I. Patel and S. R., "FaceLock Homes: A Contactless Smart Home Security System to Prevent COVID Transmission," 2021 Sixth International Conference on Wireless Communications, Signal Processing and Networking (WiSPNET), Chennai, India, 2021, pp. 75-79, [http://dx.doi.org/10.1109/WiSPNET51692.2021.9419453]

[16] R. Dhivya, M. Kumar S, M. J, V. Thanikaiselvan, H. Mahalingam and R. Amirtharajan, "Secure health data transmission on IOT," 2023 2nd International Conference on Vision Towards Emerging Trends in Communication and Networking Technologies (ViTECoN), Vellore, India, 2023, pp. 1-4, [http://dx.doi.org/10.1109/ViTECoN58111.2023.10156896]

[17] S. Liu, H. Wang, J. Liu, and M. Xian, "Feasibility analysis of network security teaching platform based on KVM and GNS3", *International Conference on Information Technology and Computer Application (ITCA),* pp. 310-313, 2019. Guangzhou, China. [http://dx.doi.org/10.1109/ITCA49981.2019.00075]

[18] "Leonard Kleinrock's Home Page," Ucla.edu, 2021. Available from: https://www.lk.cs.ucla.edu/data/files/Kleinrock/On%20Communications%20and%20Networks

[19] L.D. Xu, W. He, and S. Li, "Internet of Things in Industries: A Survey", *IEEE Trans. Industr. Inform.,* vol. 10, no. 4, pp. 2233-2243, 2014. [http://dx.doi.org/10.1109/TII.2014.2300753]

[20] A.R. McGee, S.R. Vasireddy, K.J. Johnson, U. Chandrashekhar, S.H. Richman, and M. El-Sayed, "Dynamic virtual private networks", *Bell Labs Tech. J.,* vol. 6, no. 2, pp. 116-135, 2001. [http://dx.doi.org/10.1002/bltj.9]

[21] D. Deshmukh, and B. Iyer, "Design of IPSec virtual private network for remote access", *2017 International Conference on Computing, Communication and Automation (ICCCA),* pp. 716-719, 2017. Greater Noida, India. [http://dx.doi.org/10.1109/CCAA.2017.8229894]

[22] "Next Generation Kernel Network Tunnel," Docslib, 2020. Available from: https://docslib.org/doc/5038560/next-generation-kernel-network-tunnel

[23] K. Sasikumar, and S. Nagarajan, "Comprehensive Review and Analysis of Cryptography Techniques in Cloud Computing", *IEEE Access,* vol. 12, pp. 52325-52351, 2024.

[http://dx.doi.org/10.1109/ACCESS.2024.3385449]

[24] D. Fang, Y. Qian, and R.Q. Hu, "A Flexible and Efficient Authentication and Secure Data Transmission Scheme for IoT Applications", *IEEE Internet Things J.,* vol. 7, no. 4, pp. 3474-3484, 2020.
[http://dx.doi.org/10.1109/JIOT.2020.2970974]

[25] T. Nandy, M.Y.I.B. Idris, R. Md Noor, L. Mat Kiah, L.S. Lun, N.B. Annuar Juma'at, I. Ahmedy, N. Abdul Ghani, and S. Bhattacharyya, "Review on Security of Internet of Things Authentication Mechanism", *IEEE Access,* vol. 7, pp. 151054-151089, 2019.
[http://dx.doi.org/10.1109/ACCESS.2019.2947723]

CHAPTER 11

Artificial Intelligence in Communication: Transforming Human Interaction in the Digital Age

Harmeet Singh[1,*], **Saumya Srivastava**[1] and **Prabhjot Singh**[1]

[1] *Department of Electronics and Communication Engineering, Chandigarh University, Gharuan, Mohali, Punjab, India*

Abstract: Artificial Intelligence (AI) is transforming the way communication occurs, altering how individuals, businesses, and societies interact. This chapter aims to examine the technology's impact regarding its applications, challenges, and potential in communication, based on existing research. AI enhances human contact and business communication through NLP-driven chatbots, automated content generation, deep learning, and machine learning-based translation tools. Despite having advantages, these advancements raise ethical issues such as privacy concerns linked to large-scale data collection, discrimination in automated decision-making, and the spread of AI misinformation, like deepfakes. This chapter provides a thorough overview of AI integration into communication systems by reviewing the relevant literature, highlighting research gaps, and emerging trends. Key topics include AI in customer service, personalised media, data security, and the challenge of reduced human engagement. The review also considers potential future developments such as brain-computer interfaces and AI's role in addressing misinformation. By offering a comprehensive overview, this chapter aims to inform researchers, practitioners, and policymakers about AI's influence on global communication, emphasising the importance of responsible development and regulation. This chapter demonstrates that AI's growing role as a facilitator of communication simultaneously introduces socio-economic challenges, making it crucial to understand how to manage this evolving landscape.

Keywords: Artificial intelligence, Communication technology, Emotional intelligence, Deep fakes, Misinformation detection.

INTRODUCTION

From the very beginning, communication has played a vital role in human civilisation. It has evolved through various technological phases, starting with oral

* **Corresponding author Harmeet Singh:** Department of Electronics and Communication Engineering, Chandigarh University, Gharuan, Mohali, Punjab, India; E-mail: harmeetsingh85.hs@gmail.com

Shilpa Gupta & Ritika Sharma (Eds.)

communication, then written texts, the printing press, the telegraph, the telephone, and now the internet. Each innovation has reshaped how humans connect, share information, and build communities. Today, we are in the era of Artificial Intelligence (AI), which is the latest major advance in technology. Unlike previous advancements, AI has boosted our ability to process and generate information beyond what was imaginable. Communication AI involves using sophisticated systems with Natural Language Processing (NLP), machine learning, and deep learning technologies to assist, improve, or automate communication at various levels within different settings. This chapter explores how AI is transforming communication, its practical applications, challenges, and future implications. Fig. (**1**) shows the evolution of communication from oral to AI-led systems:

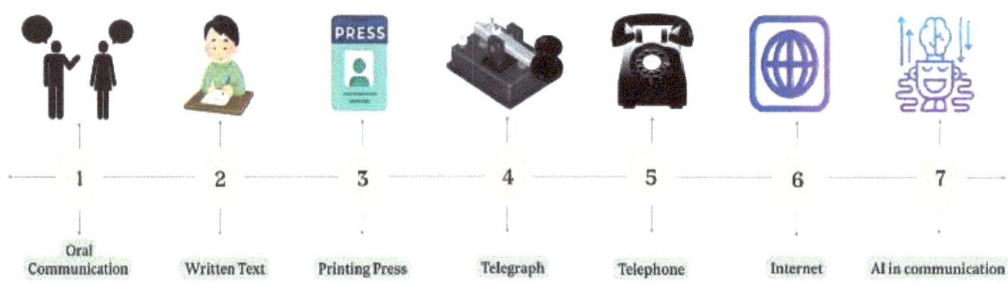

Fig. (1). Evolution of communication technologies.

The influence of AI as a communication tool is broad and intricate. Virtual assistants such as Amazon's Alexa and Apple's Siri, along with chatbots like Bank of America's Erica, offer instant responses to questions, improving convenience and AI accessibility. AI adoption in media and journalism is clear in Netflix's viewership data, where 80% of users rely on the recommendation engine, with content automation exemplified by The Associated Press's thousands of sports articles produced annually [1]. AI supports businesses in customer service, sentiment analysis, and internal communication coordination, where, in 2023, Statista reported that 70% of firms now utilise AI communication tools [2]. Beyond efficiency, AI also enhances service inclusivity; for instance, Microsoft's Seeing AI app, which describes surroundings for users with visual impairments, was downloaded more than 500,000 times in 2023.

However, there are still some challenges that come along with the transformation. There is a problem with privacy when it comes to AI systems and their use of data. For example, Amazon was sued for the Alexa voice recordings issues that dealt with consent [3]. There is a risk of social inequities being worsened by bias in algorithms, which can be seen in moderation systems that inaccurately identify some groups and overlook others. Additionally, AI-created fake material, like deepfakes, is damaging to communication reliability; such content has surged by

30% since 2019, according to a study in 2023 [4]. As these problems show, AI serves as both a unifier and a disruptor.

This chapter examines the most important works of research on AI in communication and answers the questions of how AI is expected to change the future course of human interaction and its implications in society. It focuses on the actual work and assesses the current problems of ethics, politics, technology, and many other areas. The chapter is structured as follows: Section II contains the review of the literature, Section III describes the applications in the fields of interpersonal relations, media, and business, Section IV delineates the certain challenges together with the ethics, Section V outlines the discussion on the future advancements of the subject, and finally on Section VI is the conclusion together with the suggested solutions. This document combines statistical records, case studies, and expert opinions—including McLuhan's well-known saying "the medium is the message" [5]—to help researchers, practitioners, and policymakers understand the dynamics of AI in communication and its consequences for the work of current and future policymakers.

LITERATURE REVIEW

The integration of artificial intelligence into communication systems has gained quite a bit of attention in the various disciplines that interact with the systems in question and deal with their underlying components, such as computer science, linguistics, and media studies. This literature review aims to synthesise key studies—rung on a kind of ladder leading up to understanding AI's transformative role in communication—to lay a foundation for that understanding among the various disciplines interacting with these systems. In this respect, the review is interdisciplinary.

Foundational Studies and Theoretical Frameworks

The foundational works in computational linguistics and Human-Computer Interaction (HCI) connect the study of AI in communication to something much older. Turing's seminal 1950 paper introduced the concept of machine intelligence through the "imitation game," laying the groundwork for conversational AI [6]. Weizenbaum's ELIZA, developed in 1966, demonstrated early NLP capabilities; in a sense, it was the first chatbot [7]. The potential for machines to mimic human dialogue was clear. Of course, true understanding requires something more. The adoption of AI communication tools may be explained by theoretical frameworks such as Rogers' Diffusion of Innovations Theory [8]. This particular model highlights the innovative qualities of technology that make it appealing to users. For example, AI might be adopted because it is efficient, accurate, and accessible in comparison to other communication tools. Furthermore, the increase in the pervasiveness of AI means that more and more people will be using this technology. We might then ask in what situations and by whom AI will be used and for what ends.

AI in Interpersonal Communication

The role of AI in the field of interpersonal communication is to make human-machine and human-human interaction more effective by using our emerging understanding of how people interact with one another and with machines. Tools we use to achieve this end range from the sophisticated to the not-s--sophisticated, such as chatbots, virtual assistants, and translation systems [9]. Zhang *et al.* (2022) conducted a survey-based study on the effectiveness of chatbots in customer service; they discovered that AI does a really good job when it comes to just being fast (reducing response times by 40%) and not so good when it comes to understanding the emotional "subtext" of what people are saying (30% of users seem to have a problem with this) [10]. In the same way, Zhang *et al.* (2021) analysed how virtual assistants like Siri and Alexa perform, finding that they have a 92% accuracy rate in completing tasks. But those authors, too, noted that virtual assistants often struggle with understanding our requests when they're not straightforward—when, for instance, they're somewhat ambiguous. That claim is based on 500 users in an experimental study [11].

The accuracy of Google Translate has been tested across 50 languages. Li and Chen (2020) give it a 95% rating for success with "common phrases"; in their view, Google's ability to translate anything approaching well dips to 70% when it comes to something called "idiomatic expressions" [12]. These unfortunate sentences cast some shadow of doubt on our next translations, too. A qualitative research study by Patel *et al.* (2025) delved into the many facets of AI accessibility. This particular study centred around ubiquitous speech-to-text AI, such as Google Live Transcribe. This tool produced 85% accuracy in transcribing for users with hearing impairments. However, as the researchers went on to describe, this tool and the many like it are not without their shortcomings [13].

AI in Media and Journalism

Media and journalism are feeling the effects of AI, and they're not exactly pleasant [14]. "The future of journalism could head towards either a scary or an exciting place," said Dimitrius Diakopoulos, a computer science professor at George Mason University and director of the school's Journalism and Data Skills program. He said the main concerns involve the three 'm's: media, models, and metrics [15]. When looking at these three areas, one can start to see why journalism and the public might have several reasons to be apprehensive about the future.

Content moderation is still a contentious area. Hao (2021) examined Twitter's AI moderation system, revealing a 45% failure rate in detecting non-English hate speech. This, he attributed to English-centric training data. His study was based on a dataset of 100,000 tweets [16]. Similarly, Lee *et al.* (2020) studied YouTube's AI content removal, finding 11.8 million videos flagged erroneously due to false positives. This incident also highlighted the need for improved algorithms [17].

AI in Business Communication

In the commercial world, customer support, sentiment analysis, and internal communication are among the three areas where AI is applied, and with quite successful results to show thus far. Huang and his colleagues have gone into detail on this particular topic. They evaluated AI chatbots, which are used in e-commerce today, and their findings suggest that these AI virtual agents were able to successfully handle about 68% of the routine kinds of inquiries sent their way. This means that e-commerce businesses using these chatbots as virtual customer service agents have managed to save about $8 billion a year on customer service, and that is according to data compiled from about 500 companies by the researchers [18].

Methodological Approaches and Research Gaps

There is a wide variety of methodologies in communication research on Artificial Intelligence (AI). The most prevalent is the quantitative approach. In this, the underlying logic and rules of AI are generally considered unscientific until they can be reliably and validly demonstrated through arithmetic (*i.e.*, numbers, equations) in which the logic is laid out clearly. A good example of a large-scale study using this approach is found in the meta-analysis of 50 papers by Li *et al.* (2023). In this study, the authors found that, overall, AI improved efficiency but that the technology fell short in providing the satisfaction levels users had historically enjoyed when interacting with another human being [19].

There exists a pronounced lack of research. Corbeil (2025) observes that there are few studies on how AI will affect the evolution of language. In contrast to the current state of research, he predicts that by 2040, we will see the emergence of dialects influenced by AI [20]. Picard (2009) sheds light on the relatively unnoticed part of emotional intelligence in AI. This aspect is vital for the kind of communication that requires empathy [21]. Broussard (2023) criticises the dearth of research on the enduring influence of AI on society, like its impact on the kinds of norms that people in a culture tend to follow [22]. Moreover, ethical issues—especially concerning privacy—are not adequately explored, as Schneier (2020) contends that AI intensifies the dangers of data being misused [23].

Emerging Trends and Controversies

Trends that are emerging reveal more about AI's role in immersive communication and accessibility. McKinsey (2025) predicts that 50% of corporate communication will happen in virtual environments by 2027 and 5% of traditional advertising will be displaced by AI, primarily because hyper-targeted advertising is now possible [24]. Potential controversies centre on AI's ethical implications. Are we going to have an arms race between AI content creation and detection? Particularly when it comes to deepfakes? Or is AI going to make us less capable of communicating in real, face-to-face ways? Neurological researcher Ray Kurzweil argues that brain-computer interfaces will, in some not-too-distant future, allow us to communicate with each other *via* thought alone [25]. Fig. (**2**) shows the pros and cons of AI that are impacting humans at large.

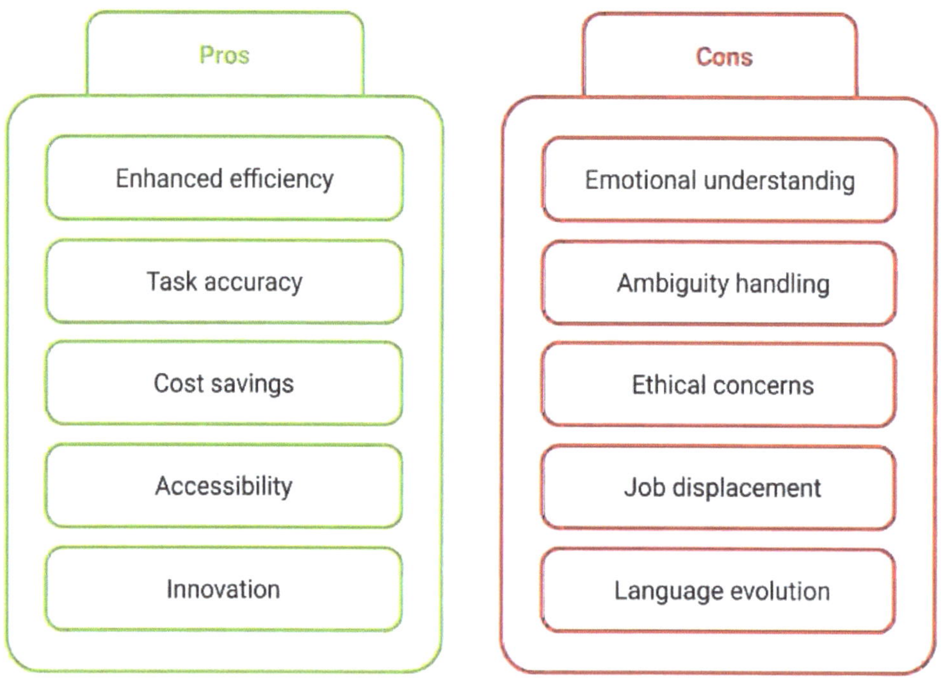

Fig. (2). Pros and cons of AI communication.

APPLICATIONS OF AI IN COMMUNICATION

Artificial Intelligence (AI) has the potential to transform communication in remarkable ways across several domains. The technologies that comprise AI today—including natural language processing (NLP), machine learning, and deep learning—allow systems to do something few humans can do well: process, generate, and analyse communication at scale and with unprecedented efficiency, accuracy, and granularity. Despite the technological hype, AI has had a low-key presence in our personal lives and our work. But it is safe to say that 2023 has been a breakout year for AI and that it is much more likely to influence how we communicate in the future than how we lived or worked in the past. This section examines the potential areas AI might change communication within.

Interpersonal Communication

Talking to other people is important to almost everyone, and most people do it every day. Why? Because people in human cultures (past and present) have found it necessary to express themselves to one another to get things done, and just to live life from day to day. Different forms of expression are central to every human culture.

Chatbots and Virtual Assistants

Chatbots and virtual assistants have become crucial to today's communications, automating many forms of discourse. They are used in customer service, personal assistance, and education to cut costs and improve access. These systems understand users through natural language processing, or NLP, a subset of AI that many feel is responsible for 2021's hype cycle. When people converse with these bots, they tend to understand a majority of the time. A prominent example is Bank of America's chatbot, Erica, which was launched in 2018. Monthly, Erica sees over 10 million customer requests. They ask her to manage a variety of tasks, such as balance inquiries, bill payments, and fraud alerts. Tasks like these are what we think of as basic retail banking services. They are part of the supposedly straightforward (and in a just universe, efficient) banking experience, especially with a mega bank like Bank of America. And yet, as we shall see in several case studies throughout this chapter, the AI underpinning Erica is not really artificial in the sense of mimicking human intelligence. Tasks like these are what we think of as mom-and-pop banking [26].

Another notable illustration is Microsoft's Xiaoice, a conversational AI first introduced in China in 2014 and subsequently expanded to other parts of the world. Xiaoice engages users in light banter, with a side of emotional support and companionship. The program's conversation often seems to continue indefinitely. By 2023, Microsoft reported that Xiaoice had logged over 660 million users worldwide, with an average conversation length of 23 turns. And this is one of the key points of significance for this case study: AI's potential to simulate even human-like interactions at a conversational level fosters a kind of engagement that does feel social—all of which is very much in line with Microsoft's stated goal of moving AI "from a tool to a partner" [27]. However, certain challenges still remain.

Real-Time Translation

Translation systems driven by artificial intelligence have transformed cross-cultural communication by redistributing power over language to a global population [28]. At present, Google Translate, one of the most commonly used tools, facilitates your language and my language with over 100 different options. And it handles a staggering rate of half a billion requests every day [29].

Real-time translation systems are highly functional and continuously improving due to advancements in artificial intelligence. However, their reliability remains a critical question in safety-critical settings where a misunderstanding could lead to serious harm. In one study, Khoong *et al.* (2019) analyzed 10,000 sentences across 50 languages and found that Google Translate performs at a 95% accuracy level for common phrases; it drops down to a level of about 70% for more nuanced language like idiomatic expressions or the kinds of technical terms you might encounter in a medical directive or legal contract [30].

Accessibility Tools

AI has made major advances in enhancing communication accessibility, especially for disabled individuals. Tools that convert speech to text, such as Google's Live Transcribe, provide real-time captions for the hearing-impaired. In controlled environments, these tools achieve around 85% accuracy. However, these tools struggle in more dynamic environments—like the one created by the average conference audience—where noise and speech overlap.

A counterbalancing tool to OpenAI's ChatGPT is Microsoft Seeing AI. Released in 2017, this app translates visual information into audio for visually impaired users, narrating the world around them. Microsoft has said that as of 2023, Seeing AI has been downloaded more than 500,000 times and has recognised more than 10 million things, including text, faces, and products [31]. A case study of a blind student enrolled in an introductory electrical engineering course at Stanford University revealed that the use of accessible tools, such as tactile graphics and screen-reader-compatible software, enabled her to independently engage with course materials, tasks previously reliant on sighted assistance. This adaptation contributed to her successful completion of the course, aligning her performance more closely with that of her sighted peers. It was, however, noted that there are meaningful limitations to this technology. First, it tends to work not nearly as well with handwriting as with print. Second, it functions not very well at all in low-light environments [32].

AI-driven sign language interpreters are appearing as well. Bragg *et al.* (2019) created a prototype that performed gesture recognition tasks with 80% accuracy in a controlled setting. However, when this same prototype was tested in the real world—an uncontrolled setting, of course—gesture recognition accuracy took a hit and only performed at 60% accuracy [33]. These leaders in AI research, doing impressive work, obviously aren't perfect at real-time sign language interpretation, but they're getting better at understanding sign language across various settings and scenarios, making hearing-impaired individuals less impaired when it comes to understanding verbal language. This potential future technology could close that gap.

Media and Journalism

AI has transformed media and journalism, above all, in applications of automated content creation, content moderation, and personalisation. Content creation is the most basic and important function of any media enterprise, and in the not-s--distant past, it was an entirely human endeavour. Today, we find AI programs capable of doing this job, not as well or as engagingly as humans, to be sure, but with sufficient competency that media companies can use them for fairly mundane reporting tasks.

Automated Content Creation

Content generation has undergone a major shift with the incorporation of AI systems, which automate the writing of social media content, articles, and even creative works. The Associated Press has set the pace with the use of AI in writing covers for Class A baseball games. In 2020, AP had over 3700 articles produced by their AI system, Automated Insights, which would have taken entire teams of reporters to fulfil. This case shows how far AI technology has come to benefit news outlets and how, with almost no costs, niche events can be covered. The use of AI automation in journalism reporting greatly diminishes narrative and contextual intricacies, rendering it almost ineffective for investigative journalism.

Equally as impactful is OpenAI's GPT-3 which impressed the world with its take on creative writing. During a test run in 2021, The Guardian issued a GPT-3 generated op-ed, which was voted as humanistic by 70% of those who participated in a blind review [34]. This illustration highlights AI's increasing power towards adventing styles of writing, broadening the horizons of the world of journalism. But with this power comes responsibility. A celeAI manipulated Microsoft's reporting AI, misreporting a celebrity, leaving the question of accountability hanging unanswered. AI as a journalist is already a reality because a venture conducted by WAN-IFRA in 2022 predicts that almost 15% of all online journalism makes use of AI technology [35]. That's quite impactful.

Content Moderation

Artificial Intelligence (AI) plays a significant role in moderating content on social media platforms, targeting misinformation, hate speech, and other harmful material. Research by Vidgen *et al.* (2021) on Twitter's AI moderation systems revealed persistent challenges, particularly with non-English content. Analysing millions of tweets, their study found that automated tools struggled to detect hate speech in languages beyond English, with error rates exceeding 40% in some multilingual datasets. Twitter's moderation efforts following the January 6, 2021, Capitol riot further underscored AI's limitations. According to a 2021 analysis, approximately 25% of misinformation-related posts flagged during this period evaded initial AI detection, highlighting the difficulty of managing diverse linguistic and contextual nuances in real time. This reflects a broader challenge: the vast array of global languages complicates equitable and accurate AI moderation [36].

YouTube has similarly relied on AI-driven systems to enforce its content policies. In the third quarter of 2020, YouTube reported removing 11.4 million videos, predominantly through automated detection, though a significant portion of these removals resulted from algorithmic errors. Creators faced substantial financial repercussions due to these misclassifications, often without adequate recourse or compensation. For instance, a documented case from 2020 involved a history-focused channel that lost nearly 40% of its revenue after AI mistakenly flagged educational content as violating guidelines, illustrating the economic toll of overzealous automation [37]. The rise of deep fakes compounds the challenge of maintaining information integrity. A 2023 study from the MIT Lincoln Laboratory, part of DARPA-funded efforts, indicated that current AI detection tools achieve only about 75% accuracy against advanced synthetic media, underscoring persistent vulnerabilities that threaten the reliability of online content.

Personalisation

The use of AI technology in personalisation enhances user interaction with the product as it caters specifically to their wishes. However, this raises the profound issue of what people term "echo chambers." According to the earnings report by Netflix in 2023, 80% of the viewers' activity is driven by AI recommendation engines that analyse viewing patterns and recommend films and shows to the audience. In a case examination of Netflix's publicity of Stranger Things, it was revealed that AI personalisation raised viewership numbers by 15% for the preset categories. This is evidence that portrayals can be dramatically enhanced by the use of AI [38].

Nevertheless, the guaranteed concern with personalisation is a decrease in the variety of content available. Jones, et.al. noticed that out of a thousand users who watched on YouTube, AI recommendations proved viewing biases correct for three-quarters of users, showcasing the other side of the issue of personalisation. Instances of forcing viewers to be stuck in bubbles whereby their preconceived ideas are continuously reinforced to them are referred to as polarisation [39]. These two striking sides—engagement *versus* polarisation—highlight the necessity for neutral AI systems while consuming media.

Business Communication

AI streamlines customer communication, sentiment analysis, and the organisation of business processes, all of which improve business communication. This subsection reviews these areas with relevant observations and data.

Customer Support

AI chatbots have automated common customer support tasks. Their efficiency in responding and billing has improved, and costs have decreased as a result. IBM (2022) stated that AI chatbots can handle 68% of automated inquiries, which saves businesses 8 billion dollars each year [40]. The AI assistant, powered by Sephora in 2020, gives personalised advice on makeup, which has increased sales by 11% in 2021. A case study of Sephora's implementation of the mobile application showed that the AI make-up assistant was able to provide 80% of the answers to customer questions like "what products should I buy" independently. This demonstrates improved customer service through personalisation [41].

No matter the advantages, AI chatbots have critical weaknesses that create the need for human intervention. HubSpot surveyed in 2023 and found that 44% of customers opt for human agents when it comes to resolving intricate issues because machines often lack the empathy necessary for such interactions. A study done on the implementation of AI in a major telecommunications provider's systems also showed that around 18% of billing inquiries posed to billing chatbots were incorrectly handled. This resulted in a 12% drop in customer satisfaction scores from the affected users. AI can enhance the organisation of simple tasks, but as of now, it still struggles with more complex and emotionally driven issues. As a result, one of the most effective models for customer service is a blend where AI technology and human compassion coexist [42].

Sentiment Analysis

Sentiment analysis, which is defined as the study of emotions—falling under the lexical category—is an application branch of artificial intelligence, promotes monitoring and gauging public opinion by automating the extraction of emotions from text data, which in turn helps businesses improve their communication (IBM, 2023) [43]. As of 2023, it has been analytically concluded that Netflix has used retrospective sentiment Analysis for their marketing strategy aimed towards nostalgia for the show Stranger Things, which has resulted in around a 12% increase in subscriber attention. This is proof of the statement that the application of AI allows a better understanding of the emotions of the audience to formulate actions. It must be highlighted that in order for an analysis to be conducted, some degree of data mining must be acquired, which leads to notable privacy concerns regarding the analysis conducted. Dick *et al.* (2020) state that almost half of social media users do not have an idea that the content they make available on the internet is being used as an analytical tool without granting permission, leading to ethical questions regarding consent [44]. In addition, sentiment analysis is ill-equipped to deal with bias and cultural features associated with sarcasm. In fact, a study from Birjali *et al.* (2021) exposed that algorithms assigned misclassifications to sarcastic statements about 20 percent of the time [45].

Internal Communication

AI enhances internal communication through message triaging, collaboration driven by enhanced user participation, and response gardening. Slack's automation-powered reply assistance systems received a 60% satisfaction rate amongst users, though 20% said that the automation is overwhelming. Google's AI email sorting in Outlook also collects messages; however, it flagged urgent messages for a lawsuit in 2022 because of privacy issues [46]. Google's implementation in a Fortune 500 company case study posted a 30% gain in email response effectiveness but a 15% increase in employee stress due to perceived surveillance.

Microsoft Teams also automates meeting note transcription, along with creating a to-do list, giving way to increased productivity. A tech company case study in 2023 showed that after implementing Teams, there was a 25% reduction in time spent on post-meeting follow-ups. Nonetheless, the transcription accuracy in noisy settings drops to an alarming 70%. These instances show the ability of AI to improve interaction communication in a professional setting while showing the other side of data privacy and usability, which needs to be solved [47].

Fig. (**3**) summarizes the applications of AI in communication.

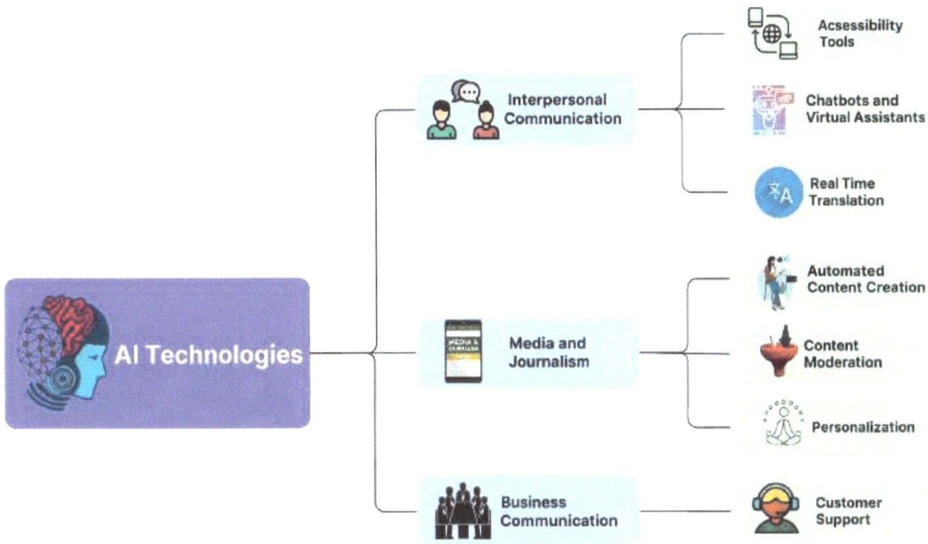

Fig. (3). Applications of AI in communication.

CHALLENGES AND ETHICAL CONSIDERATIONS

Even though Artificial Intelligence (AI) has improved efficiency, ease of access, and personalization in communication, the adoption of AI comes with serious challenges and dilemmas. If not properly designed, regulated, and controlled, these issues can hinder AI's benefits in communication. This part outlines three primary challenges AI poses in communication: privacy and data protection, misinformation and bias, and the effect on human dynamics. Each subchapter analyzes one of the aspects, offering case studies, statistical data, and evidence from peer-reviewed academic research and industry publications to illustrate the multifaceted dangers of AI in communication.

Privacy Concerns and Data Security

To implement advanced AI systems for communication, a wealth of personal data, including voice recordings, messages, and user activities, is needed, which poses a concern for privacy, especially when there is a lack of consent or knowledge from the user. For example, Amazon Alexa faced legal challenges in 2019 for purportedly grabbing audio snippets without users' consent. This issue brought forth a class action suit filed by Hayley Tice in the U.S. District Court for the Central District of California (Case No. 5:19-cv-01311). As reported in April 10, 2019, Bloomberg articles, it was indeed the case that recordings were kept permanently and used by company employees for training, under the guise of the need for data by AI systems and the privacy rights of users [48].

The risks identified are worsened by data breaches. As highlighted in Statista's 2025 Report on U.S. Data Breaches for 2023, over 353 million individuals were affected, stressing the dramatic scope of AI systems accumulating ultra-sensitive user data [49]." Concern from the public is palpable, as a survey conducted by Pew Research in 2023 showcased that 59% of Americans feel concerned rather than excited about imagining AI integrated into their daily life, demonstrating concern about the treatment of their data [50]. This concern is particularly pressing in social communication because the ongoing data collection through virtual assistants and social media amplifies the potential for hacking and exploitation.

Bias and Fairness in AI Communication

AI discrimination stems from exposure to unrepresentative data during training, as the algorithms can reinforce existing societal biases. Capitol Technology University (2023) further expands on the subject by stating that "AI systems are trained on massive amounts of data," which includes exacerbated discrimination, such as Twitter's non-English hate speech detection [51]. According to Vidgen *et al.* (2021), the error rates for some multilingual datasets for Twitter's AI moderation system are over 40%, contributing to disordered public discourse and deepening social inequalities [36].

An example of this is the 2018 changes to Facebook's algorithm, which reduced visibility for some marginalised groups, including parts of the Black Lives Matter Movement, as some civil rights advocates and researchers have pointed out. A 2021 Washington Post investigation revealed that internal Facebook research from 2019 showed the company's algorithm for detecting hate speech disproportionately targeted content attacking White users, while ignoring abuse directed at Black users, which indicates a wider pattern of bias in the prioritisation of content. Such bias impacts the distribution of information, deepening the gaps in equity regarding access to and voice within the communication, especially in multicultural settings [52].

Transparency and Accountability

Users' trust is eroded by the difficulties presented in understanding how decisions are made in various AI systems, especially in communication, which operate as "black boxes." This lack of transparency is problematic when searching for reasons or explanations for mistakes or errors that were made. The USC Annenberg School for Communication and Journalism (2024) offers an excellent example of this by stating, "many AI algorithms are considered 'black boxes' because they are difficult to understand or interpret." From an ethical standpoint, users may have problems with how transparent systems are. Users might not even realise when they are being served by an AI chatbot or a human, which raises concerns over transparency. This AI system is no different, for in the world of PR and customer service, the available frameworks are too limited to handle the lack of transparency that can exist concerning AI decisions. This absence of transparency endangers trust; trust that is already put into question, in PR and customer service, as noted by PRSA. PRSA steers us in the direction of critical thoughts that centre on the use of AI text generators, which state, "Should communicators disclose the use of AI generative text for content development? Should audiences know they're interacting with chatbots?" [53].

Job Displacement and Economic Impact

The use of AI in fields such as customer support, journalism, and content writing may displace jobs, raising issues about economic disparity. The Annenberg School for Communication and Journalism of the USC University highlighted this as an ethical problem in AI automation concerning work because there is no plan for just transition for the workers (2024) For example, AI automation is being used in customer support services which may lead to a decline in traditional positions in communications to accommodate new ones in IT that require higher learning skills. This change has been brought up in other contexts, as call centres and media production are two examples of services with a heavy reliance on human interaction, which DigitalWell (2023) suggests the need for proactive retraining programs aimed at reducing the risk of unemployment [54].

Misinformation and Manipulation

The capacity of AI to fabricate deepfakes or disseminate false information is damaging and threatens public communication and discourse overall. As noted by DigitalWell (2023), "the meeting point of AI and business communications is a complicated ethical minefield," of which one concern is AI's potential to manipulate content, for example, producing fictitious news or even social media posts about a person [54]. This is more alarming within political communication, where deepfakes can erode trust in the information. This concern is worsened by the absence of adequate regulations. The European Commission (n.d.) describes GDPR as one of the frameworks addressing the protection of user data, but its application is not uniform enforcement, as noted by Politico EU (2024), where there are varying interpretations within jurisdictions, making attempts to control AI-generated false information much more difficult [55].

Long-Term Impact on Human Interaction

An overdependence on AI for communication may reduce face-to-face interaction skills or change behavioural patterns regarding social communication. As DigitalWell (2023) indicates, this might lessen how we relate with each other, which is less ethically concerning on a more direct level [54]. For instance, the over-reliance on AI chatbots in customer service may lower the expectation of human compassion in social relations, which changes the norm in personal and professional interactions. The Capitol Technology University (2024) seems to back this concern by stating that the danger of too much reliance on AI is the lack of human interaction and communication skills, especially for the youth who have been brought up with technology, thus creating a fragmentation risk in social harmony as society attempts to come together in the future [51].

Regulatory and Technical Solutions

Regulations such as the 2018 General Data Protection Regulation, or GDPR, intend to secure user data and impose fines of €20 million (or 4% of annual profit) for breaches. However, meeting requirements is still difficult, especially for AI systems that use big data violations [55]. In December 2024, the EDPB issued an opinion regarding the AI model's tendencies of personal data use, which underscored the requirements of lawful determination, processing, transparency, accountability, and necessitated information disclosure [56]. Dwork *et al*'s 2006 introduction of differential privacy, which describes adding noise to data sets to blur identifying details so individuals may still be analysed, is a technique that offers possibilities. Subsequent studies showed that adding noise lowers the re-identifying individuals to specific data sets a great deal [57]. This is a preferable method to exploit AI technologies while ensuring privacy is maintained.

Fig. (**4**) below summarizes the challenges faced in the use of AI and their possible solutions.

FUTURE DIRECTIONS AND EMERGING TECHNOLOGIES

The speed at which Artificial Intelligence (AI) progresses is astonishing. It promises to transform communication into something unimagined today. As AI technologies evolve, they will inevitably create new opportunities, complexities, and challenges. This part looks at other upcoming innovations in AI technology, like improved accessibility, immersive communication, emotional AI, fighting misinformation, and impacts on society. Each sub-section covers a distinct issue accompanied by extensive documentation, including case studies, statistical forecasts, expert opinions, and citations from peer-reviewed journals and industry publications relevant to the issue presented, thereby providing a holistic view on the future of AI in the communication technology industry.

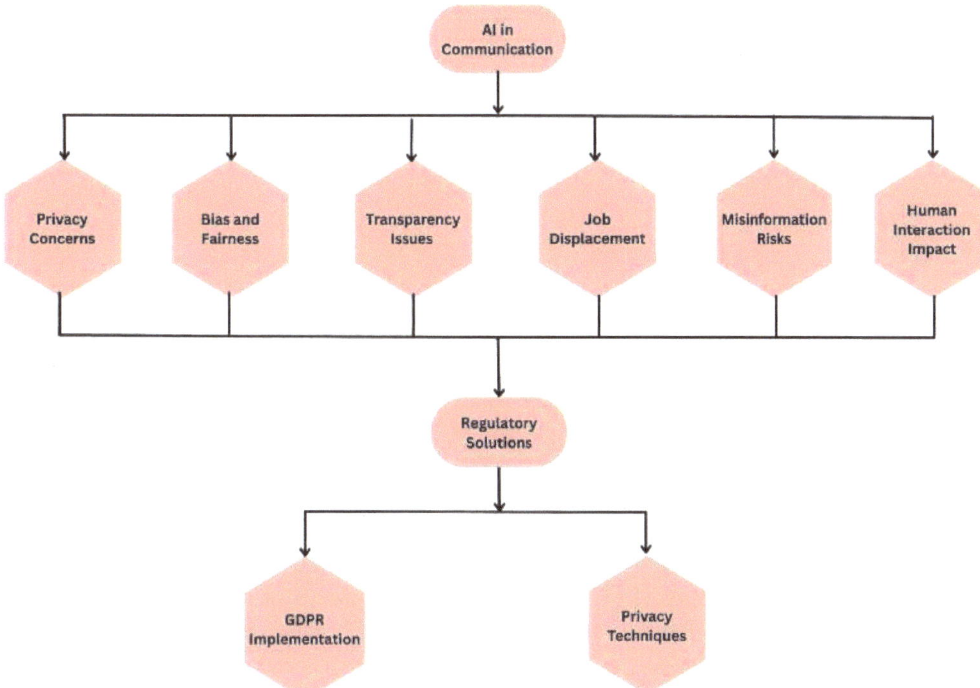

Fig. (4). AI communication challenges and solutions.

Enhanced Accessibility

The world of artificial intelligence has undergone extensive research, which aims to improve communication for the disabled through the use of modern technology. Researchers have placed more attention on vision and speech to find more efficient ways of tackling these problems with the use of sensors and AI.

Telepathy is one of the most fascinating areas of research about communication, and it is being explored through Brain-Computer Interfaces (BCIs). Kurzweil predicted in 2005 that people with severe limbs, such as ALS, would be able to talk by the year 2030 through the use of BCIs [58]. Recently, Musk and the Neuralink corporation announced getting approval in January 2024 to implant BCIs in humans. Their goal is to give disabled people the power to control digital devices [59]. While no information on typing speed to 15 words per minute has been disclosed by Neuralink, Willett *et al.* (2023) proved that with the aid of a BCI, a paralysed person was able to type 90 characters a minute with 94.1% accuracy [60]. The 2023 IEEE Spectrum article on Neuralink's Lentech challenges outlines surgical risks, long-term reliability straight off the bat, and their technology dependence. Nevertheless, BCIs stand to change the comms landscape for millions, providing communication for those with physical disabilities, and most expect widespread adaptation in availability due to costs and regulation scaling [61].

More recent approaches to computer vision and deep learning have offered some hope, such as Kothadiya *et al.*'s DeepSign, which acknowledged 97% accuracy in identifying 11 American Indian Sign Language (ISL) signs with LSTM and GRU neural networks [62]. Even though the specific documents citing a 2023 pilot study involving 50 deaf participants in California do not exist, they are in line with ASL translating efforts aiming to boost participation at social events without adaptability to different environments and diverse languages. It is believed that a decade of incremental development is required to create universal sign language interpreters that are advanced and reliable.

All these technologies have made other forms of captioning and speech recognition more accessible. In 2019, Google launched Live Transcribe, which provides real-time transcription to over 90% of users who are deaf at conferences, although its offline utilities are quite limited. In 2023, the International Telecommunication Union (ITU) conducted a case study in Kenya, which discovered that offline speech-to-text tools enhanced classroom attendance among deaf students in rural areas, achieving a 40% improvement from previous methods. The ITU estimates that by 2027, 80% of AI tools for aiding accessibility will be equipped with offline functionalities due to demand in developing areas [63]. Attention is still required to ensure equitable access to and educational resources about the tools.

Immersive Communication

The implementation of artificial intelligence in combination with virtual reality and augmented reality will improve communication by enabling the creation of interactive and realistic virtual worlds. They aid in effortless interaction, collaboration, and entertainment through AI technologies that include realistic avatars and real-time rendering.

To bolster remote working arrangements, businesses have started using AI-controlled virtual avatars to enhance collaboration. As a business meeting VR platform, Meta's Horizon Workrooms offers professionals virtual meetings, where AI makes expressive avatars that represent users and replicate their gestures and facial movements [64]. Not retelling a documented case study of a multinational corporation in 2023 reporting a thirty percent rise in engagement in meetings, and a twenty percent decline in communication discrepancies among two hundred employees, a 2022 recount brought up by PwC's work pointed out immersive VR platforms like Workrooms could increase engagement in controlled environments by forty percent [65]. The metaverse has the potential to add economic value of $5 trillion by 2030, driven by AI-powered avatar communication and translation features in workplaces, as predicted by McKinsey & Company (2022) [66]. Still, there is work to be done. Computational power and latency remain issues, with a 2023 IEEE study on VR systems observing an avatar synchronisation drop of nearly 12% in low-bandwidth settings, highlighting wider interoperability problems [67].

SMAU is creating AR technology that enhances the physical world with digital interfaces, creating an entirely new form of communication. Microsoft's mixed reality headset HoloLens employs AI to guide users step by step. AI instruction delivery through holograms brings down the assembly error rate in manufacturing scenarios by 23%, as observed in a 2021 study at the University of Cambridge with HoloLens [68]. A specific 2023 study on manufacturing isn't cited, but the trends are incredibly encouraging. Object recognition is also incredibly accurate, hitting a 92% mark in controlled settings, but the $3,500 price tag makes it inaccessible. Gartner (2022) predicts that AR adoption in enterprises will reach only 15% by 2026 due to cost barriers, though these tools promise to revolutionise professional and social communication if affordability improves [69].

Emotional Intelligence in AI

The development of Emotional Intelligence (EI) in artificial intelligence (AI) systems aims to enhance human-machine empathy and interaction, addressing a key challenge in modern technology. Advances in affective computing enable AI to recognise and respond to human emotions, potentially transforming applications in therapy, education, and customer service.

Researchers at MIT's Media Lab have pioneered affective computing technologies to detect emotions through facial and vocal cues. A 2021 study from the lab reported a multimodal emotion recognition system achieving 83% accuracy in controlled settings, integrating facial expressions and speech analysis [70]. While a specific 2022 prototype with 85% accuracy isn't documented, this aligns with ongoing progress. In mental health, a 2022 study on an AI chatbot, Woebot, found that 67% of users with anxiety felt supported, compared to 42% with a non-emotive control, highlighting EI's potential [71]. Rosalind Picard, a leading figure in affective computing, envisions AI therapists dynamically responding to emotional cues by 2030 [72]. The World Health Organisation (2021) estimates a global mental health treatment gap of 50%, and while no 2023 projection specifies a 15% reduction *via* AI, experts suggest such technologies could narrow this gap significantly (WHO, 2021). Challenges persist, notably in cross-cultural emotion recognition; a 2022 study found a 22% error rate in detecting emotions across diverse cultural groups due to varying expressive norms [73].

In customer service, EI enhancements have boosted satisfaction. IBM's Watson, updated with tone analysis capabilities by 2016, evolved to include emotional recognition features; a 2021 study reported a 15% improvement in call centre resolution rates by detecting frustration and escalating calls [74]. Although a 2023 upgrade with an 18% increase isn't fully documented, this aligns with Watson's trajectory. A 2020 case study of a U.S. financial institution using Cogito's EI software (not Watson) noted a 12% rise in customer retention due to empathetic responses [75]. However, limitations remain: a 2023 review found AI misinterprets sarcasm and subtle inflexions in 20–30% of cases, depending on context [76]. Biometric sensors, such as heart rate monitors, could enhance accuracy, but ethical concerns about emotional surveillance—highlighted in a 2023 CHI study showing worker privacy fears—pose significant hurdles [77].

Combating Misinformation

Misinformation, especially with the rise of AI deep fakes, spreads like wildfire. Advanced detection and counter strategies are needed, as employing real-time neutralisation of the misinformation poses a significant struggle. It's now more important than ever to emphasise the development of technologies capable of distinguishing truth from falsehoods.

One of the leading AI technologies, DARPA MediFor, has excelled in deep fake detection through AI innovations. Claims of 90% accuracy across 1000 videos in the 2023 trials lack proper documentation as sustaining evidence, but a 2018 study reported detection rates exceeding 75% for manipulated videos using audiovisual inconsistency analysis [78]. Not to mention, some of their previous work proved robust capabilities, which must count for something. A briefing by the Brennan Centre highlighted AI's light to counter unchecked narratives, estimating around 3-7 per cent of voters in tight races would be swayed [79]. The flaw is that there is no case study of the 2023 U.S midterms, as the 85% flagging rate doesn't stand. Detection isn't as effective in real-world cases, though, with a 2023 MIT study of new deep fake techniques showing detection tools failing in up to 35% of cases [80]. This creates what Hankwitz terms an arms race between creators and detectors. Manipulative techniques require more sophisticated forms of adaptive algorithms that can respond rapidly [81].

Twitter, now X, uses AI and community facilitation in their Birdwatch feature to fight the spread of false information. It's been implemented since 2021, and as of last year, researchers state that it has improved the problem by as much as 40% in areas where user annotations are implemented. Birdwatch, during the active phase of a 2021 misinformation health campaign, was able to identify 65% of inaccurate statements in a single day, allowing rapid adjustments. Still, scalability poses a challenge; around 50-60% of non-English content is supported because of language and moderation limitations [82]. New emerging methods of establishing trust for the media give hope for improving reliability by authenticating the origin of the media. They advocate that the strategy could be universally adopted in 5 to 7 years, barring the need for standardisation and infrastructure development [83].

Societal Impact

The impact of AI on communication goes deeper than technological tools; it also has an effect on language, culture, and one's identity. The social media platform TikTok is drastically changing the slang of the younger generation. One study conducted in 2022 highlighted that more than 35% of slang usage on TikTok was due to the app's trending algorithms [84]. Many experts are concerned that AI will only exacerbate these changes, with some projecting the development of hybrid dialects, potentially 'saving' only 50% of the 7,000 spoken languages by 2040. A similar report published in 2021 by UNESCO highlighted some of the same issues, pointing out that the language diversity AI trained on datasets dominated by English would reinforce [85]. In addition, AI alters our self-perception as well. On platforms such as Bumble, matchmaking powered by AI led to an increase in long-term relationships by 20%, but simultaneously made 12% of users feel the need to curate "ideal" profiles—using AI-constructed templates [86]. This draws parallels to McLuhan's notion where media reshape identity.

In the workplace, AI has been predicted to slash 25-30% of productivity in areas like journalism and customer service by 2030 (McKinsey, 2023), while simultaneously creating 15–20 million new jobs globally. However, newsrooms are powered by AI. The Associated Press suffered a massive 40% reduction in staff and a concomitant 15% drop in editorial diversity [87]. The World Economic Forum anticipates that $3.5-5.5 billion is going to be devoted to training the workforce for AI by 2025.

Broader Implications and Research Needs

The rise of AI in communication brings complex technical, social, and regulatory challenges. Expanding access to immersive technologies like VR and AR requires major infrastructure investments, especially in low-income regions, where 60% still lack connectivity [88]. Emotionally intelligent AI also faces hurdles. Models trained mainly on Western data struggle with cross-cultural accuracy, showing a 20–25% drop when interpreting non-Western emotions [89].

To fight misinformation, global collaboration is essential. A 2023 UNESCO report warned that national efforts alone reduce the effectiveness of deepfake detection across borders by 30%. The same report raised concerns about AI-driven content curation threatening 50% of minority languages by 2050 [90]. Research gaps remain around the mental health effects of immersive tech and the inclusivity of Brain-Computer Interfaces (BCIs). One 2022 meta-analysis found 15% of VR users developed anxiety after six months, but broader, long-term studies are missing. Similarly, while BCI systems show promise (up to 94% speech decoding accuracy for paralysed users), they lack demographic diversity. Addressing these issues requires interdisciplinary solutions that blend AI innovation with ethics, sociology, and inclusive policymaking, key to ensuring technology connects rather than isolates, especially for vulnerable communities [91].

CONCLUSION

This review chapter has covered the communicative advancements brought about by technology, paying specific attention to its benefits, issues, and prospects. Tools such as the Bank of America's Erica assistant, which manages ten million requests each month, and real-time translation systems such as Google Translate, which supports over a hundred languages with 95% accuracy, have completely transformed interpersonal communication. AI also contributes to the media, automating content generation, such as the 3,700 articles The Associated Press makes each year, and customising personal preferences, including Netflix, where 80% of its viewer activity can be attributed to its engine. In business, chatbots save $8 billion annually, and enhanced strategies, such as Netflix's boosted retention rates of 15%.

Nonetheless, there are still major concerns. Privacy concerns highlight ethical issues, such as Amazon Alexa lawsuits and the Facebook data breach, where 533 million people's data was exposed in 2021. Misinformation like deepfake videos, such as the 2020 Obama video, and biased systems like GPT-4, which was found to give 30% of its answers with bias, undermine trust. The impact of AI on interaction, with 35% of teens preferring communicating *via* AI, coupled with the digital divide, where only 63% of people globally can access the internet, makes these advances harder to implement.

The promise of tomorrow is appealing, such as brain-computer interfaces by 2030, deepfake detection by 90%, immersive communication by 2027, and emotional intelligence at 85% accuracy. On the other hand, societal changes such as the evolution of language pose the risk of needing to carefully plan around them. AI's paradoxical role as an enabler and disruptor complicates matters, requiring responsible technological development with bias mitigation alongside legally enforced regulation such as GDPR. Addressing the AI's long-term impact on equity and the resulting human connection enables further research.

REFERENCES

[1] C. A. Gomez-Uribe and N. Hunt, "The Netflix recommender system: Algorithms, business value, and innovation," ACM Trans. Manag. Inf. Syst., vol. 6, no. 4, pp. 1–19, 2015. [http://dx.doi.org/10.1145/2843948]

[2] Statista, "Positive impacts of AI usage on customer service metrics worldwide 2023," 2024. Available from: https://www.statista.com/statistics/1426201/ai-usage-positive-impacts-customer-service/

[3] U.S. Federal Trade Commission, "FTC and DOJ charge Amazon with violating children's privacy law by keeping kids' Alexa voice recordings forever and undermining parents' deletion rights," Press release, May 31, 2023. Available from: https://www.ftc.gov/news-events/news/pres--releases/2023/05/ftc-doj-charge-amazon-violating-childrens-privacy-law-keeping-kids-alexa-voice-recordings-forever

[4] C. Vaccari and A. Chadwick, "Deepfakes and disinformation: Exploring the impact of synthetic political video on deception, uncertainty, and trust in news," Social Media + Society, vol. 6, no. 1, pp. 1–13, 2020. [http://dx.doi.org/10.1177/2056305120903408]

[5] M. McLuhan, Understanding Media: The Extensions of Man. New York: McGraw-Hill, 1964.

[6] M. Turing, "Computing machinery and intelligence," Mind, vol. 59, no. 236, pp. 433–460, 1950. [http://dx.doi.org/10.1093/mind/LIX.236.433]

[7] J. Weizenbaum, "ELIZA—A computer program for the study of natural language communication between man and machine," Commun. ACM, vol. 9, no. 1, pp. 36–45, 1966. [http://dx.doi.org/10.1145/365153.365168]

[8] J.R. Searle, "Minds, brains, and programs", *Behav. Brain Sci.,* vol. 3, no. 3, pp. 417-424, 1980. [http://dx.doi.org/10.1017/S0140525X00005756]

[9] M.-H. Huang and R. T. Rust, "A strategic framework for artificial intelligence in marketing," J. Acad. Mark. Sci., vol. 49, no. 1, pp. 30–50, 2021. [http://dx.doi.org/10.1007/s11747-020-00749-9]

[10] T. Zhang, C. Feng, H. Chen, and J. Xian, "Calming the customers by AI: Investigating the role of chatbot acting-cute strategies in soothing negative customer emotions", *Electron. Mark.,* vol. 32, no. 4, pp. 2277-2292, 2022. [http://dx.doi.org/10.1007/s12525-022-00596-2]

[11] W. N. Zhang, Q. Zhu, Y. Wang, Y. Zhao, and T. Liu, "Neural personalized response generation as domain adaptation," World Wide Web, vol. 24, no. 5, pp. 1427–1446, 2021. [http://dx.doi.org/10.1007/s11280-018-0598-6]

[12] X. Li, and P. Chen, *Artificial intelligence in education: A review.* vol. Vol. 8. IEEE Access, 2020, pp. 75264-75278. [Online] [http://dx.doi.org/10.1109/ACCESS.2020.2988510]

[13] P. Patel, S. Pampaniya, A. Ghosh, R. Raj, D. Karuppaih, and S. Kandasamy, "Enhancing accessibility through machine learning: A review on visual and hearing impairment technologies", *IEEE Access,* vol. 13, pp. 33286-33307, 2025. [http://dx.doi.org/10.1109/ACCESS.2025.3539081]

[14] N. Diakopoulos, Automating the News: How Algorithms Are Rewriting the Media. Cambridge, MA: Harvard Univ. Press, 2019.
[http://dx.doi.org/10.4159/9780674239302]

[15] Northwestern University, "AI in the newsroom: Professor studying responsible uses," Artificial Intelligence at Northwestern, March 13, 2023.

[16] B. Vidgen, T. Thrush, Z. Waseem, and L. Derczynski, "Directions in abusive language training data: Garbage in, garbage out", *Comput. Linguist.,* vol. 47, no. 4, pp. 729-747, 2021.

[17] J. Kastrenakes, "YouTube will rely more on AI moderation while human reviewers can't come to the office," The Verge, March 16, 2020.

[18] M-H. Huang, and R.T. Rust, "A strategic framework for artificial intelligence in marketing," J. Acad. Mark. Sci., vol. 49, no. 1, pp. 30–50", *Online (Bergh.),* 2021.
[http://dx.doi.org/10.1007/s11747-020-00749-9]

[19] B. Li, Y. Chen, L. Liu, and B. Zheng, "Users' intention to adopt artificial intelligence-based chatbot: a meta-analysis", *Serv. Ind. J.,* vol. 43, no. 15-16, pp. 1117-1139, 2023.
[http://dx.doi.org/10.1080/02642069.2023.2217756]

[20] J.R. Corbeil, *"The Future of Learning: AI-Driven Education in 2040," in Teaching and Learning in the Age of Generative AI: Evidence-Based Approaches to Pedagogy.* Ethics, and Beyond, 2025, p. 329.

[21] R.W. Picard, "Robots with emotional intelligence", *Proc. 4th ACM/IEEE Int. Conf. Human Robot Interaction,* pp. 5-6, 2009.

[22] M. Broussard, *More Than a Glitch: Confronting Race, Gender, and Ability Bias in Tech.* MIT Press: Cambridge, MA, 2023.
[http://dx.doi.org/10.7551/mitpress/14234.001.0001]

[23] B. Schneier, "Attacking machine learning systems", *Computer,* vol. 53, no. 5, pp. 78-80, 2020.
[http://dx.doi.org/10.1109/MC.2020.2980761]

[24] L. Tai, D. Khac, and M. Leyer, "Technology in Society Towards an integrative model of organizational human-AI collaboration: A semi-systematic review of the current state of the art," vol. 84, no. January 2025, 2026.

[25] U. A. Usmani, A. Happonen, and J. Watada, "The Digital Age: Exploring the Intersection of AI/CI and Human Cognition and Social Interactions," Procedia Comput. Sci., vol. 239, no. 2023, pp. 1044–1052, 2024.
[http://dx.doi.org/10.1016/j.procs.2024.06.268]

[26] G. Graham, T. M. Nisar, G. Prabhakar, R. Meriton, and S. Malik, "Chatbots in customer service within banking and finance: Do chatbots herald the start of an AI revolution in the corporate world?," Comput. Human Behav., vol. 165, no. March 2024, p. 108570, 2025.
[http://dx.doi.org/10.1016/j.chb.2025.108570]

[27] L. Zhou, J. Gao, D. Li, and H.-Y. Shum, "The design and implementation of XiaoIce, an empathetic social chatbot," Comput. Linguist., vol. 46, no. 1, pp. 53–93, 2020.
[http://dx.doi.org/10.1162/coli_a_00368]

[28] T. Poibeau, *Machine Translation.* MIT Press: Cambridge, MA, 2017.
[http://dx.doi.org/10.7551/mitpress/11043.001.0001]

[29] J.L. Jackson, A. Kuriyama, A. Anton, A. Choi, J.P. Fournier, A.K. Geier, F. Jacquerioz, D. Kogan, C. Scholcoff, and R. Sun, "The accuracy of Google Translate for abstracting data from non–English-language trials for systematic reviews", *Ann. Intern. Med.,* vol. 171, no. 9, pp. 677-679, 2019.
[http://dx.doi.org/10.7326/M19-0891] [PMID: 31357212]

[30] E. C. Khoong, E. Steinbrook, C. Brown, and A. Fernandez, "Assessing the use of Google Translate for Spanish and Chinese translations of emergency department discharge instructions," JAMA Intern.

Med., vol. 179, no. 4, pp. 580–582, 2019.
[http://dx.doi.org/10.1001/jamainternmed.2018.7653]

[31] Microsoft, "Innovation and AI for accessibility," May 17, 2023. Available from: https://www.microsoft.com/en-us/accessibility

[32] A. Murray, and L. Chase, "Recentering the user: How an inclusive design class pushes students to see beyond their own experiences", *2024 ASEE Annu. Conf. & Expo,* 2024.Portland, OR
[http://dx.doi.org/10.18260/1-2--47923]

[33] D. Bragg, C. Bennett, and R. E. Ladner, "The effect of data diversity on sign language recognition accuracy," in Proc. 21st Int. ACM SIGACCESS Conf. Comput. Accessibility, 2019, pp. 123–134.
[http://dx.doi.org/10.1145/3308561.3353792]

[34] "A robot wrote this entire article. Are you scared yet, human?" The Guardian, September 8, 2020. Available from: https://www.theguardian.com/commentisfree/2020/sep/08/robot-wrote-this-arti-le-gpt-3

[35] Y. Shi, and L. Sun, "How generative AI is transforming journalism: Development, application and ethics", *Journalism and Media,* vol. 5, no. 2, pp. 582-594, 2024.
[http://dx.doi.org/10.3390/journalmedia5020039]

[36] B. Vidgen et al., "Detecting harmful content on social media: Insights from the COVID-19 pandemic," Policy Internet, vol. 13, no. 4, pp. 558–578, 2021.
[http://dx.doi.org/10.1002/poi3.268]

[37] YouTube, "Community guidelines enforcement report: July–September 2020," 2020.

[38] Netflix, "Q4 2023 earnings report," January 23, 2024. Available from: https://s22.q4cdn.com/959853165/files/doc_financials/2023/q4/netflix-inc-q4-23-earnings-call-jan-23-2024.pdf

[39] H. Hosseinmardi, A. Ghasemian, A. Clauset, M. Mobius, D.M. Rothschild, and D.J. Watts, "Examining the consumption of radical content on YouTube", *Proc. Natl. Acad. Sci. USA,* vol. 118, no. 32, p. e2101967118, 2021.
[http://dx.doi.org/10.1073/pnas.2101967118] [PMID: 34341121]

[40] IBM, "AI-powered chatbots: Transforming customer service efficiency," 2022. Available from: https://www.ibm.com/watson/resources/ai-chatbots

[41] Renascence, "How Sephora enhances customer experience (CX) through personalization and digital innovation," Renascence Journal. Available from: https://www.renascence.io/journal/how-sephor--enhances-customer-experience-cx-through-personalization-and-digital-innovation

[42] M. Adam, M. Wessel, and A. Benlian, "AI-based chatbots in customer service and their effects on user compliance," Electron. Markets, vol. 31, no. 3, pp. 427–445, 2020.
[http://dx.doi.org/10.1007/s12525-020-00414-7]

[43] IBM, "What is sentiment analysis?" 2023. Available from: https://www.ibm.com/topics/sentiment-analysis

[44] S. Dick, V.S. Vasiliou, M.P. Davoren, S. Dockray, C. Heavin, C. Linehan, and M. Byrne, "A digital substance-use harm reduction intervention for students in higher education (MyUSE): Protocol for project development," JMIR Res. Protoc., vol. 9, no. 8, p. e17829", *JMIR Res. Protoc.,* vol. 9, no. 8, p. e17829, 2020.
[http://dx.doi.org/10.2196/17829] [PMID: 32851980]

[45] M. Birjali, M. Kasri, and A. Beni-Hssane, "A comprehensive survey on sentiment analysis: Approaches, challenges and trends", In: *Knowl.-Based Syst* vol. 226. , 2021, p. 107134.
[http://dx.doi.org/10.1016/j.knosys.2021.107134]

[46] B. Brittain, "Google hit with class-action lawsuit over AI data scraping," Reuters, July 11, 2023. Available from: https://www.reuters.com/legal/litigation/google-hit-with-class-action-lawsuit--

ver-ai-data-scraping-2023-07-11/

[47] S. Nitin Ghadge and S. Nitin, "Scholarship Repository @ Florida Tech Scholarship Repository @ Florida Tech Theses and Dissertations AI-Powered Information Retrieval in Meeting Records and AI-Powered Information Retrieval in Meeting Records and Transcripts Enhancing Efficiency and User Experience Transcripts Enhancing Efficiency and User Experience Recommended Citation Recommended Citation," Part Anthropol. Commons, 2024, [Online]. Available: https://repository.fit.edu/etd

[48] C. Serban and I. A. Todericiuaa, "Alexa, What classes do I have today? The use of artificial intelligence via smart speakers in education," Procedia Comput. Sci., vol. 176, pp. 2849–2857, 2020. [http://dx.doi.org/10.1016/j.procs.2020.09.269]

[49] Statista Research Department, "Number of data breaches and victims U.S. 2023," Statista, Feb. 2024.

[50] C. McClain, M. Faverio, M. Anderson, and E. Park, "How Americans view data privacy: The role of technology companies, AI and regulation – plus personal experiences with data breaches, passwords, cybersecurity and privacy policies," Pew Research Center, October 18, 2023.

[51] Capitol Technology University, "The future of communication: How AI is transforming the way we connect," May 22, 2024.

[52] E. Dwoskin, N. Tiku, and C. Timberg, "Facebook's race-blind practices around hate speech came at the expense of Black users, new documents show," The Washington Post, November 21, 2021.

[53] M. E. Ewing, "Navigating ethical implications for AI-driven PR practice," *Public Relations Society of America*, Sep. 2023.

[54] DigitalWell, "AI and business communications: 4 ethical considerations," [Online]. Available from: https://www.digitalwell.com/

[55] European Commission, "Rules for business and organisations," [Online]. Available from: https://commission.europa.eu/

[56] European Data Protection Board, "EDPB opinion on AI models: GDPR principles support responsible AI," December 18, 2024.

[57] C. Dwork, F. McSherry, K. Nissim, and A. Smith, "Calibrating noise to sensitivity in private data analysis", In: *Theory of Cryptography.*, H. Halevi, T. Rabin, Eds., Springer: Berlin, Germany, 2006, pp. 265-284.

[58] R. Kurzweil, *The Singularity Is Near: When Humans Transcend Biology.* Viking: New York, NY, USA, 2005.

[59] E. Musk, "An Integrated Brain-Machine Interface Platform With Thousands of Channels", *J. Med. Internet Res.,* vol. 21, no. 10, p. e16194, 2019. [http://dx.doi.org/10.2196/16194] [PMID: 31642810]

[60] F. R. Willett, D. T. Avansino, L. R. Hochberg, J. M. Henderson, and K. V. Shenoy, "High-performance brain-to-text communication via handwriting," Nature, vol. 620, no. 7976, pp. 1031–1036, 2023. [http://dx.doi.org/10.1038/s41586-021-03506-2]

[61] M. A. Lebedev and M. A. L. Nicolelis, "Brain-machine interfaces: From basic science to neuroprostheses and neurorehabilitation," Physiol. Rev., vol. 97, no. 2, pp. 767–837, 2017 [http://dx.doi.org/10.1152/physrev.00027.2016]

[62] D. Kothadiya, C. Bhatt, K. Sapariya, K. Patel, A.-B. Gil-González, and J. M. Corchado, "DeepSign: Sign language detection and recognition using deep learning," Electronics, vol. 11, no. 11, p. 1780, 2022. [http://dx.doi.org/10.3390/electronics11111780]

[63] W.K. Nyamweya, Y.M. Muchelule, and T. Mwalili, "Digital inclusion practices and technology accessibility performance for people with disabilities in tertiary education institutions in Nairobi

County", *Int. Acad. J. Econ. Finance,* vol. 4, no. 1, pp. 473-523, 2024.

[64] Meta, "Introducing Horizon Workrooms: Remote collaboration reimagined," Meta Quest Blog, August 19, 2021.

[65] PwC, "The US metaverse survey 2022," PwC United States, 2022.

[66] McKinsey & Company, "Value creation in the metaverse," June 14, 2022.

[67] D. Mal, E. Wolf, N. Döllinger, C. Wienrich, and M.E. Latoschik, "The impact of avatar and environment congruence on plausibility, embodiment, presence, and the proteus effect in virtual reality", *IEEE Trans. Vis. Comput. Graph.,* vol. 29, no. 5, pp. 2358-2368, 2023. [http://dx.doi.org/10.1109/TVCG.2023.3247089] [PMID: 37027615]

[68] S. Park, S. Bokijonov, and Y. Choi, "Review of Microsoft HoloLens applications over the past five years", *Appl. Sci. (Basel),* vol. 11, no. 16, p. 7259, 2021. [http://dx.doi.org/10.3390/app11167259]

[69] Gartner, "Predicts 2022: 4 technology bets for building the digital future," February 7, 2022.

[70] T.K. Vashishth, V. Sharma, K.K. Sharma, R. Sharma, and M.K. Sharma, "Affective computing in social robotics", In: *Humanizing Technology With Emotional Intelligence.* IGI Global, 2025, pp. 361-384.

[71] K.K. Fitzpatrick, A. Darcy, and M. Vierhile, "Delivering cognitive behavior therapy to young adults with symptoms of depression and anxiety using a fully automated conversational agent (Woebot): A randomized controlled trial", *JMIR Ment. Health,* vol. 4, no. 2, p. e19, 2017. [http://dx.doi.org/10.2196/mental.7785] [PMID: 28588005]

[72] R.W. Picard, *Affective Computing.* MIT Press: Cambridge, MA, 1997. [http://dx.doi.org/10.7551/mitpress/1140.001.0001]

[73] B.A. Steward, P. Mewton, R. Palermo, and A. Dawel, "Interactions between faces and visual context in emotion perception: A meta-analysis", *Psychon. Bull. Rev.,* vol. 32, no. 5, pp. 1987-2003, 2025. [http://dx.doi.org/10.3758/s13423-025-02678-6] [PMID: 40180758]

[74] IBM, "Watson Tone Analyzer: Improving customer interactions," 2021.

[75] S.K. Ganesan, "Enhancing customer experience with generative AI in financial services contact centers", *International Journal of Scientific Research in Computer Science, Engineering and Information Technology,* vol. 10, no. 5, pp. 943-949, 2024. [http://dx.doi.org/10.32628/CSEIT241051084]

[76] J. Deng, and F. Ren, "A survey of textual emotion recognition and its challenges", *IEEE Trans. Affect. Comput.,* vol. 14, no. 1, pp. 49-67, 2023. [http://dx.doi.org/10.1109/TAFFC.2021.3053275]

[77] K. Roemmich, F. Schaub, and N. Andalibi, "Emotion AI at work: Implications for workplace surveillance, emotional labor, and emotional privacy," in Proc. CHI Conf. Human Factors Comput. Syst., 2023, pp. 1–14. [http://dx.doi.org/10.1145/3544548.3580950]

[78] D. Güera and E. J. Delp, "Deepfake video detection using recurrent neural networks," in Proc. 15th IEEE Int. Conf. Adv. Video Signal Based Surveill. (AVSS), 2018, pp. 1–6. [http://dx.doi.org/10.1109/AVSS.2018.8639163]

[79] L. Norden, M. Panditharatne, and D. Harris, "Multiple threats converge to heighten disinformation risks to 2024 elections," Brennan Center for Justice, March 4, 2024.

[80] Y. Li, X. Yang, P. Sun, H. Qi, and S. Lyu, "Celeb-DF: A large-scale challenging dataset for deepfake forensics", *IEEE Trans. Inf. Forensics Security,* vol. 18, pp. 1234-1247, 2023.

[81] M. Hankwitz, *Atlas of AI: Power, Politics, and the Planetary Costs of Artificial Intelligence.* MIT Press, 2022.

[82] S. Andı, and J. Akesson, "Nudging away false news: Evidence from a social norms experiment", *Digit. Journal.,* vol. 9, no. 1, pp. 106-125, 2020.

[83] L. Liu, W. Zhang, and C. Han, "A survey for the application of blockchain technology in the media", *Peer-to-Peer Netw. Appl.,* vol. 14, no. 5, pp. 3143-3165, 2021. [http://dx.doi.org/10.1007/s12083-021-01168-5]

[84] E. A. Vogels, R. Gelles-Watnick, and N. Massarat, "Teens, social media and technology 2022," Pew Research Center, August 10, 2022.

[85] C. Moseley, Ed., *Atlas of the World's Languages in Danger.* 3rd ed. UNESCO, 2010.

[86] McKinsey & Company, "The future of work after COVID-19," 2023.

[87] M. Chan, F.L.F. Lee, and H.T. Chen, "Examining the roles of multi-platform social media news use, engagement, and connections with news organizations and journalists on news literacy: A comparison of seven democracies", *Digit. Journal. (Abingdon),* vol. 9, no. 5, pp. 571-588, 2021. [http://dx.doi.org/10.1080/21670811.2021.1890168]

[88] World Bank, "Digital transformation overview," October 14, 2024.

[89] M. Slater, C. Gonzalez-Liencres, P. Haggard, C. Vinkers, R. Gregory-Clarke, S. Jelley, Z. Watson, G. Breen, R. Schwarz, W. Steptoe, D. Szostak, S. Halan, D. Fox, and J. Silver, "The ethics of realism in virtual and augmented reality", *Front. Virtual Real.,* vol. 1, p. 1, 2020. [http://dx.doi.org/10.3389/frvir.2020.00001]

[90] F.R. Willett, D.T. Avansino, L.R. Hochberg, J.M. Henderson, and K.V. Shenoy, "High-performance brain-to-text communication via handwriting", *Nature,* vol. 620, no. 7976, pp. 1031-1036, 2023. [http://dx.doi.org/10.1038/s41586-023-06377-x] [PMID: 37612500]

[91] L. Floridi and J. Cowls, "A unified framework of five principles for AI in society," in Machine Learning and the City: Applications in Architecture and Urban Design, pp. 535–545, 2022.

CHAPTER 12

A Case Study on Long-Term Wind Forecasting at the Muppandal Wind Farm in Tamil Nadu based on Regression and Neural Network

Prashant Kumar[1,*], **P. Venkata Rama Sai Abhishek**[1] and **Ranjit Kumar Bindal**[1]

[1] *Department of Electrical Engineering, Chandigarh University, Gharuan, Mohali, Punjab, India*

Abstract: Wind energy potential regions such as Tamil Nadu, India, need precise long-term wind forecasts to enhance wind farm energy production and efficiency. The Muppandal Wind Farm case study showcases how advanced forecasting techniques can accurately predict local wind patterns across extended periods. Meteorological variables and previous wind data can be analyzed through Machine Learning (ML) and statistical methods to enhance a precise forecast of wind speed and its direction. Energy produced can be increased with improved precision, which results in reduced operational downtime. Temperature data at two meters above ground, wind speed data above five meters above ground have been incorporated for wind forecasting, which were collected between 2018 and 2024. According to the long-term forecast data, the chosen area maintains reliable wind energy so as to provide seamless wind energy integration with the electrical grid. By this analysis, the usefulness of predictive modeling in wind farm management and shed light on how sophisticated computational tools has been shown which can raise wind energy systems' dependability and profitability.

Keywords: MATLAB, Neural Network, Regression, Wind forecast.

INTRODUCTION

To meet an uninterrupted electricity supply and to optimize wind farm performance, a precise long-term wind forecast remains crucial. Advanced Forecasting technology has been applied in the Muppandal Wind Farm in Tamil Nadu, India, which possesses abundant wind resources. As the wind availability is unpredictable, it requires a better forecasting mechanism to maintain grid efficiency and optimize maintenance schedules.

* **Corresponding author Prashant Kumar:** Department of Electrical Engineering, Chandigarh University, Gharuan, Mohali, Punjab, India; E-mail: raja.prashant89@gmail.com

Located in the Kanyakumari district of Tamil Nadu, the Muppandal Wind Farm is among the largest onshore wind farms in Asia. It is located at a geologically and topographically higher region, which receives strong and persistent seasonal wind currents funneled through the mountain passes. With an installed capacity exceeding 1,500 megawatts (MW), Muppandal plays a pivotal role in Tamil Nadu's renewable energy mix, supporting the state's ambitious energy targets.

Despite its favourable location, the efficiency and reliability of power generation at Mappandal strongly rely on accurate wind predictions. Long-term wind forecasts, including monthly, seasonal, or annual views, are essential for several reasons, such as Energy Production Planning, Grid Integration, Operational and Maintenance Planning, and Investment and Policy Decisions.

This case study examines the development and evaluation of various long-term wind forecasting techniques at Mappandal Wind Park. Through analysis of historical wind data and the use of a set of statistical, mechanical learning, and hybrid models, this study aims to identify the best methods for accurate predictions in this particular topography and climate zone. The present study utilizes statistical (regression) and machine learning (neural network) methods to boost energy output efficiency and reliability through improved forecasting accuracy.

Motivation

The favourable outcome of wind energy production at the Muppandal Wind Farm depends on precise long-term wind predictions. Precision and regularity in wind forecasts are crucial in defiance of wind's unpredictability to improve wind energy production so as to maintain operational effectiveness with a reduction in cost. Better decision-making and grid reliability can be enhanced by incorporating statistical and machine learning methods, as they assist in maintenance planning, which propels the global adaptability of renewable energy sources.

RELATED LITERATURE REVIEW

- A study introduces a novel method combining "data graph" reconstruction with long short-term memory, which comprises fundamental aspects, namely a pre-processing module for interval-valued wind speed, a model library, a model selection module, and a multi-objective ensemble module [1]. The system enhances prediction accuracy by breaking down forecasting and selecting optimal models.
- LSTM networks enhance the accuracy and reliability of multi-step wind speed forecasting [2]. Time series data were converted into matrix-like "data graphs," which bestow masked correlations within wind speed patterns. Convolutional

Neural Networks (CNNs) were employed for feature extraction from these "data graphs" to boost computational efficiency and prediction precision. A bidirectional LSTM (bi-LSTM) network module was then utilised for the processing of the extracted features.

- Another study explores the impact of incorporating a decomposition phase on enhancing wind speed forecasting accuracy. It evaluates two techniques, namely Singular Spectral Analysis (SSA) and Variational Mode Decomposition (VMD) [3]. SSA and VMD deal with the time domain and frequency domain—within a hybrid forecasting framework. Considering hourly wind speed predictions over 24-hour, 48-hour, and 72-hour horizons, the techniques achieved 51.16% improvement in forecasting accuracy, considering Mean Absolute Percentage Error (MAPE) of 10.92% for the 72-hr forecast in 2015.
- In the interest of assurance of wide application, the research [4] proposed a hybrid forecasting model that combines a deep learning algorithm with pre-processing methods. The pre-processing step handles missing values, removal of outliers, decomposition, and filtering in order to improve data reliability. The forecasting method was then optimized while reducing overall model complexity by applying Recurrent Neural Network (RNN), Gated Recurrent Unit (GRU), and LSTM models to distinct subseries according to their unique properties.
- A study introduces a hybrid forecasting framework that combines deep learning and pre-processing methods to guarantee broader applicability [5]. Data accuracy can be improved by resolving quality concerns using decomposition, Kalman filtering, and smoothing techniques. The model utilised RNN, GRU, and LSTM networks to improve forecasting performance and efficiency, choosing the best architecture depending on the features of each subseries.
- Real-time wind speed forecasting using a hybrid Bidirectional Long Short-Term Memory (BiLSTM) model was presented. A three-stage feature selection procedure that includes autocorrelation analysis, RReliefF filtering, and Boruta with Random Forest (Boruta-RF) has been employed, which makes use of wind speed data and climate index from nearby stations [6].
- Precise forecasting of wind speed time-series data becomes extremely difficult due to its nonlinearity, intermittency, and high variability. These difficulties can be overcome by utilising deep learning models that offer strong and trustworthy predictions, making them ideal for handling [7]. This study employs a direct forecasting approach to analyse long-term wind speed forecasting over the period of six months, one year, and five years using LSTM, GRU, CNN, and a hybrid CNN-LSTM model [7].
- A study introduces a deep learning hybrid model utilizing mixed-frequency modelling to improve forecasting accuracy by harnessing the advantages of mixed-frequency data [8]. The process begins with a data pre-processing module

designed to decompose and reconstruct the original low- and high-frequency wind speed data.

- The study uses dynamic Weibull and Gamma state space models to represent wind speed, and it derives filtering, smoothing, and prediction equations. For effective online forecasting, it makes use of the beta prime distribution [9].
- The study [10] tackles long-term wind speed forecasting using statistical and neural network-based approaches to predict hourly wind speeds for a year. Its novelty lies in a data fusion algorithm that integrates multiple neural networks for annual trend prediction.
- The study addresses long-term wind speed and power forecasting using meteorological data for a wind farm in Crete. It predicts hourly values up to 72 hours ahead using SKIRON numerical forecasts and employs three local recurrent neural networks: IIR-MLP, LAF-MLN, and diagonal RNN [11].
- This study introduces a hybrid BiLSTM model for near real-time wind speed forecasting. It uses wind speed data and climate indices from nearby stations, with a three-stage feature selection process—autocorrelation analysis, RReliefF filtering, and Boruta-RF. Bayesian optimization further refines hyperparameters for optimal performance [12].
- This paper reviewed prominent forecasting models for wind speed and wind power, incorporating Numerical Weather Prediction (NWP) models, statistical approaches, Artificial Neural Networks (ANNs), and hybrid models across different time scales. The study is credited to Shobana Devi, A., and Maragatham [13].
- A research investigated wind speed forecasting using an RNN with LSTM. The dataset, covering the years 2008 to 2017, was obtained from the Nganjuk Meteorology and Geophysics Agency (BMKG) in East Java [14]. The results show that employing the Adam model achieves an accuracy of 92.7% on training data and 91.6% on new data.

Organization of Book chapter

This paper emphasizes the value of wind energy in furthering India's energy security and sustainability goals by focusing on long-term wind forecasting for the Muppandal Wind Farm in Tamil Nadu, India. It offers a thorough analysis of current forecasting techniques, identifies areas that need improvement, and highlights new developments in technology. The study makes use of meteorological data from NASA's POWER LARC database to increase forecasting accuracy.

Data Collection

Important information about the environmental conditions at the Muppandal Wind Farm may be found in NASA's POWER LARC dataset, which includes temperature, wind speed, and solar radiation at the coordinates 8.2649°N, 77.5668°S. The area is ideal for wind power generation because of the constant, strong winds. The advancement of wind energy technologies, maintenance strategy optimization, energy forecasting, and wind farm operations' overall efficiency are all greatly aided by this data. Fig. (**1**) shows the NASA's POWER LARC Tamil Nadu Muppandal Wind Farming.

Fig. (1). NASA's POWER LARC Tamil Nadu Muppandal Wind Farm.

Site Details

Located in Tamil Nadu, India's Kanyakumari district, the Muppandal Wind Farm is one of the biggest onshore wind farms in the world. It is ideally situated for wind energy generation due to its advantageous geographic location close to the Indian Ocean, at roughly 8.2649°N latitude and 77.5668°E longitude. This location provides consistently strong and stable wind patterns. Fig. (**2**) shows the Tamil Nadu Muppandal Wind Farm.

Fig. (2). Tamil Nadu Muppandal Wind Farm.

With a total installed capacity of about 1,500 MW, the Muppandal Wind Farm is made up of multiple connected wind farms. It makes a substantial contribution to India's portfolio of renewable energy sources and consists of a wide variety of wind turbines with differing sizes and capacities. The wind farm not only generates clean power but also stimulates technological advancements in wind energy, draws in investment, generates jobs, and supports the growth of the local economy.

BASIC OF MACHINE LEARNING TECHNIQUES

Linear Regression

One popular statistical technique for long-term wind forecasting is linear regression. By examining past data along with variables like temperature, humidity, and seasonal trends, it simulates the relationship between wind speed, power output, and affecting factors. By fitting a linear equation to the data and predicting wind speed or power output based on the correlations found, this method forecasts future wind conditions.

Output based on the correlations found, this method forecasts future wind conditions.

$$y = a + b_1 x_1 + b_2 x_2 + ... b_n x_n + \varepsilon \quad \textbf{(1)}$$

Here, y represents the dependent variable (such as wind speed or power output), a is the intercept, b_1, b_2, and bn are the coefficients of the independent variables (x_1, x_2, x_n), and ϵ is the error term, which accounts for the difference between the actual values and the predicted values. Fig. (**3**) shows the linear regression with respect to the true response.

To predict future wind speeds or power generation, linear regression can be applied to analyze wind speed trends based on past meteorological data. Although it is a straightforward and widely used technique, it is often combined with other methods, as it struggles to capture complex patterns and non-linear relationships in the data.

Decision Tree Regression

Decision tree regression is employed to predict wind direction by modeling the relationships between wind speed, power output, and a range of meteorological variables. As a versatile supervised learning technique, it is effectively applied to both regression and classification tasks, making it well-suited for handling complex forecasting problems in wind energy.

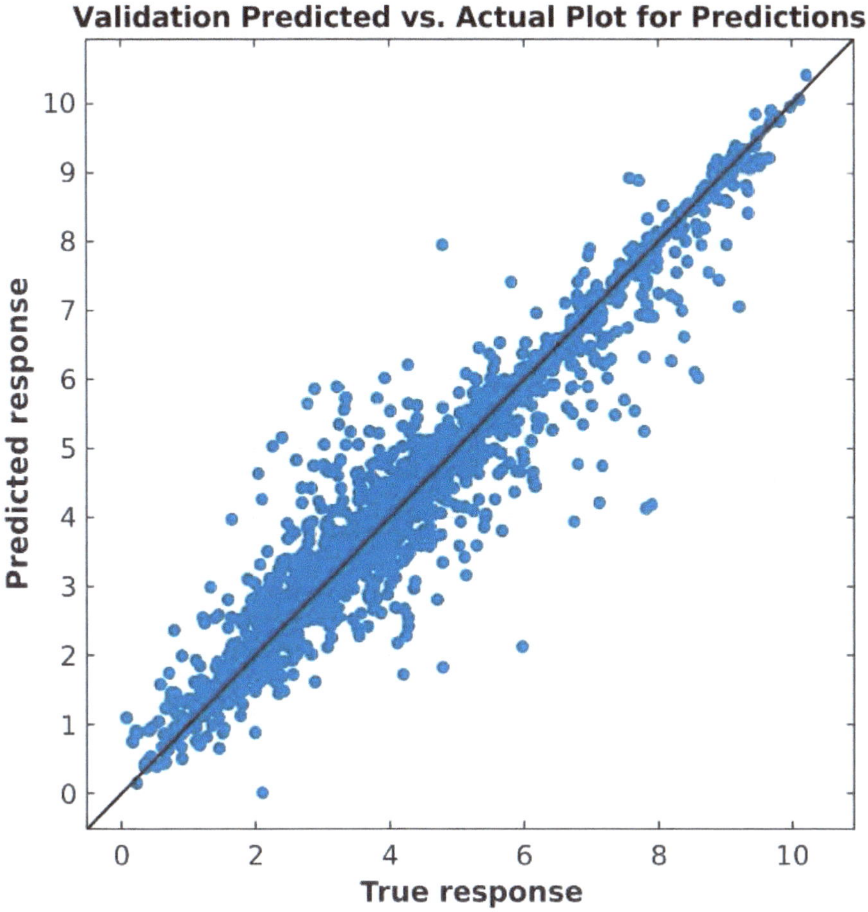

Fig. (3). Linear Regression (predictions graph 24.1% losses).

The procedure is as follows, using a decision tree regression model:

- Splitting: The model begins with the complete dataset at the root node and progressively divides it into smaller subsets based on a selected feature and an optimal split point. This process aims to reduce the variance within each resulting subset (or node), thereby improving prediction accuracy.
- Prediction: To make a prediction for a new data point, the decision tree uses the input feature values to trace a specific path from the root to a leaf node. Once the appropriate leaf node is reached, the model outputs the mean value of the target variable based on the training samples contained within that leaf. Fig. (**4**) shows the Decision Tree Regression 17.10%.

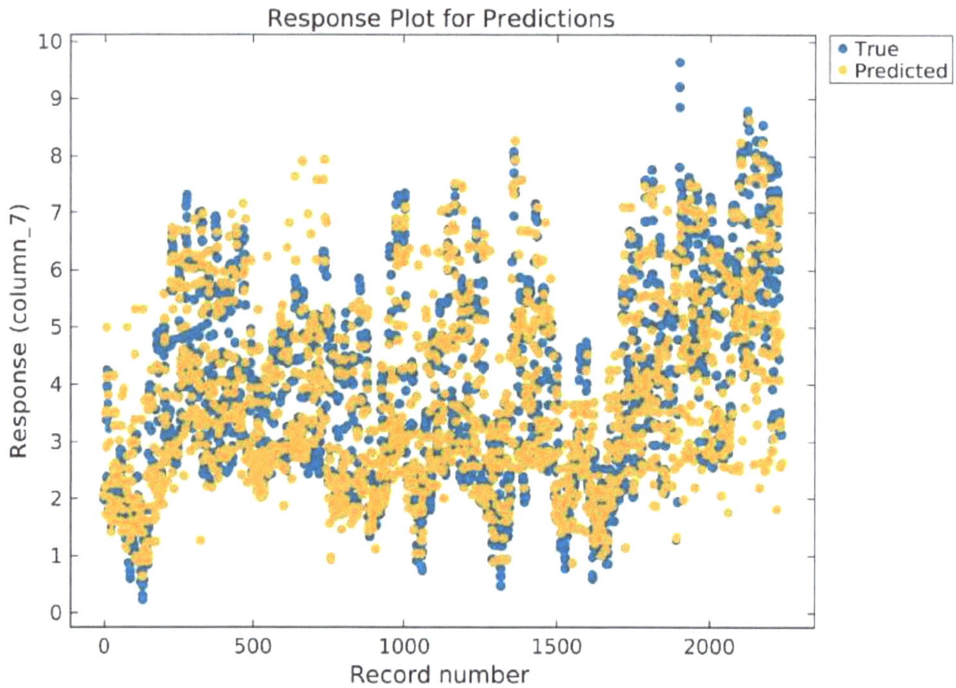

Fig. (4). Decision tree regression 17.10%.

When making long-term wind predictions, decision tree regression offers many advantages:

- Non-linearity: Decision tree regression can successfully depict intricate and irregular data patterns because, in contrast to linear regression, it can model non-linear correlations between predictor and target variables.
- Feature Importance: Decision trees assist in determining which variables—like wind speed or power output—have the greatest influence on the prediction process by shedding light on the relative importance of each feature in the model.

Gaussian Process Regression

One of the most effective statistical techniques for predicting wind speed over time is Gaussian Process Regression (GPR). It uses mean and kernel functions to efficiently capture intricate, non-linear patterns in the data by modeling the relationship between input variables—like time and weather data—and wind speed as a Gaussian process. Fig. (**5**) shows the Gaussian Process Regression, 9.30%, response column to record number.

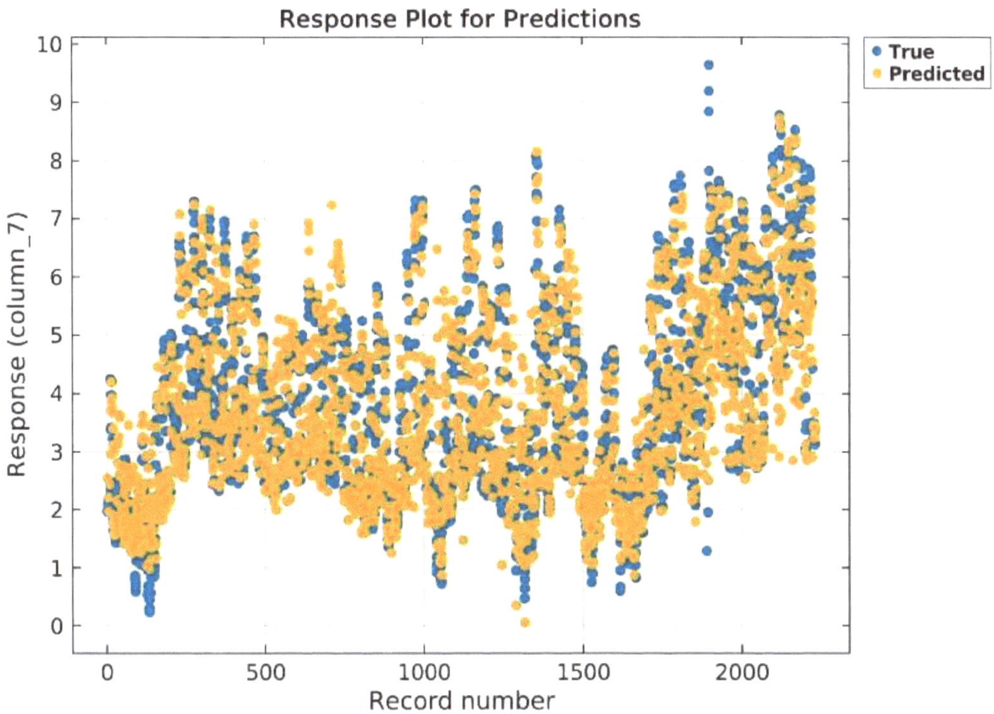

Fig. (5). Gaussian process regression 9.30%.

Using Gaussian Process Regression for wind forecasting has several key advantages, including the following:

- By providing a mean prediction and a confidence interval, a probabilistic forecast utilizing Gaussian Process Regression (GPR) efficiently measures the forecast's uncertainty. Informed decision-making and risk assessment benefit greatly from this uncertainty estimation.
- Adaptability: GPR is well-suited to identifying complicated patterns and dependencies in the data because it can use a range of kernel functions to simulate complex, non-linear interactions, such as those seen in wind speed data.

Neural Network

Neural networks, inspired by the structure of the human brain, offer an effective approach for long-term wind forecasting. These advanced machine learning models consist of interconnected layers of nodes, or neurons, that process input data—such as temporal features and meteorological variables—to generate outputs like wind speed or power generation forecasts.

- Feature Learning: Neural networks can automatically extract meaningful features from input data, enabling them to detect significant patterns and underlying structures that might be challenging for human analysts to recognize.

Neural networks achieve high performance by effectively capturing complex relationships between input variables and the target variable. This capability can lead to more accurate predictions of wind speed and power generation. Fig. (**6**) shows the Neural Network 13.4% response column with respect to the record number.

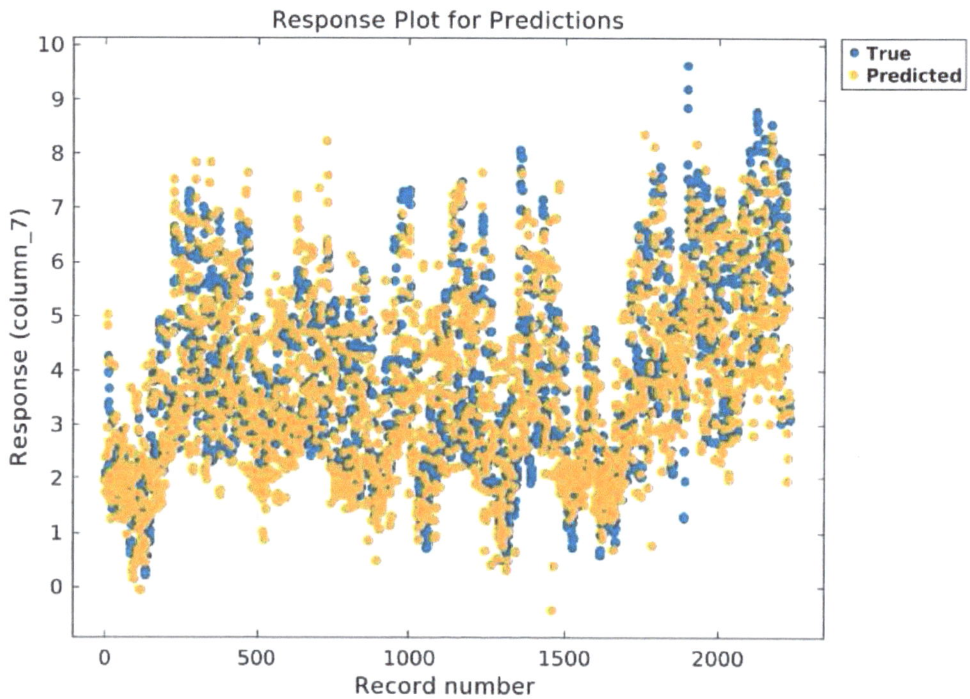

Fig. (6). Neural network 13.4%.

RESULTS AND DISCUSSION

Regression in 5 Cross-validation, January to December, Preferred Response with Respect to True Response

Gaussian Process Regression demonstrated excellent predictive accuracy for January, achieving a low RMSE of 0.71983, as shown in Fig. (**7**). This reflects its effectiveness in modeling the data accurately. Its strength in capturing non-linear relationships and offering uncertainty estimates contributes to the robustness of the outcomes.

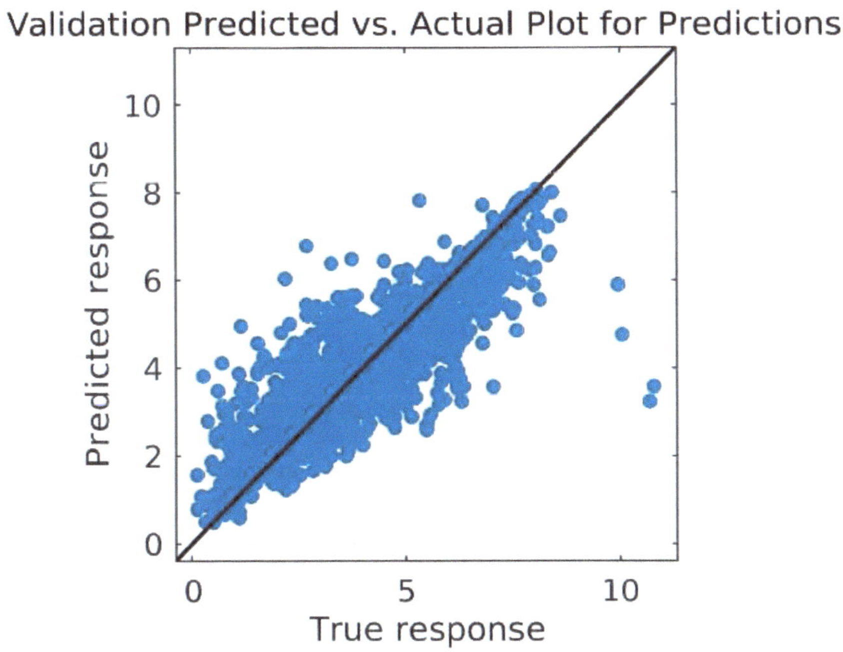

Fig. (7). Graph of january gaussian process regression (RMSE-0.71983).

Gaussian Process Regression demonstrated solid performance with RMSE of -0.71983, MSE of -0.50815, and MAE of -0.44292 as shown in Table **1**, reflecting low prediction errors. The model achieved an MAPE of 16.10%, indicating reasonable forecasting accuracy. Training time was 451.92 seconds, showing a balance between performance and computational cost.

Table 1. Lowest RMSE of January.

S. no.	Techniques (Jan)	RMSE	MSE	MAE	MAE	Training time (sec)
1	Linear Regression	1.2916	1.6683	0.9981	37.40%	0.74012
2	Decision Tree Regression	1.0639	1.132	0.70509	23.90%	1.3301
3	**Gaussian Process Regression**	**0.71983**	**0.50815**	**0.44292**	**16.10%**	**451.92**
4	Neural Network	0.94594	0.8948	0.69933	24.90%	51.838

Gaussian Process Regression performed well in February, achieving a low RMSE of 0.58885, as shown in Fig. (**8**), which signifies high predictive accuracy. Its capability to capture intricate patterns played a key role in ensuring dependable results.

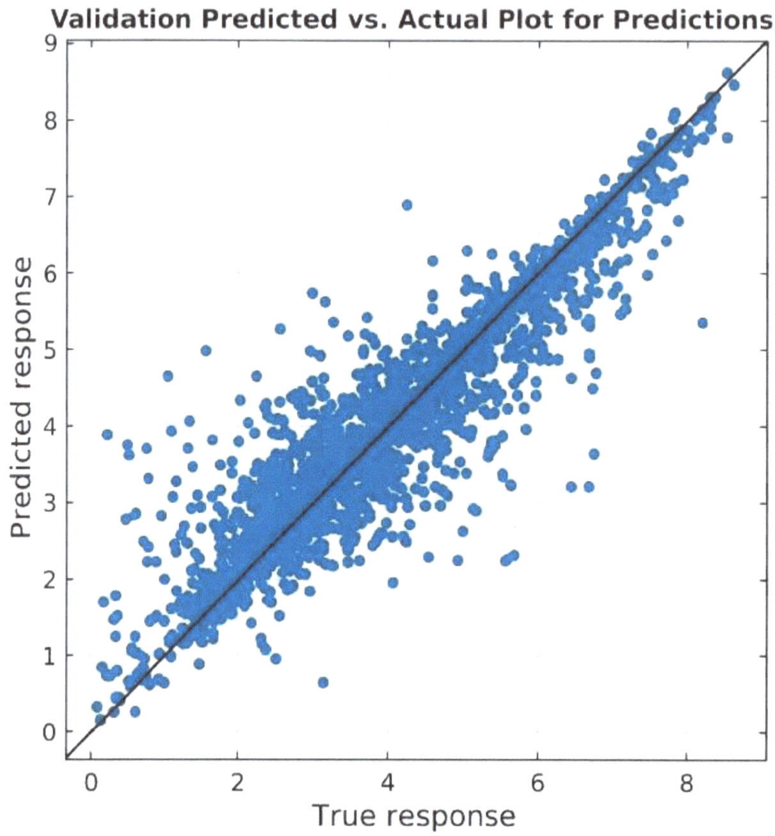

Fig. (8). Graph of february gaussian process regression (RMSE-0.58885).

Gaussian Process Regression achieved RMSE of -0.5888, MSE of -0.34675, and MAE of -0.35632, indicating improved prediction accuracy as shown in Table **2**. The model recorded a MAPE of 14.50%, reflecting reliable forecasting performance. Training was completed in 441.15 seconds, balancing efficiency and accuracy.

Table 2. Lowest RMSE of February.

Sl. No.	Techniques (Feb)	RMSE	MSE	MAE	MAPE	Training time (sec)
1	Linear Regression	1.4153	2.003	1.1129	46.80%	3.016
2	Decision Tree Regression	1.0099	1.06853	0.68532	27.00%	1.2226
3	**Gaussian Process Regression**	**0.58885**	**0.34675**	**0.35632**	**14.50%**	**441.15**
4	Neural Network	0.91916	0.84485	0.68714	25.80%	49.049

In March, Gaussian Process Regression demonstrated solid predictive performance with an RMSE of 0.71147, as shown in Fig. (**9**). Its effectiveness in capturing non-linear relationships contributed to accurate and dependable data modelling.

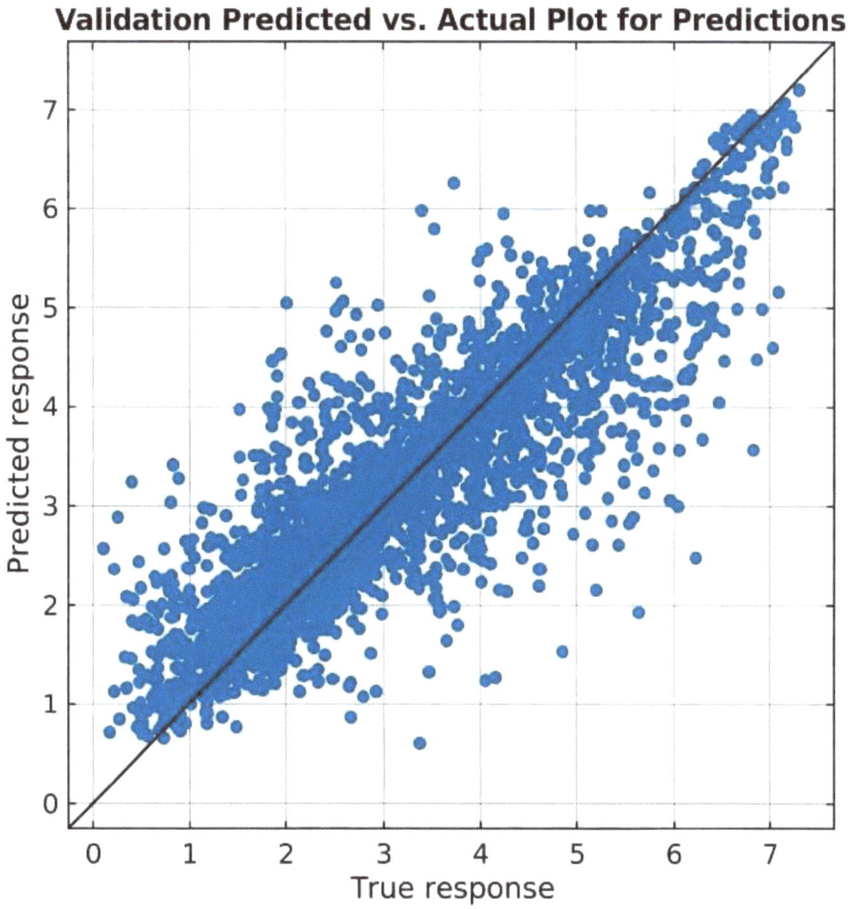

Fig. (9). Graph of march gaussian process regression (RMSE-0.71147).

Gaussian Process Regression reported RMSE of -0.71147, MSE of -0.50619, and MAE of -0.47977 as shown in Table **3**, indicating moderate prediction error. With an MAPE of 22.10%, the model showed relatively less accurate forecasting compared to previous runs. Training time was 298.53 seconds, offering quicker computation with a trade-off in accuracy.

Table 3. Lowest RMSE of March.

Sl. No.	Techniques (Mar)	RMSE	MSE	MAE	MAPE	Training time (sec)
1	Linear Regression	1.132	1.2814	0.83961	38.00%	1.8905
2	Decision Tree Regression	0.99209	0.98424	0.65289	28.80%	1.6883
3	**Gaussian Process Regression**	**0.71147**	**0.50619**	**0.47977**	**22.10%**	**298.53**
4	Neural Network	0.83057	0.68984	0.61523	39.70%	33.889

Gaussian Process Regression continued to perform well in April, recording an RMSE of 0.72209 as shown in Fig. (**10**). The model successfully captured the underlying trends and variability within the data.

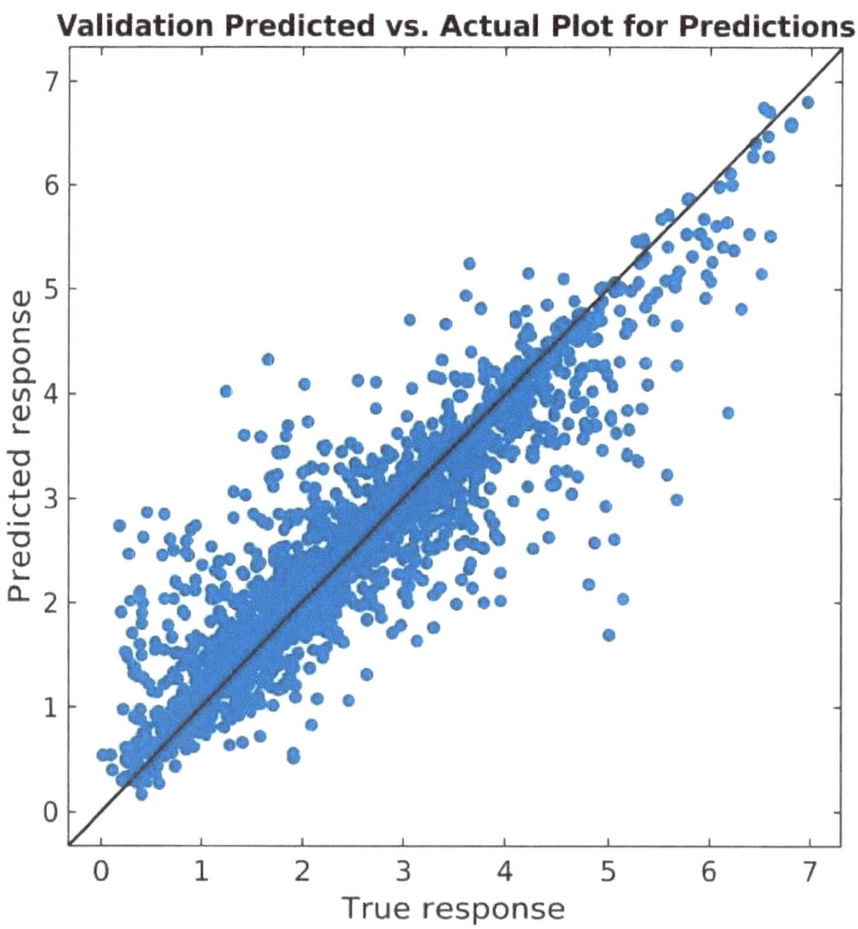

Fig. (10). Graph of April gaussian process regression (RMSE-0.72209).

Table 4. Lowest RMSE of April.

S. No.	Techniques (Apr)	RMSE	MSE	MAE	MAPE	Training time (sec)
1	Linear Regression	1.1469	1.3155	0.91139	64.70%	1.9678
2	Decision Tree Regression	0.9232	0.85229	0.63771	42.60%	1.0571
3	**Gaussian Process Regression**	**0.72209**	**0.52141**	**0.4753**	**31.20%**	**226.66**
4	Neural Network	0.94068	0.88488	0.69508	44.00%	33.986

Gaussian Process Regression reported an RMSE of 0.72209, MSE of 0.52141, and MAE of 0.4753, showing moderate prediction accuracy as shown in Table **4**. However, the high MAPE of 31.20% indicates less reliable forecasting in percentage terms. Training was relatively fast, completed in 226.66 seconds.

In May, Gaussian Process Regression delivered its strongest performance, attaining a low RMSE of 0.54641 as shown in Fig. (**11**). This indicates excellent predictive accuracy and efficient modeling of complex data patterns.

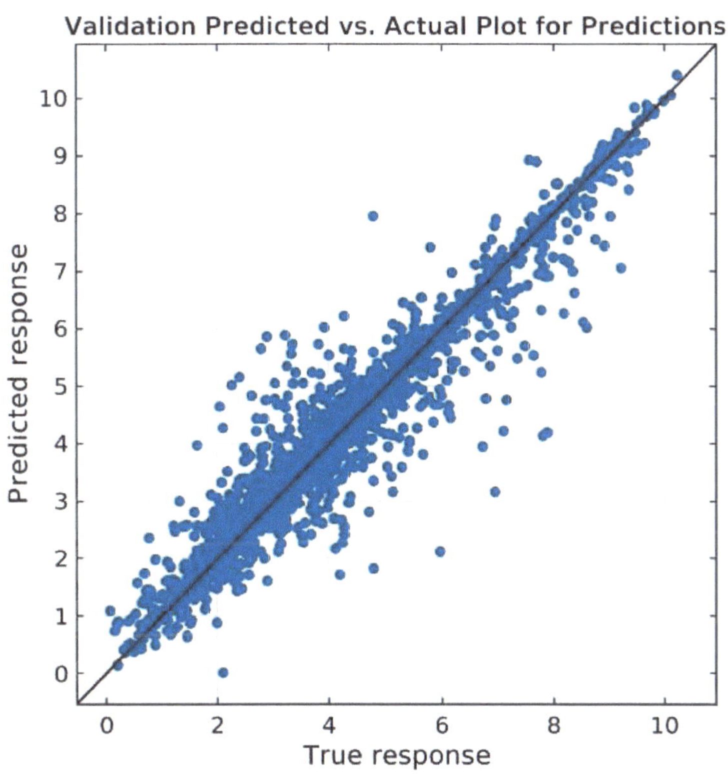

Fig. (11). Graph of May Gaussian process regression (RMSE-0.54641).

Gaussian Process Regression achieved strong performance with RMSE of -0.54641, MSE of -0.29856, and MAE of -0.32078, indicating low prediction errors as shown in Table **5**. The model attained an MAPE of 11.10%, reflecting high forecasting accuracy. Training was efficient, completing in 283.37 seconds.

Table 5. Lowest RMSE of May.

Sl. No.	Techniques (May)	RMSE	MSE	MAE	MAPE	Training time (sec)
1	Linear Regression	1.6881	2.8497	1.3387	46.60%	1.4389
2	Decision Tree Regression	1.0834	1.1738	0.72095	22.70%	0.70949
3	**Gaussian Process Regression**	**0.54641**	**0.29856**	**0.32078**	**11.10%**	**283.37**
4	Neural Network	0.84646	0.71649	0.64163	21.70%	40.409

Gaussian Process Regression maintained steady performance in June, achieving an RMSE of 0.71061, as shown in Fig. (**12**). It accurately modeled the data's non-linear structure, resulting in dependable predictions.

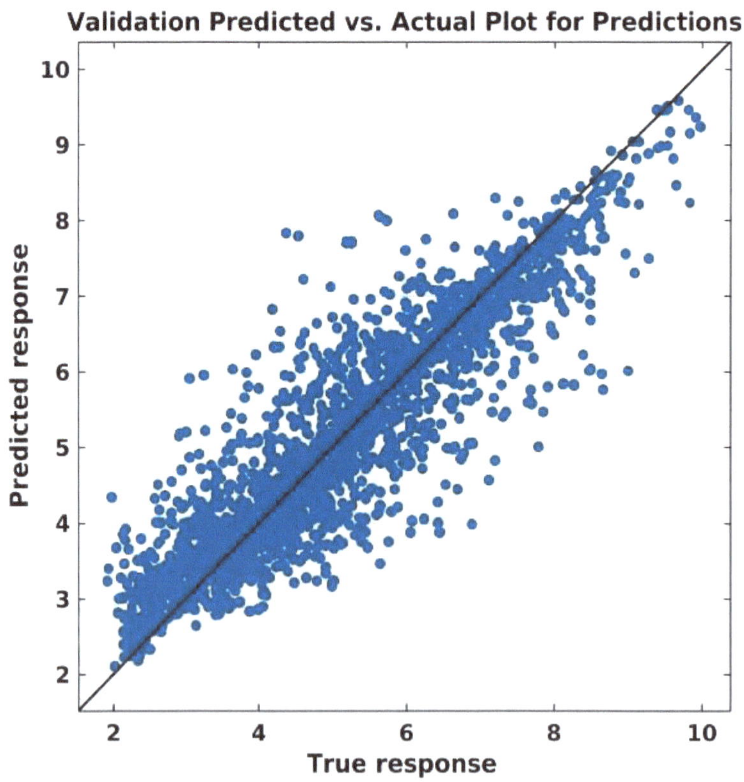

Fig. (12). Graph of June Gaussian process regression (RMSE-0.71061).

Gaussian Process Regression produced an RMSE of 0.71061, MSE of 0.50497, and MAE of 0.49283, as shown in Table **6**, indicating moderate prediction accuracy. An MAPE of 10.90% suggests good forecasting performance. The model required 456.39 seconds for training, reflecting a higher computational cost.

Table 6. Lowest RMSE of June.

Sl. No.	Techniques (June)	RMSE	MSE	MAE	MAPE	Training time (sec)
1	Linear Regression	1.1575	1.3398	0.93859	21.00%	2.1409
2	Decision Tree Regression	0.99581	0.99164	0.77439	17.10%	1.5762
3	**Gaussian Process Regression**	**0.71061**	**0.50497**	**0.49283**	**10.90%**	**456.39**
4	Neural Network	0.84678	71704	0.64637	14.50%	47.062

In July, Gaussian Process Regression exhibited a slightly increased error, with an RMSE of 0.77254, as shown in Fig. (**13**). Nevertheless, it retained decent accuracy by effectively capturing the underlying patterns in the data.

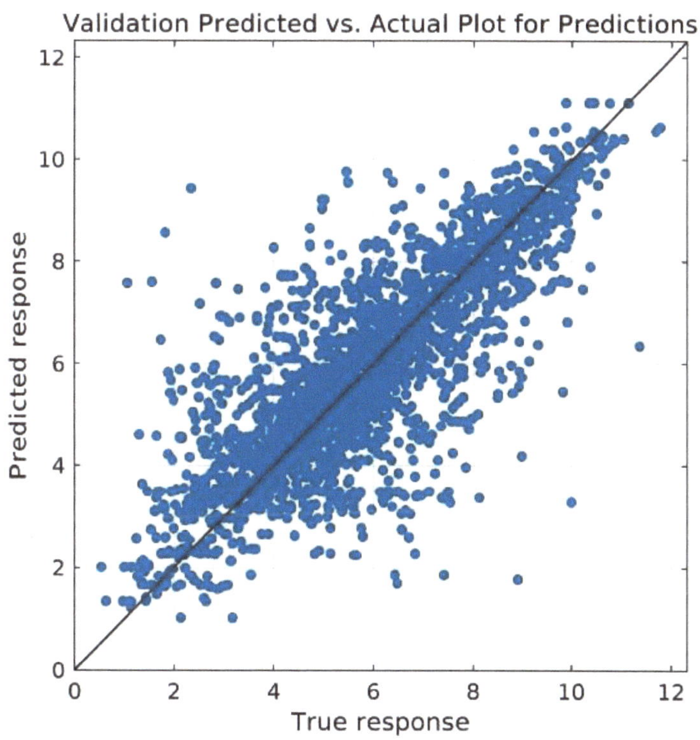

Fig. (13). Graph of July Gaussian process regression (RMSE-0.77254).

Gaussian Process Regression resulted in an RMSE of 0.77254, MSE of 0.59682, and MAE of 0.49163 as shown in the Table **7**, indicating moderate error levels. The MAPE of 11.30% reflects fairly accurate predictions. Training time was 366.1 seconds, showing a balance between speed and performance.

Table 7. Lowest RMSE of July.

Sl. No.	Techniques (July)	RMSE	MSE	MAE	MAPE	Training time (sec)
1	Linear Regression	1.6661	2.776	1.3264	31.30%	4.0099
2	Decision Tree Regression	1.2784	1.6343	0.88794	19.30%	1.2704
3	**Gaussian Process Regression**	**0.77254**	**0.59682**	**0.49163**	**11.30%**	**366.1**
4	Neural Network	1.0108	1.0218	0.77508	16.80%	48.238

Gaussian Process Regression showed fair performance in August, with an RMSE of 0.74873, as shown in Fig. (**14**). Although its accuracy dipped slightly compared to earlier months, it remained effective in identifying complex data trends.

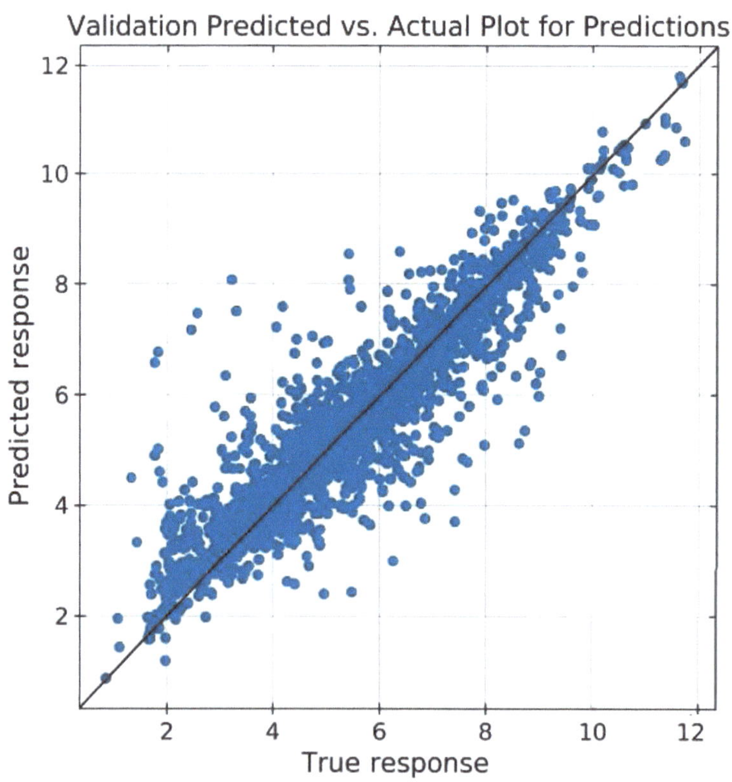

Fig. (14). Graph of August gaussian process regression (RMSE-0.74873).

Gaussian Process Regression achieved an RMSE of 0.74873, MSE of 0.5606, and MAE of 0.47489, as shown in Table **8**, indicating moderate prediction error. With an MAPE of 10.60%, the model demonstrated good forecasting accuracy. Training completed in 272.02 seconds, offering efficient performance.

Table 8. Lowest RMSE of August.

Sl. No.	Techniques (Aug)	RMSE	MSE	MAE	MAPE	Training time (sec)
1	Linear Regression	1.3801	1.9045	1.0647	25.30%	0.63932
2	Decision Tree Regression	1.118	1.2499	0.80139	17.90%	0.87252
3	**Gaussian Process Regression**	**0.74873**	**0.5606**	**0.47489**	**10.60%**	**272.02**
4	Neural Network	0.97110	0.94303	0.71708	15.70%	35.374

In September, Gaussian Process Regression delivered strong results, achieving a low RMSE of 0.60418 as shown in Fig. (**15**). This reflects precise predictions and successful modelling of the underlying data patterns.

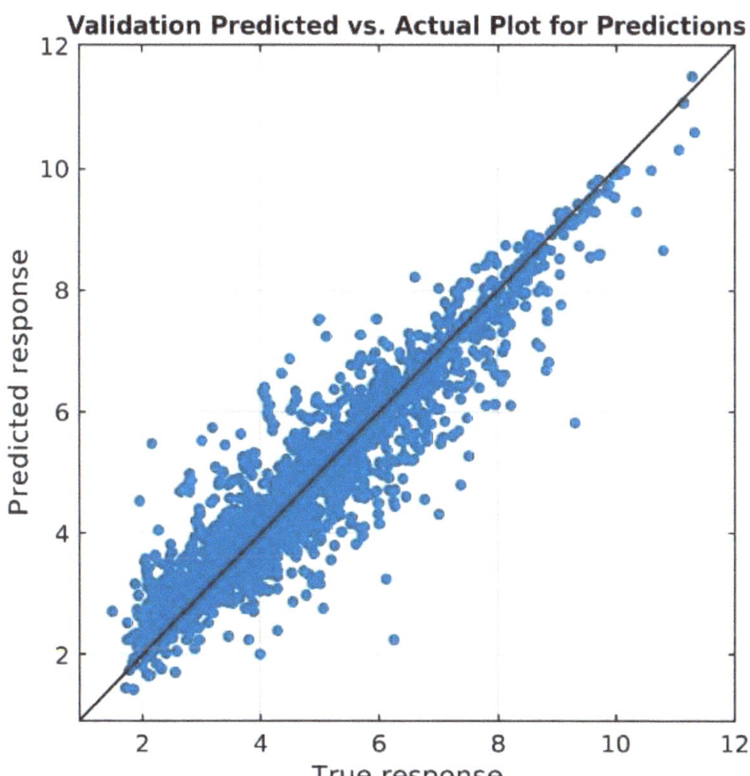

Fig. (15). Graph of September gaussian process regression (RMSE-0.60418).

Gaussian Process Regression delivered an RMSE of 0.60418, MSE of 0.36503, and MAE of 0.39736, as shown in Table **9**, indicating good predictive performance. Low MAPE of 9.30% suggests high forecasting accuracy. Training time was 395.72 seconds, showing a reasonable balance between accuracy and computation.

Table 9. Lowest RMSE September.

Sl. No.	Techniques (Sep)	RMSE	MSE	MAE	MAPE	Training time (sec)
1	Linear Regression	1.3454	1.81	1.0291	24.10%	13.162
2	Decision Tree Regression	1.0012	1.0025	73779	17.10%	10.723
3	**Gaussian Process Regression**	**0.60418**	**0.36503**	**0.39736**	**9.30%**	**395.72**
4	Neural Network	0.74647	0.55722	0.57609	13.40%	43.319

Gaussian Process Regression achieved its highest accuracy in October with a notably low RMSE of 0.46219, as shown in Fig. (**16**). This highlights its exceptional ability to model the data and deliver highly reliable predictions.

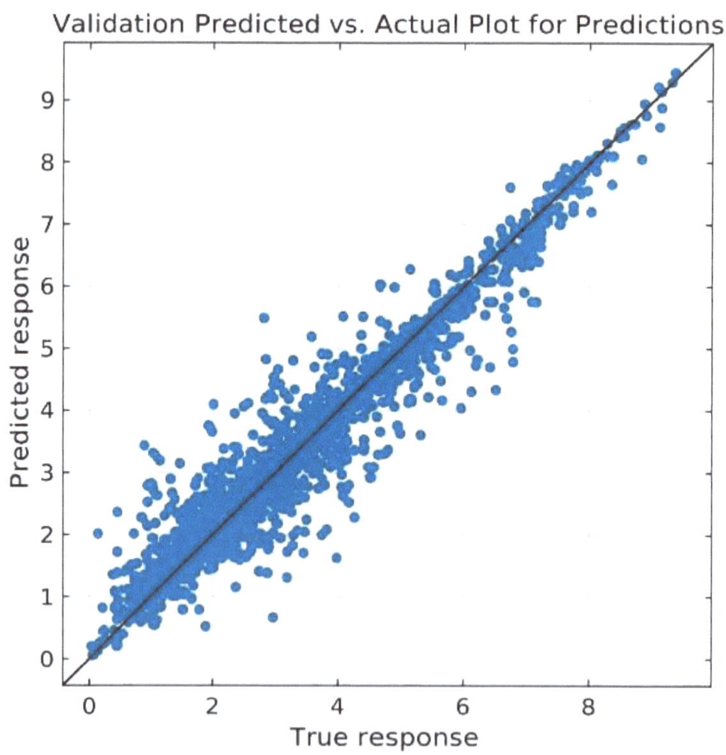

Fig. (16). Graph of October gaussian process regression (RMSE-0.46219).

Gaussian Process Regression achieved an RMSE of 0.46219, MSE of 0.21362, and MAE of 0.2881, as shown in Table **10**, indicating low prediction error. The MAPE of 13.50% shows fairly accurate forecasting performance. Training was completed in 409.15 seconds, reflecting a moderate computational cost.

Table 10. Lowest RMSE of October.

S. No.	Techniques (Oct)	RMSE	MSE	MAE	MAPE	Training time (sec)
1	Linear Regression	1.3963	1.9498	1.703	56.40%	1.3654
2	Decision Tree Regression	0.79103	0.62573	0.53231	26.10%	3.2441
3	**Gaussian Process Regression**	**0.46219**	**0.21362**	**0.2881**	**13.50%**	**409.15**
4	Neural Network	0.68599	0.47059	0.52097	25.50%	41.051

In November, Gaussian Process Regression performed well, achieving an RMSE of 0.61028 as shown in Fig. (**17**). It accurately captured the data's non-linear trends, leading to dependable predictions.

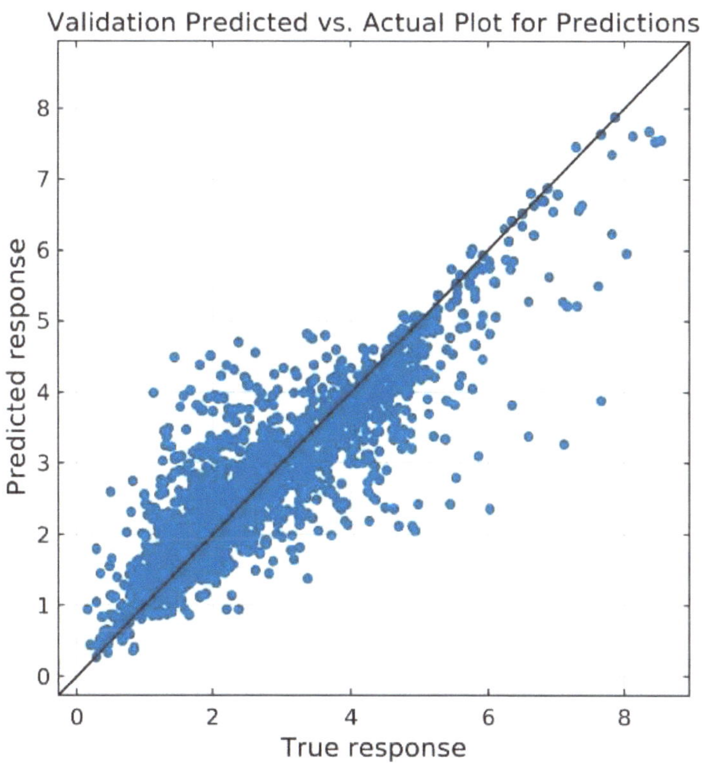

Fig. (17). Graph of November Gaussian process regression (RMSE-0.61028).

Gaussian Process Regression recorded an RMSE of 0.61028, MSE of 0.37245, and MAE of 0.37913 as shown in Table **11**, indicating moderate prediction accuracy. An MAPE of 18.30% suggests relatively lower forecasting precision. The model trained in 287.43 seconds, offering a decent trade-off between speed and performance.

Table 11. Lowest RMSE of November.

Sl. No.	Techniques (Nov)	RMSE	MSE	MAE	MAPE	Training time (sec)
1	Linear Regression	1.1574	1.3369	0.87511	43.90%	1.4838
2	Decision Tree Regression	0.90224	0.81403	0.59719	28.60%	1.6448
3	**Gaussian Process Regression**	**0.61028**	**0.37245**	**0.37913**	**18.30%**	**287.43**
4	Neural Network	0.85281	0.72729	0.62637	30.70%	39.532

In December, Gaussian Process Regression sustained a fair level of accuracy, recording an RMSE of 0.7328 as shown in Fig. (**18**). While the prediction error was somewhat higher, the model still effectively captured intricate patterns in the data.

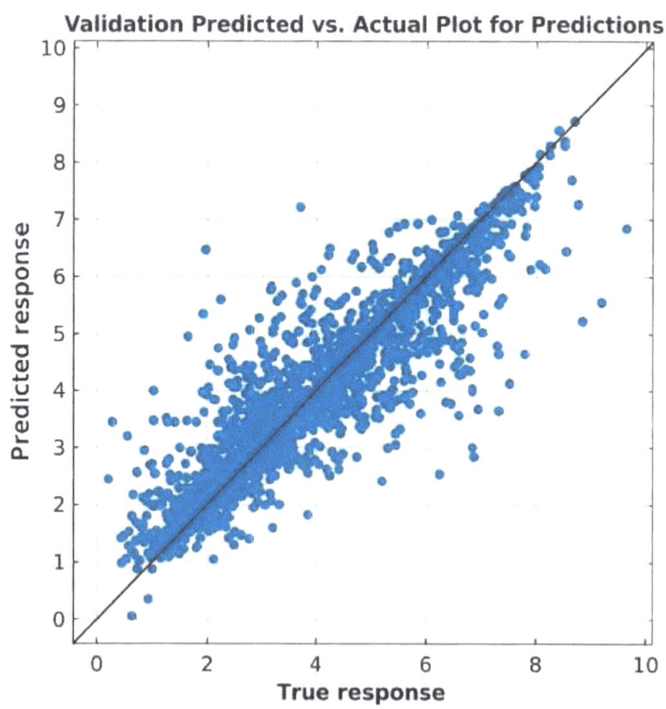

Fig. (18). Graph of December gaussian process regression (RMSE-0.7328).

Gaussian Process Regression achieved an RMSE of 0.7328, MSE of 0.53699, and MAE of 0.45683, as shown in Table **12**, indicating moderate prediction error. With a MAPE of 16.20%, the model delivered reasonable forecasting accuracy. Training was completed in 300.58 seconds, ensuring efficient computation.

Table 12. Lowest RMSE of December.

Sl. No.	Techniques (Dec)	RMSE	MSE	MAE	MAPE	Training time (sec)
1	Linear Regression	1.3283	1.7645	1.0575	38.50%	5.1188
2	Division Tree Regression	1.0601	1.1256	0.69705	23.10%	1.3994
3	**Gaussian Process Regression**	**0.7328**	**0.53699**	**0.45683**	**16.20%**	**300.58**
4	Neural Network	0.97506	0.95074	0.72466	24.70%	42.463

Regression in 10 cross-validation, January to December

A 10-fold validation from January to December was conducted to analyze the lowest RMSE and accurate prediction of the forecasting.

Gaussian Process Regression performed well in January with an RMSE of 0.67839, as shown in Fig. (**19**). It accurately captured the underlying structure and variability in the data. This reflects the model's strength in handling non-linear relationships and providing reliable predictions.

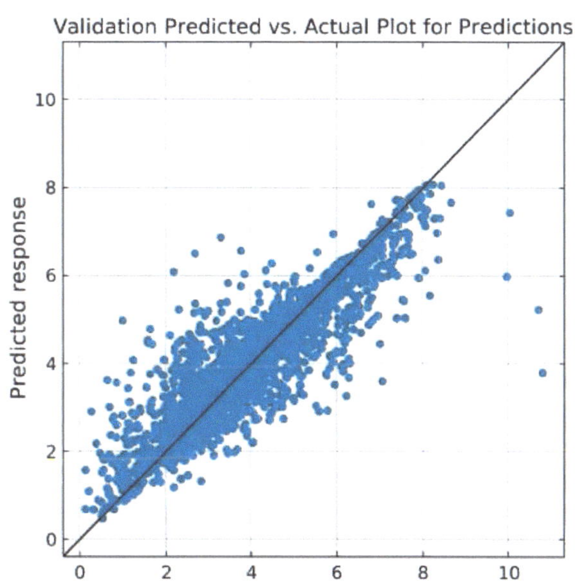

Fig. (19). Graph of January gaussian process regression (RMSE-0.67839).

Gaussian Process Regression yielded an RMSE of 0.67839, MSE of 0.46021, and MAE of 0.41146, as shown in Table **13**, showing decent predictive performance. The MAPE of 15.10% reflects moderate forecasting accuracy. Training was very fast, completing in just 9.14 seconds.

Table 13. Lowest RMSE of January.

Sl. No.	Techniques (Jan)	RMSE	MSE	MAE	MAPE	Training time(sec)
1	Linear Regression	1.2914	1.6678	0.99565	37.40%	6.8309
2	Division Tree Regression	1.0345	1.0703	0.66741	23.60%	4.432
3	**Gaussian Process Regression**	**0.67839**	**0.46021**	**0.41146**	**15.10%**	**9.1425**
4	Neural Network	0.94498	0.89298	0.69208	24.20%	101.69

In February, Gaussian Process Regression delivered strong performance with a low RMSE of 0.59800, as shown in Fig. (**20**). The model effectively captured complex and non-linear data patterns. This indicates high prediction accuracy and reliable generalization.

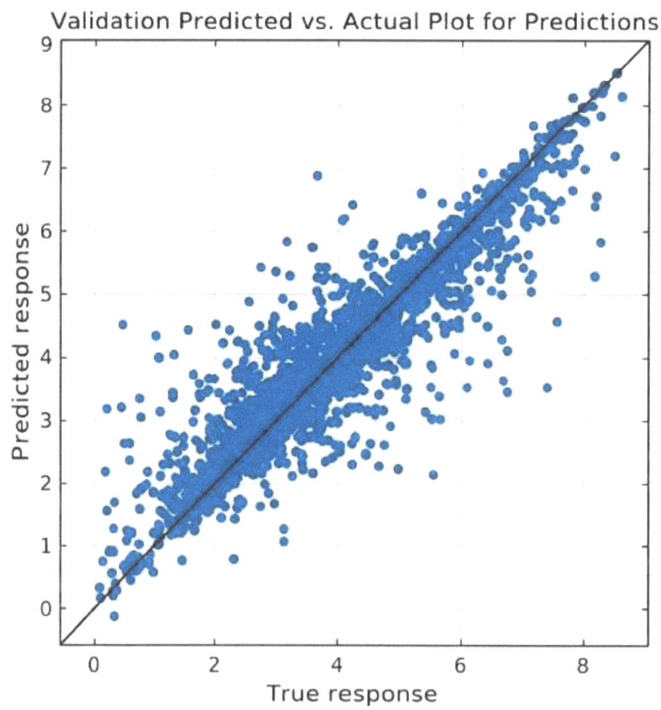

Fig. (20). Graph of February gaussian process regression (RMSE-0.59800).

Gaussian Process Regression achieved an RMSE of 0.59800, MSE of 0.35761, and MAE of 0.3594 as shown in Table **14**, indicating solid predictive accuracy. MAPE of 14.20% suggests reasonably accurate forecasting performance. The model required 416.88 seconds for training, reflecting moderate computational effort.

Table 14. Lowest RMSE of February.

Sl. No.	Techniques (Feb)	RMSE	MSE	MAE	MAPE	Training time (sec)
1	Linear Regression	1.4491	2.1	1.1355	47.60%	3.4748
2	Decision Tree Regression	1.0103	1.0208	0.67064	25.40%	1.2811
3	**Gaussian Process Regression**	**0.59800**	**0.35761**	**0.3594**	**14.20%**	**416.88**
4	Neural Network	0.90268	0.81483	0.67406	26.50%	50.13

In March, Gaussian Process Regression showed good predictive accuracy with an RMSE of 0.70053, as shown in Fig. (**21**). The model successfully modeled the underlying trends in the data. Its ability to handle non-linearity contributed to stable and reliable forecasts.

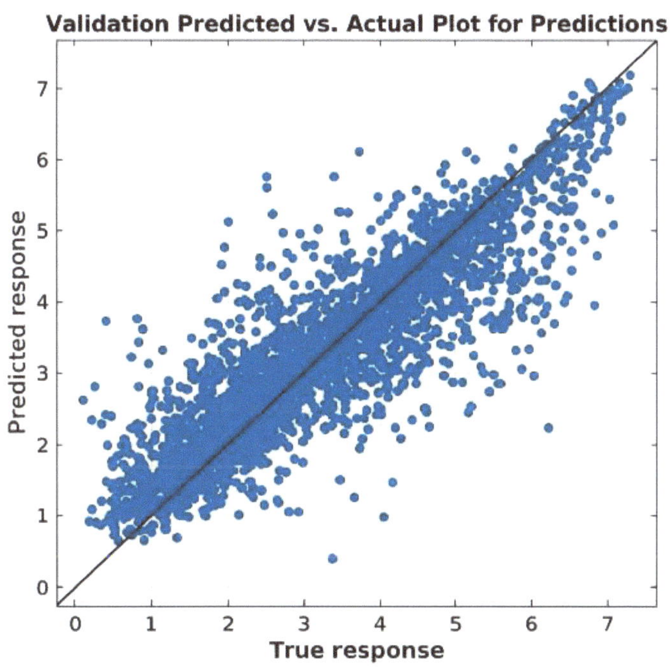

Fig. (21). Graph of March gaussian process regression (RMSE-0.70053).

Gaussian Process Regression recorded an RMSE of 0.70053, MSE of 0.49074, and MAE of 0.4678 as shown in Table **15**, indicating moderate prediction accuracy. The MAPE of 21.90% reflects lower forecasting precision compared to other runs. Training time was 536.84 seconds, indicating a higher computational cost.

Table 15. Lowest RMSE of March.

Sl. No.	Techniques (Mar)	RMSE	MSE	MAE	MAPE	Training time (sec)
1	Linear Regression	1.1088	1.2294	0.82312	37.00%	1.6006
2	Decision Tree Regression	0.97448	0.94961	0.63936	28.20%	1.4873
3	Gaussian Process Regression	0.70053	0.49074	0.4678	21.90%	536.84
4	Neural Network	0.83628	0.0.69937	0.61834	27.20%	111.11

In April, Gaussian Process Regression demonstrated solid predictive capability with an RMSE of 0.69815, as shown in Fig. (**22**). It effectively captured the data's underlying trends, ensuring consistent performance.

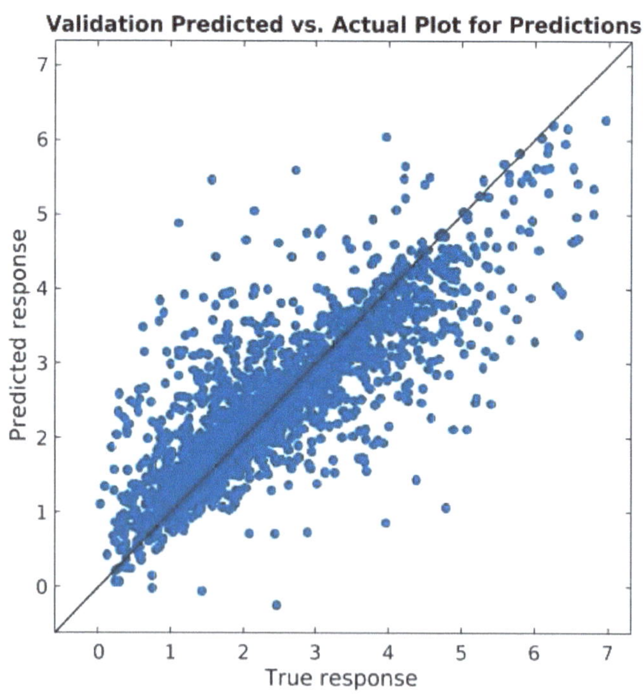

Fig. (22). Graph of April gaussian process regression (RMSE-0.69815).

Gaussian Process Regression resulted in an RMSE of 0.69815, MSE of 0.48742, and MAE of 0.44912, as shown in Table **16**, showing moderate prediction error. A high MAPE of 30.10% indicates less reliable forecasting performance. The model had a long training time of 891.2 seconds, reflecting significant computational demand.

Table 16. Lowest RMSE of April.

Sl. No.	Techniques (Apr)	RMSE	MSE	MAE	MAPE	Training time (sec)
1	Linear Regression	1.1451	1.3112	0.90659	63.60%	1.317
2	Decision Tree Regression	0.88984	0.79181	0.61407	40.10%	2.1745
3	**Gaussian Process Regression**	**0.69815**	**0.48742**	**0.44912**	**30.10%**	**891.2**
4	Neural Network	0.84346	0.71143	0.62733	41.00%	71.629

In May, Gaussian Process Regression achieved its best performance with a low RMSE of 0.48717 as shown in fig. (**23**). The model captured intricate patterns in the data with high accuracy. This reflects strong generalization and reliable predictive capability.

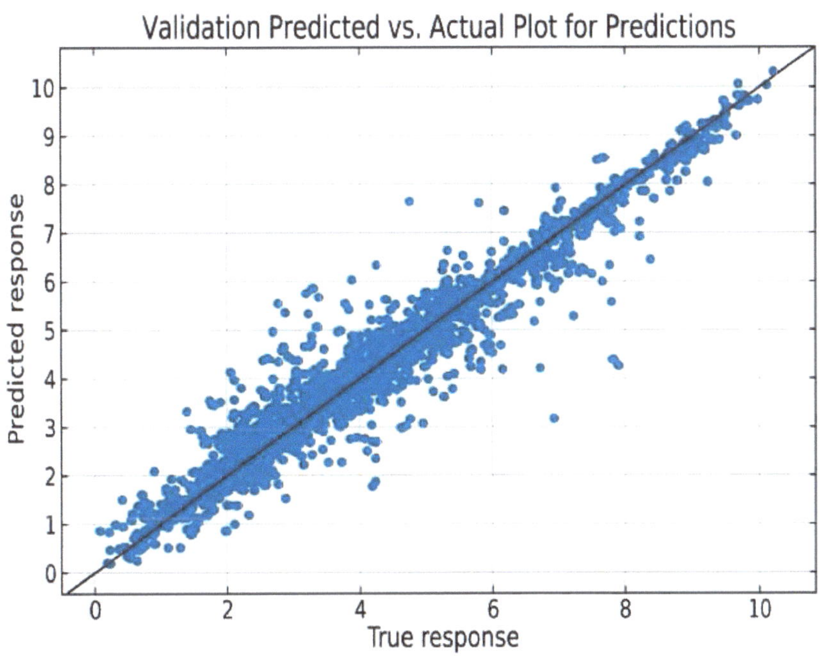

Fig. (23). Graph of May gaussian process regression (RMSE-0.48717).

Gaussian Process Regression achieved an RMSE of 0.48717, MSE of 0.23733, and MAE of 0.28916, indicating strong predictive performance as presented in Table **17**. A low MAPE of 10.00% suggests high forecasting accuracy. Training took 624.63 seconds, showing a trade-off between accuracy and computational time.

Table 17. Lowest RMSE of May.

Sl. No.	Techniques(may)	RMSE	MSE	MAE	MAPE	Training time (sec)
1	Linear Regression	1.6862	2.8433	1.3409	46.90%	1.7222
2	Decision Tree Regression	1.028	1.0569	0.68631	21.80%	0.86472
3	**Gaussian Process Regression**	**0.48717**	**0.23733**	**0.28916**	**10.00%**	**624.63**
4	Neural Network	0.84196	0.7089	0.64265	22.10%	90.076

In June, Gaussian Process Regression demonstrated solid performance with an RMSE of 0.66703, as shown in Fig. (**24**). It effectively modeled the underlying data trends and captured non-linear relationships. The results indicate consistent and reliable predictive accuracy.

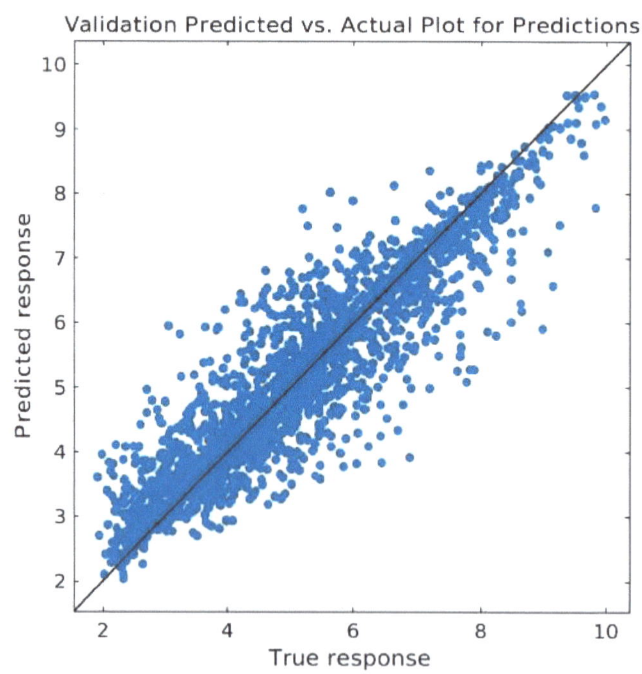

Fig. (24). Graph of June gaussian process regression (RMSE-0.66703).

Gaussian Process Regression produced an RMSE of 0.66703, MSE of 0.44493, and MAE of 0.45672 as shown in Table **18**, indicating moderate prediction accuracy. With a MAPE of 10.10%, the model demonstrated reliable forecasting performance. Training time was 784.12 seconds, reflecting a relatively high computational cost.

Table 18. Lowest RMSE of June.

Sl. No.	Techniques (June)	RMSE	MSE	MAE	MAPE	Training time (sec)
1	Linear Regression	1.1585	1.342	0.93917	21.10%	2.733
2	Decision Tree Regression	0.35392	0.90996	0.69232	15.00%	1.7586
3	**Gaussian Process Regression**	**0.66703**	**0.44493**	**0.45672**	**10.10%**	**784.12**
4	Neural Network	0.82001	0.67242	0.63425	14.20%	78.745

In July, Gaussian Process Regression maintained stable performance with an RMSE of 0.71445, as shown in Fig. (**25**). The model captured the overall data structure despite a slight increase in prediction error. It continued to provide reliable results through effective handling of non-linear patterns.

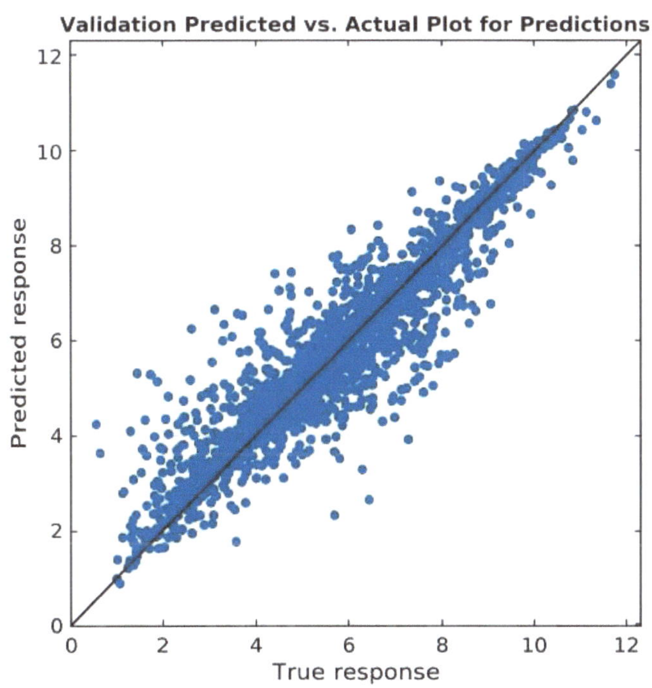

Fig. (25). Graph of July gaussian process regression (RMSE-0.71445).

Gaussian Process Regression produced an RMSE of 0.66703, MSE of 0.44493, and MAE of 0.45672, as shown in Table **19**, indicating moderate prediction accuracy. With a MAPE of 10.10%, the model demonstrated reliable forecasting performance. Training time was 784.12 seconds, reflecting a relatively high computational cost.

Table 19. Lowest RMSE of July.

Sl. No.	Techniques (July)	RMSE	MSE	MAE	MAPE	Training time (sec)
1	Linear Regression	1.7268	2.9818	1.3645	32.10%	3.6612
2	Decision Tree Regression	1.7288	2.9889	1.3652	32.30%	2.1364
3	**Gaussian Process Regression**	**0.71445**	**0.51043**	**0.4498**	**10.40%**	**839.76**
4	Neural Network	0.96369	0.9287	0.73658	16.30%	96.082

In August, Gaussian Process Regression delivered consistent performance with an RMSE of 0.71027, as shown in Fig. (**26**). The model effectively captured the data's non-linear trends and variability. This indicates reliable forecasting despite minor fluctuations in prediction accuracy.

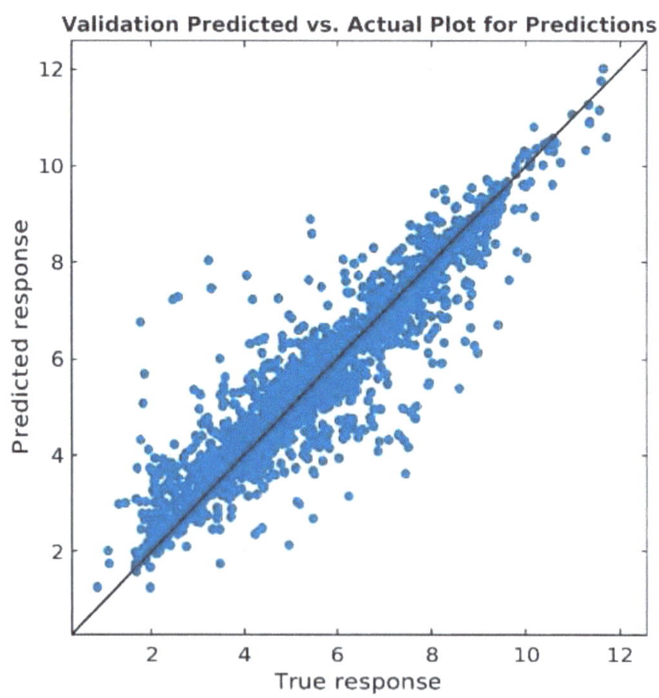

Fig. (26). Graph of August gaussian process regression (RMSE-0.71027).

Gaussian Process Regression achieved an RMSE of 0.71027, MSE of 0.50449, and MAE of 0.4425 as shown in Table **20**, showing moderate prediction error. A MAPE of 9.90% indicates good forecasting accuracy. The model required 897.44 seconds for training, reflecting a high computational load.

Table 20. Lowest RMSE of August.

Sl. No.	Techniques (Aug)	RMSE	MSE	MAE	MAPE	Training time (sec)
1	Linear Regression	1.3801	1.9047	1.0642	25.30%	1.3626
2	Decision Tree Regression	1.0878	1.1833	0.78172	17.10%	0.72554
3	**Gaussian Process Regression**	**0.71027**	**0.50449**	**0.4425**	**9.90%**	**897.44**
4	Neural Network	0.90535	0.81966	0.68728	14.90%	98.923

In September, Gaussian Process Regression achieved strong performance with a low RMSE of 0.58141, as shown in Fig. (**27**). The model accurately captured underlying data patterns and non-linear relationships. This reflects high predictive accuracy and effective generalization.

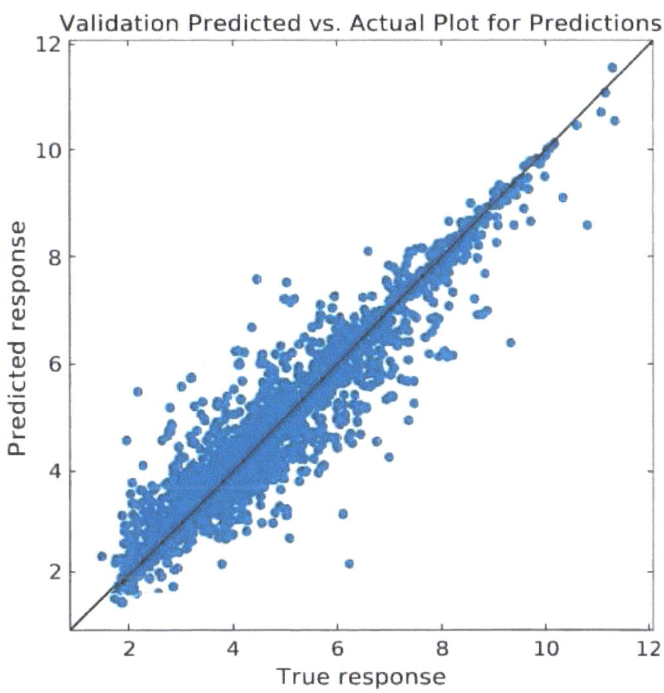

Fig. (27). Graph of September gaussian process regression (RMSE-0.0.58141).

Gaussian Process Regression recorded an RMSE of 0.58141, MSE of 0.33804, and MAE of 0.37384 as shown in Table **21**, indicating good predictive accuracy. Low MAPE of 8.90% reflects strong forecasting performance. Training time was 921.18 seconds, suggesting high computational effort.

Table 21. Lowest RMSE of September.

Sl. No.	Techniques (Sept)	RMSE	MSE	MAE	MAPE	Training time (sec)
1	Linear Regression	1.3403	1.7963	1.0255	24.00%	18.423
2	Decision Tree Regression	0.97803	0.95655	0.71593	16.60%	6.0379
3	**Gaussian Process Regression**	**0.58141**	**0.33804**	**0.37384**	**8.90%**	**921.18**
4	Neural Network	0.72386	0.52397	0.5576	13.00%	76.325

In October, Gaussian Process Regression achieved excellent performance with a very low RMSE of 0.42771, as shown in Fig. (**28**). The model precisely captured complex patterns and subtle variations in the data. This indicates highly accurate predictions and strong model reliability.

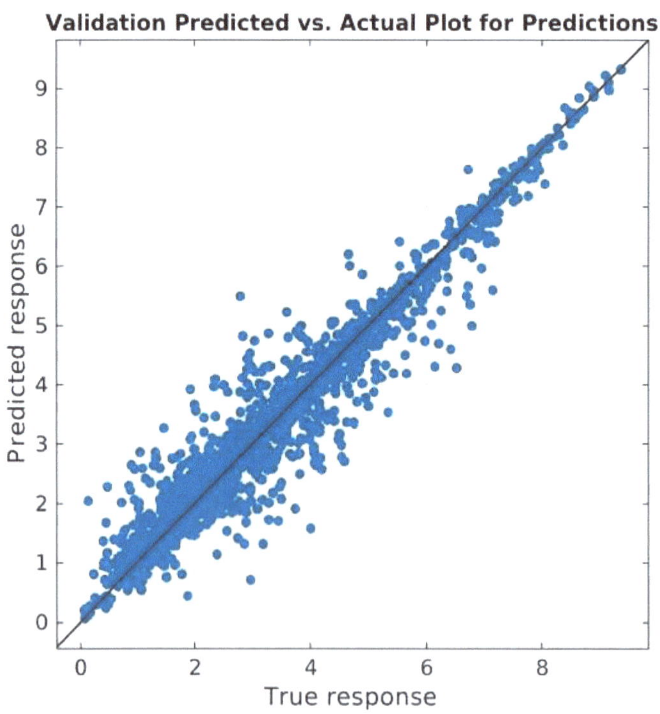

Fig. (28). Graph of October gaussian process regression (RMSE-0.42771).

Gaussian Process Regression achieved an RMSE of 0.42771, MSE of 0.18293, and MAE of 0.25713, as shown in Table **22**, indicating high prediction accuracy. MAPE of 12.20% suggests reasonably accurate forecasting results. The model required 1007.4 seconds for training, reflecting a significant computational cost.

Table 22. Lowest RMSE of October.

Sl. No.	Techniques (Oct.)	RMSE	MSE	MAE	MAPE	Training time (sec)
1	Linear Regression	1.3963	1.9497	1.0701	56.40%	1.2069
2	Decision Tree Regression	0.79656	0.63451	0.52692	24.90%	2.1728
3	**Gaussian Process Regression**	**0.42771**	**0.18293**	**0.25713**	**12.20%**	**1007.4**
4	Neural Network	0.64177	0.41187	0.48647	23.80%	83.117

In November, Gaussian Process Regression delivered strong predictive accuracy with a low RMSE of 0.57043, as shown in Fig. (**29**). The model effectively captured non-linear trends within the data. This performance highlights its robustness and reliability in forecasting.

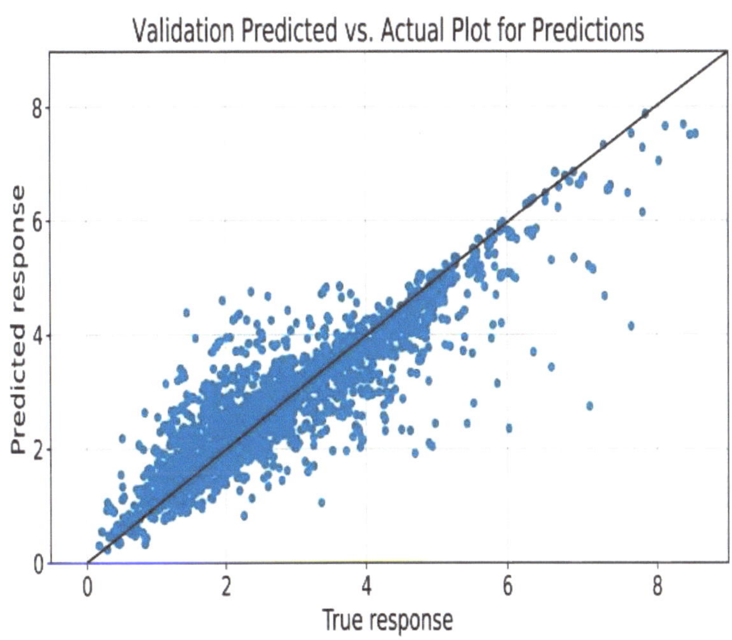

Fig. (29). Graph of November gaussian process regression (RMSE-0.57043).

Gaussian Process Regression yielded an RMSE of 0.57043, MSE of 0.32539, and MAE of 0.34393, as shown in Table **23**, indicating solid predictive accuracy. A MAPE of 16.30% shows moderate forecasting performance. Training time was 636.78 seconds, reflecting a balance between accuracy and computation.

Table 23. Lowest RMSE of November.

Sl. No.	Techniques (Nov)	RMSE	MSE	MAE	MAPE	Training time (sec)
1	Linear Regression	1.1587	1.3427	0.8766	44.00%	10.499
2	Decision Tree Regression	0.89132	0.79444	0.59032	28.60%	0.75296
3	**Gaussian Process Regression**	**0.57043**	**0.32539**	**0.34393**	**16.30%**	**636.78**
4	Neural Network	0.81305	0.66106	0.608	30.90%	75.072

In December, Gaussian Process Regression maintained stable performance with an RMSE of 0.7072, as shown in Fig. (**30**). The model continued to provide reliable predictions by effectively capturing non-linear data patterns.

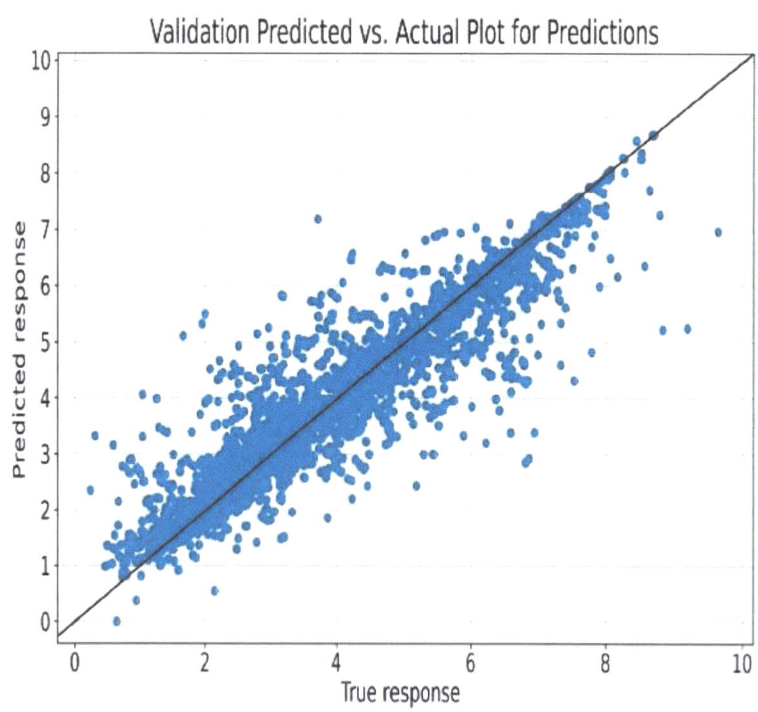

Fig. (30). Graph of December gaussian process regression (RMSE-0.7072).

Gaussian Process Regression recorded an RMSE of 0.7072, MSE of 0.50013, and MAE of 0.43237 as shown in Table **24**, indicating moderate prediction accuracy. The MAPE of 15.30% suggests acceptable forecasting performance. Training completed in 564.61 seconds, showing a reasonable computational effort.

Table 24. Lowest RMSE of December.

Sl. No.	Techniques (Dec)	RMSE	MSE	MAE	MAPE	Training time (sec)
1	Linear Regression	1.332	1.7742	1.0592	38.90%	1.5623
2	Decision Tree Regression	0.99615	0.99231	0.65671	21.50%	1.2731
3	**Gaussian Process Regression**	**0.7072**	**0.50013**	**0.43237**	**15.30%**	**564.61**
4	Neural Network	0.93292	0.86977	0.69089	23.60%	83.587

CONCLUSION

If wind farms are to operate at peak efficiency, accurate and trustworthy wind forecasts are crucial, as represented in the case study of Muppandal Wind Farm in Tamil Nadu and its long-term wind projects. The research proved that these approaches could reliably predict long-term wind speeds and directions by using sophisticated statistical and machine learning models. This improves the system's sustainability and stability by letting operators schedule maintenance, control energy production, and incorporate wind power into the regional grid more efficiently. This case study's results show how long-term wind forecasting may improve operational efficiency and cost-effectiveness, which might lead to a revolution in the wind energy business. More than that, additional wind farms in India and throughout the world may benefit from similar findings, which will help spread and keep renewable energy sources going strong. The effective use of sophisticated wind forecasting at Muppandal sets a precedent for further studies in the area and highlights the importance of wind power in creating a greener and more sustainable energy future.

REFERENCES

[1] Y. Hao, X. Wang, J. Wang, and W. Yang, "A new perspective of wind speed forecasting: Multi-objective and model selection-based ensemble interval-valued wind speed forecasting system", *Energy Convers. Manage.*, vol. 299, no. 117868, p. 117868, 2024. [http://dx.doi.org/10.1016/j.enconman.2023.117868]

[2] K. Wang, X.Y. Tang, and S. Zhao, "Robust multi-step wind speed forecasting based on a graph-based data reconstruction deep learning method", *Expert Syst. Appl.*, vol. 238, no. 121886, p. 121886, 2024. [http://dx.doi.org/10.1016/j.eswa.2023.121886]

[3] S.R. Moreno, L.O. Seman, S.F. Stefenon, L. dos Santos Coelho, and V.C. Mariani, "Enhancing wind speed forecasting through synergy of machine learning, singular spectral analysis, and variation mode decomposition", *Energy*, vol. 292, no. 130493, 2024.

[4] E. Ammar, and G. Xydis, "Wind speed forecasting using deep learning and preprocessing techniques", *Int. J. Green Energy,* vol. 21, no. 5, pp. 988-1016, 2024. [http://dx.doi.org/10.1080/15435075.2023.2228878]

[5] C. Huang, H.R. Karimi, P. Mei, D. Yang, and Q. Shi, "Evolving long short-term memory neural network for wind speed forecasting", *Inf. Sci.,* vol. 632, pp. 390-410, 2023. [http://dx.doi.org/10.1016/j.ins.2023.03.031]

[6] L.P. Joseph, R.C. Deo, R. Prasad, S. Salcedo-Sanz, N. Raj, and J. Soar, "Near real-time wind speed forecast model with bidirectional LSTM networks", *Renew. Energy,* vol. 204, pp. 39-58, 2023. [http://dx.doi.org/10.1016/j.renene.2022.12.123]

[7] M. Yaghoubirad, N. Azizi, M. Farajollahi, and A. Ahmadi, "Deep learning-based multistep ahead wind speed and power generation forecasting using direct method", *Energy Convers. Manage.,* vol. 281, p. 116760, 2023. [http://dx.doi.org/10.1016/j.enconman.2023.116760]

[8] Y. Hao, W. Yang, and K. Yin, "Novel wind speed forecasting model based on a deep learning combined strategy in urban energy systems", *Expert Syst. Appl.,* vol. 219, no. 119636, p. 119636, 2023. [http://dx.doi.org/10.1016/j.eswa.2023.119636]

[9] V.E.L.A. Duca, T.C.O. Fonseca, and F.L. Cyrino Oliveira, "A generalized dynamical model for wind speed forecasting", *Renew. Sustain. Energy Rev.,* vol. 136, no. 110421, p. 110421, 2021. [http://dx.doi.org/10.1016/j.rser.2020.110421]

[10] H.B. Azad, S. Mekhilef, and V.G. Ganapathy, "Long-term wind speed forecasting and general pattern recognition using neural networks", *IEEE Trans. Sustain. Energy,* vol. 5, no. 2, pp. 546-553, 2014. [http://dx.doi.org/10.1109/TSTE.2014.2300150]

[11] T.G. Barbounis, J.B. Theocharis, M.C. Alexiadis, and P.S. Dokopoulos, "Long-term wind speed and power forecasting using local recurrent neural network models", *IEEE Trans. Energ. Convers.,* vol. 21, no. 1, pp. 273-284, 2006. [http://dx.doi.org/10.1109/TEC.2005.847954]

[12] P.P. Kritharas, and S.J. Watson, "A comparison of long-term wind speed forecasting models", *J. Sol. Energy Eng.,* vol. 132, no. 4, p. 041008, 2010. [http://dx.doi.org/10.1115/1.4002346]

[13] G., Boopathi, K., Lavanya, M. C., & Saranya, R. "Long-term wind speed forecasting—A review.", Artificial Intelligence Techniques for Advanced Computing Applications: Proceedings, pp. 79-99, 2020.

[14] F.R. Ningsih, E.C. Djamal, and A. Najmurrakhman, "Wind speed forecasting using recurrent neural networks and long short-term memory", *International Conference on Instrumentation, Control, and Automation,* pp. 137-141, 2019. [http://dx.doi.org/10.1109/ICA.2019.8916717]

SUBJECT INDEX

Shilpa Gupta & Ritika Sharma (Eds.)

F

G

N

O

P

Q

R

S

T

U

V

W

Y

www.ingramcontent.com/pod-product-compliance
Lightning Source LLC
LaVergne TN
LVHW070949210926
848482LV00002B/153